TELL

TELL

LOVE, DEFIANCE, AND THE MILITARY TRIAL AT THE TIPPING POINT FOR GAY RIGHTS

MAJOR MARGARET WITT

with Tim Connor

ForeEdge

ForeEdge
An imprint of University Press of New England
www.upne.com
© 2017 Margaret Witt
All rights reserved
Manufactured in the United States of America
Designed by Mindy Basinger Hill
Typeset in Cochin LT Std

Library of Congress Cataloging-in-Publication Data

Names: Witt, Margaret, 1964- author.
Title: Tell : love, defiance, and the military trial at the tipping point for
gay rights / Major Margaret Witt, with Tim Connor.
Description: Lebanon NH : ForeEdge, an imprint of University Press of
New England, 2017. | Includes bibliographical references and index.
Identifiers: LCCN 2017006241 (print) | LCCN 2017011336 (ebook) |
ISBN 9781611688429 (cloth) | ISBN 9781512601114 (epub, mobi, & pdf)
Subjects: LCSH: Witt, Margaret, 1964 — Trials, litigation, etc. | United States.
Department of the Air Force — Trials, litigation, etc. | Trials (Military
offenses) — United States. | Gay military personnel — Legal status, laws, etc. —
United States. | Gay rights — United States. | Military discharge — United States. |
Gay military personnel — Government policy — United States.
Classification: LCC KF229.W58 .W58 2017 (print) | LCC KF229.W58 (ebook) |
DDC 343.73/014 — dc23
LC record available at https://lccn.loc.gov/2017006241

5 4 3 2 1

In memory of Sher Kung *and* Darren Manzella

CONTENTS

Photographs follow page 122.

FOREWORD

Colonel Margarethe Cammermeyer | *RN, PhD, USAR retired*

Major Witt's determination, stamina, integrity, and loyalty are brought to life in *Tell*, the story of her successful four-year battle to challenge the constitutional validity of her dismissal from the U.S. Air Force under the law and policy known as Don't Ask, Don't Tell. Throughout the years, thousands of others have walked in her shoes, bravely serving in the military while hiding their sexual orientation: many served full careers in silence, while many others were dishonorably discharged because of their homosexuality. However, few had the impact her case has had on changing the military to open service. In effect, Major Witt successfully challenged 240 years of policy and law that prohibited or limited homosexuals serving in the military.

A BIT OF HISTORY

To understand Major Witt's story, readers need to understand that homosexuality has always been considered incompatible with military service, despite the fact that General Friedrich von Steuben, a known homosexual, is the creator of American military organization, discipline, training, and supply organization. In fact, von Steuben organized the Continental army effectively enough to win the Revolutionary War. Ironically, at the same time, Lieutenant Frederick Gotthold Enslin, who was with Washington at Valley Forge, was drummed out of the military, disgraced and humiliated for homosexual conduct in 1778.

Since those revolutionary times, contradictory attitudes and treatment have continued to plague gays in the military; regulations and laws have evolved over the years based on social trends dealing with homosexuality. For instance, during World War I, homosexual conduct would result in a court-martial; also, at that time witch hunts were conducted to ferret out homosexuals from the military. Sodomy was a crime punishable by incarceration. Physical characteristics, "stigmata of degeneration," were used to determine sexuality and to prevent individuals from joining the military because they were deemed "unfit for service." For instance, in 1921, the disqualification standard included men with female physical characteristics such as sloping shoulders, broad hips, an absence of facial and body hair, etc.

By World War II, "homosexual proclivity" was the disqualifier for the draft. Military psychiatrists determined that homosexuals had "psychopathic personality disorder" and were unfit to fight. Those already serving would be discharged and denied veterans' benefits regardless of their accomplishments or skills.

During the Korean War, homosexuals were classified into three categories based on behavior, ranging from criminal behavior to denial of homosexual behavior, which determined their type of discharge. In addition, sodomy became defined under the Uniform Code of Military Justice, Article 125, and would result in imprisonment. During the 1950s, homosexuals were regarded as security risks, impeding national security, and President Eisenhower signed Executive Order 10450 prohibiting homosexuals from being employed by the federal government.

Homophobic attitudes survived the more liberal years of civil rights for minorities and women; by 1972, regulations continued to establish policies for discharging enlisted personnel found to be unfit or unsuitable for duty because of homosexuality only, even if their service was commendable. However, contradictions continued, as there was discretion by commanders, so some known homosexuals were able to continue their careers. Consequently, treatment of individual cases was uneven, which resulted in lawsuits after service members were discharged. By 1981, the Department of Defense flatly stated that "homosexuality is incompatible with military service"; therefore, mandatory discharge applied to all known homosexuals. This directive was reaffirmed in 1982, 1993, and 2008.

However, by 1993, after many advocates, civilians, and President Clinton had put forth considerable effort to attain open service, there was a compromise that created the law Don't Ask, Don't Tell (DADT). In effect, homosexuality was still considered unacceptable to morale, good order, discipline, and unit cohesion, but the law recognized that homosexuals were actively serving and therefore allowed them to continue doing so as long as this was a silent characteristic (no disclosure). During its tenure, DADT resulted in the discharge of over fourteen thousand service members.

By 2010, President Obama decided it was time for the demise of Don't Ask, Don't Tell. Fighting extreme odds and the long history of anti-homosexual agendas, many supporters lobbied against the biased policy; finally, with involvement of the courts and senior military leadership, Congress acted, voting to repeal DADT, and on December 22, 2010, President Obama signed the repeal.

Although another eight months passed before the enactment of the repeal, on September 10, 2011, all legal bias against homosexuals disappeared from the books; the United States, for the first time ever, provided open service for homosexuals.

As the final coup de grâce, On June 28, 2013, the United States Supreme Court struck down the Defense of Marriage Act. Finally, homosexuals, including military personnel, were recognized as having equal rights to marry; same-sex marriage has become legal throughout the United States.

In addition, progressive ideals finally were expanded to others: after another four years, on June 30, 2016, transgender service members were also granted the right to serve without constraint.

SIGNIFICANCE OF MAJOR WITT'S STORY

While reading *Tell*, Margaret Witt's story, think of it as multilevel love story. Witt not only loves and wants to serve her country; she also does so with distinction and dedication, despite discrimination under that country's laws. This is also the love story of a nurse who not only cares for fellow service members, but also does so with compassion, dedication, and skill. Finally, *Tell* becomes the love story of a service member whose mission is not only to fight for her own career, but also to fight to expand and change the opportunities for all homosexual service members, allowing them to serve with integrity and honor.

The caveat to Witt's successful lawsuit challenging her discharge is that now she will live in infamy, forever connected to antigay military regulations: the "*Witt* standard" is now the basis by which the military must prove why someone who is homosexual should not serve in the military! The *Witt* standard is unwinnable for the military, because the military could never demonstrate why sexual orientation should make any difference in the ability of a service member to continue to serve.

In fact, Major Witt's case demonstrated her effectiveness in maintaining good order, discipline, morale, and unit cohesiveness, clearly illustrating how she was an asset to the military and now to all who can serve with dignity.

I salute you, Major Witt.

TELL

Chapter 1

▪▪▪▪▪▪▪▪▪▪▪▪▪▪

HOMECOMING

It was 5:46 a.m. Pacific time, and the late-summer sunrise was still a half hour away. Margie Witt was in her bed in Spokane, Washington, a midsize city that unfolds against the northern Rockies to the east and the basalt-columned canyon lands of the Columbia River basin to the west. The alarm clock radio was set to prod her from sleep at the top of the hour. Because she didn't actually have to be at work until eight o'clock, the opening report from the alarm could be received as a suggestion and cut short by a tap to the snooze button. But on this breezeless and blue morning the newscaster's voice was reporting that a small plane had struck one of the massive towers in Lower Manhattan. With only the barest of facts being provided in those early minutes, radio listeners were left to fill in the gaps of what seemed to be a tragic airplane crash—a newsworthy but not necessarily earth-shattering accident.

If most would have received this as ordinary news, Margie (the "g" is hard) did not. The thirty-seven-year-old physical therapist quickly rolled out of bed, walked briskly to her living room, and cued the television to bring up CNN. It was September 11, 2001.

By happenstance, she knew New York City's World Trade Center was an inviting target for terrorists. As an Air Force flight nurse, she had been on a medical evacuation mission to Newark's Liberty International Airport on February 23, 1993. That was the day Ramzi Yousef and a group of co-conspirators detonated twelve hundred pounds of explosives packed into a Ryder truck that was parked in the basement of the World Trade Center's North Tower. The intent was to topple the North Tower into the South Tower. The towers somehow withstood the blast, but the explosion killed six people, injured more than a thousand, and left an enormous hole beneath the North Tower. On that late winter day in Newark, Margie could plainly see the Lower Manhattan skyline and the plume of smoke rising from the World Trade Center. Now, seven and a half years later, she had a strong sense that whatever was under way in Lower Manhattan was no accident.

The news reports quickly went from bad to horrifying. A second plane struck the South Tower at three minutes past 6 a.m. Pacific time.

Over the years, one of the unspoken understandings between Margie and her mother, Gloria, is that when big news happens they communicate with each other. She knew her mom would likely still be asleep at her home in Gig Harbor, just west of Tacoma. But she had to call, just as Gloria needed to call her daughter fifteen years earlier when the space shuttle *Challenger* exploded in the sky over Florida. The two of them—250 miles apart but connected by phone and by the barely believable live images of the twin towers sending thick black plumes of smoke into a cloudless sky—watched for a few minutes. Together they tried to get their minds around what they were witnessing. Then it was time for Margie to shower and fumble through the motions of getting ready to go to work at the offices of Spokane's largest school district. She finally grabbed the keys to her Subaru station wagon and headed down the long slope of Spokane's South Hill, amid heritage maples and towering ponderosa pines, driving through crisp, sun-streaked air but with a steadily sinking feeling in her stomach.

By the time she crossed the Spokane River and reached the district office, both the World Trade Center towers had collapsed, and another large jetliner had crashed into the Pentagon. By now, it should have been clear that a broader attack was under way. Yet she couldn't understand the business-as-usual atmosphere in the office. Were people oblivious to what was happening? Were they numb to it? In a large conference room where she and the other therapists were gathering, a large television was turned to CNN. The surreal events in New York and Washington, DC, were unfolding before their eyes as the meeting got under way. Supervisors doled out assignments, and the district's physical and occupational therapists coordinated their schedules. It was as though nothing out of the ordinary were occurring.

As the meeting wrapped up, her colleagues returned to their offices or left for their assignments at the district's schools around the city. Margie remained in the conference room. She had tears in her eyes and couldn't pull herself away from CNN.

By this time, she had been in the Air Force—first on active duty, and now as a reservist—for fourteen years. She had been assigned as an operating room nurse in Germany during the first Gulf War, and in the years since, she had served as a flight nurse on countless air evacuation missions around the world. By now she knew that when you're in the Air Force, the world is not so big. There is no such thing as an event or a calamity that is too far away to affect your next assignment. The sight of the twin towers sending dark plumes of smoke into a cloudless sky, and then collapsing, nightmarishly, to the ground delivered a clear message that her world was going to change. She just had no idea how life-altering the changes would be.

In the years leading up to the 9/11 attacks and to her eventual deployment to the Middle East two years later, Margie was increasingly aware of the deepening stresses and contradictions in her life. In Spokane, she had been working as a pediatric physical therapist four days a week, with shifts as a part-time registered nurse and volunteer firefighter. She was doing all this and still flying as many actual and training missions for the Air Force as she could. By now she had been decorated many times over, and in 1999 she had been promoted to the rank of major.

Her reserve unit, the 446th Aeromedical Evacuation Squadron (AES), was based at McChord Air Force Base in Tacoma, only a few miles from where she had grown up and gone to high school and college. Once a month, she would either drive or fly to McChord to attend to her reserve duties. There were no questions, by then, about her value to the Air Force and the 446th AES. More so than in the dozens of commendations, her worth as an officer, mentor, and leader was reflected in the loyalty, respect, and camaraderie of her peers in a unit internationally recognized as setting the standard for in-flight medical care.

It was in her personal life that she was struggling to find happiness in a world that wasn't quite ready to accept her on her own terms. As an American Civil Liberties Union lawyer would bluntly announce at a Seattle press conference a few years later, Major Witt was gay. For all the furious political and legal weight that this simple truth would eventually bring to bear upon her life, it was the intimate dimensions of it that she had to wake up to every day. She was approaching middle age, yet, for fear of disappointing and perhaps alienating her parents, she still hadn't spoken directly to either one of them about the fact that she was a lesbian.

Her partner at the time was Tiffany Jenson, a Spokane physical therapist whom she had met while the two were studying for their master's degrees at Eastern Washington University. They had been in a romantic relationship for four years, were sharing a home on Spokane's South Hill, and were managing very full lives, "Tiff" as a full-time physical therapist, and Margie with her schedule packed with civilian and Air Force duties.

Even if she felt the time had arrived to come out to her parents, she would still have been forced to live a lie in that large part of her life that involved the United States Air Force. Like thousands of other gay men and women serving in the U.S. military, she was in a cruel twilight zone created by the law and policy known as Don't Ask, Don't Tell (DADT).

In the rollout to the 1994 law, the American public had been invited to believe DADT somehow protected gay service members so long as they didn't publicly reveal they were homosexual. But those who believed gay service members were now safe from recriminations if they didn't talk or write about their sexual orientation had been misled. As time and events would demonstrate in Margie's case, the mere suspicion or accusation of a service member's homosexuality—delivered in any form to a superior, or even a fellow service member—was enough to trigger an investigation leading to one's expulsion from military service under DADT. In other words, you could be silently obedient in upholding your end of the Don't Ask, Don't Tell double-wink game and still be ordered off the base and out of the military. By September 2001, more than seven thousand service members had been discharged under DADT in the six years since it had gone into effect.

For Margie, the thought of being forced to leave the Air Force was horrifying. After nearly fifteen years of service, her identity as a flight nurse had become deeply woven into her sense of self. Not that it was the sum of her existence, but it was a near perfect way to be fully alive, to experience the world, the camaraderie of her peers, and the deep satisfaction of doing meaningful work for both her patients and her country. She was also very good at it, and because she was good at it, the respect she garnered from her peers reinforced her self-confidence and sense of security.

What she hadn't quite figured out was how to put the two halves of her life together. Given the nature of the commitments that both active duty and reserve service members make to the military, it is difficult enough for straight couples to give up so much control over their lives. To be a gay service member in a committed relationship also involved a nerve-racking and never-ending commitment to the art of disguise. Then, of course, there are the basic, inescapable challenges of just being in an intimate relationship, whether gay or straight.

As the winter of 2001 became the spring of 2002, there was a new source of tension and stress in Margie and Tiffany's evolving relationship. Tiff wanted to become a mother, and she was making it increasingly clear to Margie that she didn't want to wait, that she wanted to become pregnant. At least from Margie's end of that discussion, there was a thread of irony in this gathering push toward parenthood. After witnessing the tenderness Tiff displayed while babysitting a friend's young children, Margie told her she would make a fine mother. This left Margie to wonder, as the tension mounted in their labored discussions about having a child, as to whether her compliment had set her partner's clock in motion.

Even in the best of times, a conversation about whether to become parents was going to be challenging. It was all the more so now because Margie's attention—in the aftermath of the 9/11 attacks—was being pulled toward the inevitable deployment of her unit in support of the missions in southwest Asia. Yet the clear message from her partner was that she wanted to have a baby via in vitro fertilization. And she wanted to have it soon.

Under the circumstances, the idea of becoming a parent was a breathtaking proposal and one from which Margie couldn't help but recoil. What followed was a spiral of personal tumult unlike anything she had ever experienced. To better understand her visceral resistance, she sought help from professional therapists. Even so, she struggled for clarity and peace of mind. Nothing about what her partner was asking of her was easy, and to Margie, much of it made little sense. She would soon be forty years old, and neither she nor Tiff, who was in her early thirties, were out to their respective parents.

Quite apart from the dilemma of how to break such news to her parents, Margie harbored deep anxiety over whether she could play the part for which she was being cast. Like her brother and her sister, Margie felt she had been blessed with the best parents on the planet. As close as she was to her mother, Margie's ties to her devoted father, Frank, were no less strong. She well understood how important her father had been to building the person she had become. And now she would be the father to the child Tiff wanted to deliver. Could she even begin to fill a father's shoes? And even if she could successfully step into the role of the child's father, she would still be helpless to control how other people, and other children, would behave toward a child whose parents were two women. Spokane is the hub of the culturally conservative inland Northwest. The city—bisected at its downtown core by the majestic falls of the Spokane River—has its charms and plenty of good people. But it is a long way from San Francisco, let alone Seattle.

Above all, of course, was the profoundly vexing question of how Major Margaret Witt would explain her child and her child's mother to the U.S. Air Force. There may have been a lot of double-winking going on in how the military chose to enforce Don't Ask, Don't Tell, but scores of gay service men and women were being discharged every month. Was it reasonable to expect that her Air Force superiors would simply look away from her becoming a parent under these circumstances? And what if they didn't?

In January 2003, Margie led a small cadre of reservists from the 446th being deployed to the Arabian Peninsula. Their purpose was to support Operation Enduring Freedom, the effort to uproot the Taliban and al-Qaeda in Afghanistan, and Operation Southern Watch, the mission to enforce a no-fly zone in Iraq in the run-up to the invasion that now looked inevitable (and would occur in late March). By now, the personal tensions in her life were nearly unbearable. She was packing to go off into a war zone, yet even as she was gathering her equipment and personal items, her partner was reminding her of the importance of a decision and her desire to have an answer by the time Margie returned from the Middle East.

At the same time, Margie was anxious about what awaited her and her crew as she hauled all her mobility bags out the door, on her way to McChord. Among the items packed in the oversize canvas bags were her charcoal-lined chemical warfare protection suits (complete with gas mask and hood), plus a Kevlar helmet, body armor, uniforms, standard survival gear, and assorted personal items. There was a separate, heavy-duty plastic case for the chemical protection mask, suit, boots, etc., she could use in flight in the event of a chemical attack.

The trip to Oman took nearly a day and a half. She flew out of Seattle with Stacey Julian and Anna Friscia, two of the 446th's medical technicians.

Stacey and his wife Heather, a 446th flight nurse, lived in Spanaway, just east of McChord's flight line, and both were part of the close-knit family of the unit that helped make Margie's reserve duty so satisfying. She had known Anna for most of her flying career, having met her when the two were stationed at Scott Air Force Base near St. Louis. Anna had flown in Desert Storm and had a vast amount of air evacuation experience. The three spent their first night in Baltimore, where nearly all the deployment crews heading to southwest Asia were routed. The next morning, they departed for Frankfurt, Germany, and from there boarded a charter for the long, final leg to the Arabian Peninsula. Along the way, Margie and Stacey rested their heads on each other's shoulders as they tried to sleep. Given the spartan working conditions they typically endured, they felt almost pampered to be traveling in a plush, warm, and quiet commercial aircraft.

In contrast, the military aircraft they used for their medical missions (primarily C-130s, C-141s, and C-17s) were bare metal tubes with minimal amenities—sometimes not even heat. There were very few windows, and the seats, such as they were, were fashioned from nylon webbing and forced you to sit bolt upright. To alleviate the stress on her tailbone and lower back, Margie carried a twelve-inch-square self-inflating cushion on the longer flights.

As their charter flight started its final descent into Oman, a flight attendant announced the cabin lights would be extinguished so as to make the plane a less visible target for hostile ground fire. Eventually, the landing gear touched ground on the island of Masirah, in the Arabian Sea. It could hardly have been any darker. As the passengers left the plane, they were greeted at the bottom of the long stairs by the base commander and as many staff as he could wrangle up in the middle of the night. It was eerily silent, except for the hum of distant generators. The warm night air smelled of dust, saltwater, and what they later learned was frankincense.

Anna was tired and hauled her bags to the quarters assigned to enlisted women. Stacey and Margie were too amped up to sleep and curious about where they had landed. The pair staggered into the base recreation center to check it out. Where they expected to see card and foosball tables, and perhaps a Ping-Pong table or two, were instead couches and video game consoles connected to large, flat-screen TVs. They had flown halfway around the world, landed in the dark, only to stride into an electronic arcade of American youth culture. Trying to work the hand-held controllers on the video games was mind numbing, so they eventually gave up and turned to the task of hauling their own bags to what the military refers to as "transient" quarters, typically tents reserved for those who are staying just a night or two as they make their way between assignments.

Margie was assigned to a tent the size of a school cafeteria in a back corner of the compound. She couldn't quite believe her eyes when she stepped inside. The huge tent was filled with empty cots, and by the looks of things, she was the only female transient officer on the base in Masirah. She chose the cot farthest from the door, in a back corner, and slept for a few hours.

At dawn, Margie, Stacey, and Anna boarded a C-130 to fly to Seeb Air Base in Oman, a monarchy roughly the same size and population of Nevada. The northeast coast of Oman arcs northward to form a funnel between the Arabian Sea and the strategically important Strait of Hormuz, the narrow passage into the Persian Gulf, through which passes 20 percent of the world's oil. At Seeb, the training filters on their chemical warfare masks were replaced with actual filters. The team members were also issued air crew survival vests and sidearms.

Before leaving the states, they had received shots to protect them from anthrax. Now they were vaccinated with live smallpox virus. The multiple-needle injection creates a healing wound that could conceivably spread the virus on contact. To protect those who hadn't been vaccinated, this condition required that the team members be quarantined to the base for the duration of their stay—excepting, of course, when they were flying their missions. Moreover, to further reduce the possibility of infecting others, their camp had to be cleared of the immigrant workers who would normally take care of the day-to-day chores. Thus, in addition to handling their own duty assignments, the crew members now had to do their own cooking and cleaning for the duration of their deployment. The camp was not connected to the Omani power grid, so huge, trailer-size diesel generators were used to provide electricity for lighting, equipment, and the large swamp coolers and air conditioners needed to offset the desert heat. For Stacey, one unforgettable postscript to the tour is that, unknown to him, an enormous camel spider, nearly a half-foot long with enormous jaws, had taken up residence beneath his bunk. The frightening creature was found by the technician who replaced him, who sent Stacey a photograph of the eight-legged little monster—with an additional pair of leglike sensory organs—as a souvenir.

The crew assignments were in small groups of three, composed of one registered nurse and two medical technicians. When it came time to rotate crews, Margie was teamed up with her longtime buddy Jim Schaffer, a Spokane firefighter and paramedic.

Schaffer's presence in the din and dust of Oman would become a godsend for Margie. In terms of the courage, commitment, and experience that the reserves allow the country to tap into in times of need, Schaffer epitomized the best of what the military reserves are all about.

Somewhat comically, Schaffer's first experience with the Air Force had come when he was in elementary school. His family lived on a farm just outside Beale Air Force Base north of Sacramento. In the mid-1960s, Beale became the first of a select number of air bases to host the SR-71 Black-bird, an exotic spy plane that flew at speeds in excess of Mach 3. With its sleek aerodynamic contours and massive twin engines, the SR-71 would be a really cool thing for an eight-year-old to photograph. Young Jim decided he would do this by sneaking onto the base with his mom's Brownie "Hawkeye" camera—a cube with a lens and a handle on top, about the size of a coffeepot. He had hiked through a dry creek bed, walked across the base's main runway, and snapped several photos of the futuristic spy plane by the time he was detected and detained by base security. He got to keep the camera, though not the film, and was barred from visiting the base commissary (his father was by then a retired Air Force colonel) for three months.

In his teens, Schaffer became interested in firefighting after the fire-fighter husband of one of his junior high teachers spoke to the class about his experiences. Schaffer eventually decided that the Air Force, and the training it offered in firefighting, would be his "college" experience. The experience came quickly. He had barely begun to deal with the harsh environs of his first assignment—the Shemya air base on a tiny island in the westernmost reaches of Alaska's Aleutian archipelago—when a large reconnaissance plane crashed and burst into flames while attempting a landing in whiteout conditions.

"I was told in school, 'You'll probably never get an air crash.' I'm there two weeks and an RC-135 hits the deck."

Six crew members died in the crash.

Schaffer eventually wound up at Fairchild Air Force Base, a bomber and tanker base just west of Spokane, at age twenty-five. By the time he was thirty, he had transitioned to the Air Force reserves and had qualified to become a full-time paramedic with the Spokane Fire Department. His reserve duty included dangerous deployments such as Mogadishu, Somalia, in the fall of 1993.

Schaffer was serving at a makeshift medical camp in Mogadishu when the infamous "Black Hawk Down" incident occurred. Somali militants shot down two U.S. helicopters, leading to a bloody and harrowing rescue mission. In the aftermath of the battle, Schaffer and the other medical personnel found themselves working desperately with rudimentary medical equipment trying to treat the dozens of badly wounded soldiers. They referred to it as "Bloody Sunday." Schaffer received two Air Force commendation medals for his service in Somalia.

Master Sergeant Jim Schaffer would meet Captain Margaret Witt in early 1996. At the time, Margie was not only transitioning from active duty into the reserves but also moving to Spokane to pursue a master's degree in physical therapy at Eastern Washington University. The 446th draws its reservists from all over the northwestern states, and many arrived at McChord on dedicated Air Force flights from places as far away as Salt Lake City. There were no dedicated flights from Spokane, though, and this led to cross-state car pools. Schaffer and Witt had quickly come to respect each other as professionals, but the five-hour car rides became an opening to deepen their friendship.

It was toward the end of one of their many car trips—a year before they would be deployed to Oman—that Schaffer popped the question. There were, to be sure, some obvious clues that Margie was a lesbian. Yet, for layers of reasons—not the least of which was an official military decree not to ask, and not to tell—they had both chosen not to discuss it.

The car had exited the freeway when both noticed an impressive Harley-Davidson motorcycle.

"I used to have one of those," Jim remembers Margie saying. But, she added, she had sold it.

"Why?" he asked.

"It seemed a little too stereotypical," she answered.

To Schaffer, such a coy answer only made sense if it packed an implicit reference to a connection between lesbians and motorcycles. It made him feel awkward, and he was tired of feeling awkward. It was time to get all the cards on the table. He asked. She told.

Now, in early 2003, in the dust and isolation of their camp in Oman, the timing of their being reunited was nothing short of a godsend for Margie. By day, their missions primarily involved flying the familiar C-130 cargo planes to airfields throughout the southwest Asia "area of responsibility," from the horn of Africa to Kazakhstan. They would pick up sick and injured soldiers and Department of Defense civilian personnel and evacuate them to Oman, where they would be treated at a U.S. hospital in Seeb. The missions were always subject to change after takeoff, but included landings in combat zones in Afghanistan. After their patients arrived at Seeb, those requiring more intensive treatment would be flown from Oman to Landstuhl Regional Medical Center in southern Germany. Though most of their flights were intra-theater, Margie and Jim would occasionally make the seven-hour flights to Germany as well.

Still, Margie's deployment to the other side of the world had not shortened the distance between her and her most pressing life decision—about whether to be a parent to the baby that Tiff wanted to have. Between telephones in Spokane and Oman, life and the tormenting impasse between her and her partner still traveled at the speed of light.

The "phone bank" they were required to use was in a small trailer on the other side of the camp. Because of the time difference, the calls would usually occur after two in the morning, Omani time. Margie and Jim would walk along gravel roads in the dark to use their fifteen minutes of allotted phone time to hear about life back home. Because of the tight security attached to their mission, they were prohibited from discussing where they had flown, or why, or what they had done for the day. Moreover, the calls were routinely monitored, and it was no secret that the Air Force's Office of Special Investigations (OSI) would make use of electronic eavesdropping to initiate expulsions of gay service members under Don't Ask, Don't Tell.

The chilling effect of the security monitoring only added to the tension and difficulty of the phone conversations between Margie and Tiff. For example, whereas Margie craved bits of daily news—such as how the dogs were doing—her partner had little patience for these sorts of discussions.

At times, Tiff voiced her frustration in personal terms, the essence of the complaint being, "If you don't have anything real to talk about, then don't call me." The invasiveness of the security would have tested even a healthy romantic relationship. But their relationship was already unraveling. As time progressed, Margie became increasingly anguished by Tiff's unsparing focus on what she wanted out of the relationship. She would often leave the phone trailer in tears and walk out into the desert darkness, where Jim would embrace her and try to console her.

"We talked about all that," Jim recalls. "And basically what it all came down to is she just knew it wasn't for her."

During the early weeks after they had set up camp in Oman, the possibility that the United States could be minutes away from war with Iraq was inescapable. The tension subsided somewhat when it became clear the United Nations would be involved and the diplomatic process would require some time to play out. The sense of urgency would begin mounting again in February 2003. The pace of preparation was picking up dramatically, with bunkers and tarmacs being built and tons of chemical protection gear, medical supplies, and construction materials literally piling up. Suddenly the ground medical crews greeting them at their stops in the region were wearing flack vests, helmets, and sidearms. It was in the midst of this escalation that Margie's two-month assignment in the region was coming to an end. She and Jim flew to Al Udied Air Base in Qatar to make final preparations for the long trip home.

It was on a shuttle bus at Al Udied that Margie felt a strong wave of mixed emotions. She couldn't help but notice the forty-some soldiers with all their gear, including M-16 rifles and M-60 machine guns, heading out to an aircraft destined for who knows where. From the flight line, F-15s and F-16s were taking off continually, with refueling tankers parked on the tarmac, ready to go when needed. The part of her that was an Air Force major and flight nurse was deeply unsettled at the prospect of being sent to the sidelines, heading stateside just as the war was about to begin. The pull to stay was strong, even though both she and Jim were in physical pain. Both were going to need surgery upon their returns, Margie to repair the right knee she had injured jumping out of a flatbed truck, and Jim to repair a rotator cuff in his shoulder that he had torn trying to load a liquid oxygen tank onto a truck.

On their last night at Al Udied, Margie got assigned to what was supposed to be one of the transient air crew tents. When she found the tent and
peered inside, however, it looked to her like a teenage girl's slumber party
had run amok. All the bunk beds in the central area were covered with
clothes, uniforms, robes, stuffed animals. It was the opposite of what she
had experienced that first dark night in theater at the base on Masirah. This
time, there wasn't an empty bunk to be found, and nobody was in charge
to sort things out. Confused and frustrated, she stepped back outside the
tent, dragging her personal belongings and military gear with her. Dusk
was settling in. Feeling and looking like a weary and lost soul, she turned
and looked down the seemingly endless row of tents and pondered her next
move. As if on cue, Jim and the rest of her small crew stepped out of their
tent, two down from the one she had just exited.

"What's up?" one of them asked.

She tried to explain. The solution was at least clear to them, and they
quickly picked up her bags.

"You'll stay with us."

The large tent was dark, dusty, and filled with empty bunks and old
Ethernet cords heading in all directions. But she couldn't remember ever
feeling so welcomed and safe. Later that night, Jim walked with her to a
well-lit trailer where they could actually take showers (albeit cold ones)
and use toilets without having to hold flashlights. Under the circumstances,
the trailer was a small oasis of comfort. As they walked back to the tent,
Margie experienced another wave of strong emotions. The entire day had
been filled with the sights and sounds of the run-up to war. Now the darkness was pierced by the roar of jet fighters taking off, one after another.
She was feeling forsaken, anxious, and sad all at once when she turned to
Jim and expressed just how grateful she was for his being with her. Once
back inside the cavernous tent, she saw that the guys had found a way to
bring light to the area around her new bunk. Her sheets were turned down,
and there was a little fake potted plant beside the bed.

"Don't know if I'll sleep tonight," she wrote in her journal that evening.
"Don't know how I'll feel when boarding the plane in the morning. Do know
it wouldn't be any fun to be here. What I will remember and continue to
enjoy is looking at each moon and each sunset — and now — Orion's Belt."

Their ticket out of theater was on a wide-bodied, long-range commercial airliner headed to Frankfurt. Then they would fly to Baltimore to catch a domestic flight back to Seattle-Tacoma. Although they were leaving weapons and aircrew survival gear behind for use by their replacements, they were still hauling several huge mobility bags filled with their uniforms and protective gear, including the survival and chemical protection gear, gas masks, and other equipment they had brought with them. Ever helpful, Gloria had made little purple pom-pom tags for Margie's bags to help her keep track of them.

When their airliner lifted off from Al Udied on the morning of February 27, 2003, Margie had been in the region for nearly two months and was physically and mentally exhausted. She and Schaffer were sitting side by side as the plane climbed toward its cruising altitude. As no alcohol was allowed in Oman or Qatar, one of the perks of being airborne is that they could now enjoy a drink or two. She ordered a Bloody Mary. He ordered a screwdriver. They were ready to relax.

No such luck. Their drinks had just been delivered when there was an announcement on the plane's intercom.

"Are there any medical personnel aboard?"

A Department of Defense employee, also on his way home, had fallen seriously ill. In his distress, he had risen from his seat in the rear and staggered up the aisle before collapsing near the galley in the middle of the plane, near where Margie and Jim were seated. He was having a severe seizure, and suddenly it was up to the two of them to assess and treat him. Although Margie, as the officer and flight nurse, was nominally the team leader, the arrangement she and Jim adopted for such emergencies was that he would take the reins. That only made sense. In his civilian job, Jim is a captain and a trained paramedic with the Spokane Fire Department. He still handles emergencies like this on a near-daily basis.

Within seconds of realizing what was happening, both were on the floor—Jim trying to do an assessment on the collapsed passenger, while Margie propped the man's legs over her shoulder to keep them elevated. Margie was in such serious pain from her injured knee that she couldn't kneel. At the same time, Jim had to pull the sling up from his injured shoulder to improve his range of motion so he could work on the patient. Margie asked the cabin crew for oxygen, and Jim requested the plane's emergency medical kit. The oxygen came promptly, but the airliner's medical kit turned out to be useless, containing only a syringe, rubber gloves, and a couple of vials of epinephrine. There was nothing that could help with a seizure.

Jim was surprised by the distressed passenger's low pulse, raising the concern that he was in cardiogenic shock. Given the lack of useful medical supplies, the choice was made for them, and they quickly decided to ask that the airplane be diverted to Bahrain, where they would have access to U.S. military medical support.

It was a harrowing diversion. Their patient was incoherent, morbidly pale, his breathing shallow, and he was sweating profusely. His heartbeat was barely palpable. All they could do was work to stabilize him, lifting him up off the floor, and then securing him and themselves in the wide, middle row of the aircraft for the descent to Bahrain.

Once they were on the ground, an enormous portable stairway was quickly wheeled into position. Though it could reach to the middle door of the plane, the stairs were so sharply angled that it complicated one of the crucial tasks, which was keeping the patient level at all times. Somehow they managed to keep the stretcher horizontal as they lowered it to the tarmac. The patient turned out to be a high-ranking Department of Defense civilian. He lived, and, months later Witt and Schaffer were both presented Air Force Achievement Medals for efforts that may have saved his life.

As they again prepared to try to leave for Germany, Margie went to the bathroom to clean herself up. She could only laugh when she saw what was left of their drinks in the aircraft lavatory. Once back in the air, new drinks were delivered. Still, Margie couldn't get to sleep or even set her mind at ease. The part of her that didn't want to leave was restless, and the part that wanted to go home was mired in the dread of going back to her collapsing relationship with Tiffany. The truth is she was more anxious about her homecoming than she had been about heading into a war zone.

Chapter 2

━━━━━━━━━

YOUNG MS. EVERYTHING

Karyn Ingebritsen could be forgiven for feeling a sense of dread when she arrived for her first day at Curtis Junior High School. Winters tend to arrive early in the Pacific Northwest, and there can be a disheartening suddenness to the way the radiant foliage and cobalt-blue skies of autumn are replaced by woolen mists and a darkness that gets delivered well before dinner. And it was at this time of year, in late 1976, that Karyn's family made the move from the drier side of Washington State to the one that, in winter, gets a near-daily rinse of cold rain from the Pacific. After eight rewarding years as the pastor at Grace Lutheran Church in east Spokane, Karyn's father had come to the realization that, for his growth and for the good of the congregation, the time had come for him to step aside. He had been reassigned to Mount Cross Lutheran, in University Place, a then-unincorporated town wedged between Tacoma and the southernmost reaches of Puget Sound.

Karyn wasn't pleased to be leaving her friends and classmates in Spokane. Shy and introverted, she was especially unhappy to have to change schools well into her seventh-grade year. She was tall and thin, with long, straight, red hair, and she felt out of place and uncertain as to how she would fit in. Yet within days of starting at Curtis Junior High, Karyn had a new companion. Her name was Margie Witt.

At first, that hardly seemed possible. The two met in orchestra class, where both played violin. Karyn's first impression of Margie was framed by the contrast between herself as a "nerdy, bookish kind of kid" and this popular, athletic girl with sandy hair who seemed to know everyone and who easily navigated among the school's social circles. That contrast, by itself, was a little intimidating—though not for long, because what Karyn experienced was the embrace of a new and lasting friendship.

That Margie would take it upon herself to help a new classmate feel welcome made sense, given how closely she and her family were connected to the school. In those years, the cluster of brick buildings that housed the junior high was part of a larger campus built up over the years by the University Place school district. Margie's father, Frank, had been recruited to teach in the district in 1957, the same year the junior high opened its doors. Later, Margie's mom, Gloria, would teach in one of the district's elementary schools. Margie was born in University Place in 1964, and the campus—which would soon grow to include Curtis High School—was just a part of the environment in which she had been raised. To commemorate their contribution to the University Place community, the names of all the Witt family members were etched in a concrete curb around the junior high's athletic track. In a sense, Karyn was being welcomed into Margie's extended family, and before long Margie was being welcomed into the Ingebritsens' home as a frequent guest.

Not surprisingly, it was the pursuit of education that brought Frank and Gloria together in the first place. Frank enlisted during World War II and by the end of the war was serving in the Signal Corps as the U.S. Army liberated Korea from the Japanese. While in the Army, he began receiving mailings from Pacific Lutheran College, inviting him to consider attending the school after he had completed his service. He was puzzled by this. Growing up in Southern California, he had never expressed an interest in going to college, nor were his parents encouraging him to do so. What he learned later is that the college admissions office had been contacted by a supportive parishioner from his stateside church in Glendale, just north of Los Angeles. When the first Pacific Lutheran packet reached him in Korea, he had tossed it away. But when a second envelope arrived after he had returned to Glendale, he held on to it. By then he had begun asking himself what he was going to do with the rest of his life, and now the answer was literally in his lap. With a stipend to pay tuition and expenses, courtesy of the new GI Bill, he and a buddy decided they would go off to college in the Northwest.

Gloria arrived in Tacoma from a different direction. After graduating from high school in the small, western Minnesota town of Barrett, she had moved with one of her hometown girlfriends to Portland, Oregon. An uncle lived in Tacoma, 140 miles to the north, where he divided his time between a dental practice and teaching biology at Pacific Lutheran. When Gloria and her girlfriend made a weekend visit to Tacoma, her uncle simply asked if the two would like to try college for a while. They decided they would. Gloria enrolled at the college, moved in with her aunt and uncle, and began fitting her work as a part-time dental assistant around her class schedule.

The two met shortly before Christmas in 1948, because Frank needed a dental visit. And while Gloria was keeping her eyes open for "a clean-cut fellow, with good teeth," it was also in her criteria that he had to be smart. She was wary at first, given her and her girlfriend's shared observation that while veterans made decent football players, they didn't always pan out to be good students. But Frank did. Considering that both Gloria and Frank were being guided toward Pacific Lutheran by other church members, it was no small coincidence that they were both Lutherans. Yet they also shared an interest in science. Less than a year after they had met in her uncle's dental office, the two decided to marry. In their wedding photo, Gloria's eyes flash above a playful smile, and Frank, lean and square-jawed, smiling broadly, tips gracefully at the hips to make just enough room between them for their intertwined hands.

As a new couple, they didn't start with much. The first apartment they shared was in Parkland, an unincorporated suburb just south of Tacoma where the college (which became Pacific Lutheran University in 1960) is located. Before they made it their home, the small structure had been a chicken coop. Three decades later, when Margie was studying at PLU, one of her friends would take up residence in the same tiny dwelling.

After graduating, Frank was frustrated at being unable to find a teaching position, but his studies in biology qualified him for an opening at nearby Fort Lewis. He reluctantly took a job in pest control at the sprawling 250,000-acre Army base. After a couple of years suppressing skunks, bats, rats, and mosquitoes, he finally got his opportunity. A neighbor put him in touch with a school principal in the small, historic town of Steilacoom (in 1854 it became the first incorporated town in what was then Washington Territory), tucked along the water in western Pierce County, midway between Tacoma and the state capital of Olympia. He would start his teaching career as the Steilacoom school's first full-time sixth-grade teacher. The opportunity to join the faculty at University Place and buy a house adjacent to the growing campus would come two years later.

By the time Margie was born in 1964, the Witts, like so many other baby-boom families, were upwardly middle class and living out their American dream. A centerpiece of that dream, for Frank and Gloria, was to ensure they could afford to provide for a college education for each of their children. For that reason, the births of the Witt children were spaced years apart, with Virginia, the first, arriving in 1954, then Christopher in 1958, and finally Margie, six years later.

The military that had given Frank his opportunity to go to college was a fixture on the Pierce County landscape and a major economic pillar, primarily in the form of Fort Lewis and adjacent McChord Air Force Base. (In early 2010 the fort and base were merged into a mega-installation and the name changed to Joint Base Lewis-McChord.) Along with Tacoma's mill-town roots and bustling seaport, the long-standing military presence in the area is part of what gives the "City of Destiny" its blue-collar fabric relative to upscale Seattle, some thirty miles to the north along the burgeoning Interstate 5 corridor. For the Witts, in particular, the area had another attractive feature, one tied to Frank and Gloria's passions for science and education. Nature.

From University Place and other vantage points with open views to the west, you can't help but notice the blue-green waterscape of southern Puget Sound, the montage of densely forested islands, and the jagged, snow-covered peaks of the Olympic Mountains beyond. As a teacher of marine biology and oceanography, Frank Witt made use of the sound's tide pools as living laboratories, both for his students and his three children.

One of Margie's indelible memories is of Frank carefully lifting shoreline rocks, identifying the barnacles, limpets, sea urchins, and mussels that clung to them, and then gently placing some of the detachable specimens into her hands. Limpets were her favorites, but as a young girl she also became expert at identifying the different varieties of starfish that she would lift from the tide pools with her own hands. Another of her favorites was the moon snail, an enormous (five inches in diameter), clam-eating marine gastropod that, with the precision of a lathe, secretes a large gasket-like ring around its eggs. The beaches and sandbars of Puget Sound are also home to the world's largest burrowing clam, the Pacific geoduck (pronounced "gooey duck"). For a while when Margie was young, the Witts owned property on the southwesternmost bay in Puget Sound, at Shelton, Washington, in an area where geoducks thrive. The clams weigh upward of two pounds and have necks that can extend to three feet in length. At the top of the neck is a siphon that squirts water. When clam diggers spot the squirting siphon, that is the signal to start shoveling, furiously, in order to get down to the rapidly burrowing clam. Among her memories from the sandbars at Shelton are those of her brother Chris holding her upside down by her little green boots as she quickly excavated with her hands to try to capture the elusive giant clams.

But what most fully captured Margie's imagination, and framed her earliest memories, is a sight you can't possibly miss from Tacoma on days when the weather is clear: Mount Rainier. Even with the aid of photography, it is hard to convey how Mount Rainier dominates an open eastern sky from Tacoma. Its summit is only forty miles from the city's sea-level docks, and in that relatively short distance, the terrain surges upward over fourteen thousand feet. Rainier is a massive upwelling of glacier-cloaked rock, shaped more like an upraised fist than the classic, tapered cinder cones characterized by Japan's Mount Fuji, or Mount Hood in northern Oregon.

In 1967, when Margie was three, Frank Witt's regular summer job was as a ranger and naturalist at Mount Rainier National Park. Gloria and the children would often go with him and enjoy the privilege of exploring one of America's great natural environments during the time of year when it is brimming with color and wildlife. One of Margie's early memories is running around on the stage at the Paradise Inn while her father narrated slide shows for visitors to the lodge. To try to quell her restlessness, Frank gave her a small metal counter that she could use to count the cars of the tourists.

Paradise is on the mountain's southern flank and is usually open by late spring, as the winter snowpack subsides. By midsummer, Margie's favorite Rainier destination would become accessible. This was at Sunrise, at sixty-four hundred feet on the northeast side of the mountain. From the rangers' quarters at Sunrise she would hike east toward the pinnacles of Antler Peak, and to the west lies Shadow Lake, a destination that remains her favorite place not just on the mountain, but on the planet. By the time she was five years old, she thought of Mount Rainier as "my mountain." She remembers drinking glacial meltwater from the streams, and experiencing the wonder of finding frogs' eggs tucked under the sand shelves that form along the shoreline at Shadow Lake. She can still recite the names of the high-country wildflowers, and remembers even the hollow-thumping sound of hiking boots landing on the packed glacial dust of the mountain's upper trails.

Those memories, from "her" mountain, are intertwined with the most formative experiences she shared with her parents. When she was too young to go on the longer hikes with her siblings, her mom taught her a game based on the Norwegian fairy tale "Three Billy Goats Gruff," in which a trio of goats try to outsmart a hungry troll so they can get across a bridge to a greener pasture. Gloria would be her daughter's playmate, but she would also pack a small telescope in Margie's backpack and, like Frank, spend hours with her younger daughter exploring and teaching her about the flora and fauna of the alpine wilderness. On their car trips to Rainier and other destinations, Frank and Gloria would playfully challenge each other's knowledge of the scientific names of plants.

What her parents began to notice, with no small amount of pride and satisfaction, is how happy, well adjusted, and outgoing their younger daughter seemed. Others noticed too, among them Laura Maes, whom Margie befriended almost immediately when Laura joined Margie's first-grade class at Sunset Elementary School in University Place in the fall of 1970. As with Karyn, six years later, Laura was new to University Place and feeling uneasy about how she was going to fit in. But there to greet her, and to shepherd her in the hallways and the playground, was the five-and-a-half-year-old Margie Witt.

"I remember Margie was really, really strong," Laura says. "And if you had Margie on your team you were all set. She was going to look after the people she was close to."

The other feature about Margie, Laura recalls, is that she was just flat-out funny, even as a first grader.

Jill Spangler and Margie began playing soccer together on a club team when the two of them were fourth graders. They attended different elementary schools, but Jill's family moved into the University Place district in time for her to start seventh grade at Curtis. The Spanglers were going through a difficult period as a family that year, and Jill would often come to school feeling distressed and tense. It was the kind of stress that Margie would notice, and would use her zany sense of humor to alleviate.

"I have a friend who's like a female Robin Williams," Jill says. "She taught me how to lighten up."

Days in the life of young Margie Witt included the summer day in the mid-1970s when she and Laura Maes visited Laura's grandfather at his cabin on the Bumping River, a whitewater stream east of Mount Rainier. With them was Laura's friend Marie. In need of adventure, the three girls in their early teens asked if they could take an inflatable, canvas-bottomed raft to float down a stretch of the river near the cabin. In the pre-launch discussion they were advised the raft had a tendency to collect standing water in the bottom. This deterred them not at all.

A few minutes after they shoved off, though, the raft flipped over, sending the three girls (none wearing a lifejacket) shrieking and tumbling into the freezing, roiling water. The raft landed on top of Laura, trapping her beneath it. Marie, unaware of this, quickly clambered to get herself on top of the upside-down vessel. Swimming alongside, Margie saw what was happening. She reacted quickly by flipping the overturned raft to get it off Laura. That worked well enough to free Laura, but in the process Marie was abruptly tossed back into the icy water. It would all be funnier later. The three then drifted down the river, clinging to the inflatable parts of the raft, until they found a spot where they could pull themselves out of the stream. They headed back to the cabin on foot, holding the tattered raft above their heads. As Laura's grandfather walked out to meet them, Laura remembers dreading that she would be in trouble on account of the new gaping holes in the raft. But then Margie came to the rescue again, this time with cheerful sarcasm.

"Grandpa," Margie said, still holding up the raft with the shredded canvas bottom hanging off of it, "I think we solved the drainage problem."

If she could be difficult, she would be most difficult when she was sticking up for a friend, or a principle. Her first act of rebellion that anyone can remember came in first grade. Gloria was puzzled to get a phone call from the principal asking her to come by Margie's classroom because her daughter was being given "an afternoon assignment." More precisely, she was being disciplined for being stubborn. As the teacher explained to Gloria in the hallway outside the classroom, the day's writing assignment had been for the students to answer the question "What does your father do?" Margie decided that inasmuch as her parents did the same work—as teachers—she would write about both of them, and use the word "they" instead of "he" in what she was writing. When the teacher objected and asked her to redo the assignment, to write only about her father, Margie refused, insisting that to do so would be unfair to her mother.

In her willfulness to buck the assignment, Margie—even as a six-year-old—was insisting upon the same respect for her mother that her father had always shown for the woman he had married. It was a trait all the Witt children absorbed and which, for each of them, became part of their very close, enduring connections with their parents.

As the firstborn, Margie's sister Virginia refers to herself, humorously, as "the experiment" but bubbles with memories about how deeply engaged her parents were in the lives of all the Witt children and the "magical" childhood she enjoyed as a result.

"My parents are opposites," she says. "My dad I would call the rock; everything is very even-keeled, he doesn't get too excited, he doesn't have down periods. Always steady and very patient, he takes whatever time is needed to get it just right. My mom, on the other hand, is pretty much like me, very excitable, up and down, like a roller coaster. So the two of them are a great balance. We grew up with one who was always super high energy, and the other one who was super steady. But as parents they always, *always* worked together. They were a team. It was never, 'go see Dad because he'll say yes,' or 'go see Mom because she'll say yes.' You knew they were going to talk together about it, and you knew that the decision would be the same."

For their devotion, the two demanded effort in return, especially when it came to schoolwork and grades.

"To get a C in our family was a very big deal," Margie's brother Chris recalls. "You know, you just didn't do that."

Adds Virginia: "They wouldn't have expected anything of us than what they expected of themselves. We were taught manners. We were taught to be gracious and thankful, and there was an expectation that you do the best you can. It was not an expectation of 'be perfect.' It was 'we expect you to do the best that you can; we expect honesty and integrity.' And even though those words weren't probably used, they *were* that. They emulated that."

Still, there were soft coils of irony. In Margie's experience, her mother made no apologies for being a stoic Norwegian when it came to avoiding displays of emotion. And yet she was the parent who, through her willingness to be silly and make fun of herself, inspired her daughter's crackling sense of humor. Frank took himself very seriously as a father and a teacher. Yet beneath these projections of authority was a tender soul who, as he got older, increasingly wore his heart on his sleeve and could easily find himself wiping away tears at the movie theater.

Growing up with her father, Margie says, was like growing up with Euell Gibbons, the naturalist and wild-food advocate who became a popular national television guest during the 1970s. Among Frank's lessons was about how easy it is to find edible plants, even on short hikes into the back lots and greenbelts surrounding their neighborhood at University Place and, later, at nearby Fox Island. Margie was all in for these outings and more. When she and her close friend Jill Spangler weren't playing sports together, they loved to explore the ravines that tumble down from University Place to the railroad tracks skirting the edge of Puget Sound near Chambers Bay. The two would wear waders and carry flashlights and nets for catching frogs and other critters. They would gather blackberries, climb along fallen trees over the creeks, and then come home with tattered sweatshirts and mud on their sneakers. "Our ideas of fun, and her siblings' and my siblings' ideas of fun," Jill recalls, "were two different things."

Virginia enjoyed forays into the same ravines, but by the time Margie was seven, Virginia was a seventeen-year-old fashion model, already being paid through a talent agency to pose in clothing ads for Nordstrom and Peoples department stores. One of the memories that still causes them to laugh aloud whenever it comes up is of Margie coming home after one of her adventures, her clothes dirty and her hair smelling like grass, and pleading to climb in bed and snuggle with her older sister. But Virginia was adamant that nothing like this would happen until after a bath and a change of clothes.

As the years unfolded, Margie would gather a deeper appreciation for her father's gentler side, but his reputation in her youth was of a no-nonsense teacher who was duly feared by boys who sought to date her. The intensity and vigilance of Frank and Gloria's parenting was mostly for the good, in the ways it sustained and galvanized their bond with their daughter. Yet the one thing that neither Margie nor Gloria nor Frank knew at the time is that Margie simply couldn't grow up to be the person her parents expected her to become. She was different, and different in a way that neither she, nor they, were at all prepared to deal with.

By 1979—the spring of their ninth-grade year—Karyn Ingebritsen knew Margie Witt was gay. And though it was never directly discussed, Karyn thought her parents—who so warmly welcomed Margie into their home—also knew. If it was not obvious, even to Karyn, it was because Margie had several friends of both genders. At least one of her closest companions was a young man, a fellow band member, with whom Margie hung out and enjoyed going to parties. But for Karyn it came into focus during their ninth-grade year. Even though Margie was attractive to young men, and dated them, Karyn says she never got the sense that her close friend was gushing with romantic emotions toward any of them. What she did notice, when a close same-gender relationship ended abruptly, is that Margie seemed brokenhearted. She remembers the two of them being together in the backseat of a car being driven by her father, Pastor Ingebritsen, when a break-up song came on the car radio. Margie began to sob, Karyn recalls, and "to me that just kind of cemented it, that she was attracted, and not just in a friendship way."

Still, even as Karyn correctly surmised that her good friend was gay, Margie was unsure. Even as she began to question her sexuality, she did not stop dating young men and still assumed that she would eventually fall in love and marry someone of the opposite sex. Because that's what girls did.

As for her emerging feelings of attraction to certain young women, it was not—especially not at first—something she was experiencing as a good thing. During that tumultuous ninth-grade year, she happened one day to see a television program involving lesbianism, and she watched long enough to realize that the subject matter was about homosexuality in women.

"That's when I discovered what a lesbian was," she recalls. "And I thought I might be one."

The implications of that possibility were overwhelming, if not unthinkable. Starting with her relationship to her parents, she had organized her life with a strong desire to please those who mattered most to her. It was actually a trait that Margie and Jill Spangler—her longtime teammate and adventure companion—were proud to share and would joke about later in life.

"I mean, we ran with a pretty sedate group of kids," Jill says. "There was no way we were going to disappoint our parents, and maybe that's just our personalities."

Margie just knew that disclosing that she was gay, or even acknowledging that she was questioning her sexuality, would be painful and disruptive, to say the least. Her first experience with heartbreak grew out of a strong emotional connection, not a sexual liaison. This painful chapter, along with her emerging awareness that she was experiencing romantic feelings for women rather than for men, led her into a deep depression. It was a turn that Karyn couldn't help but notice as her normally gregarious and self-confident friend began to struggle with her emotions. There was only so much Karyn could do, but one of those things was to get together with another mutual friend and decide, out of their concern for her, that May 4, 1979, would be "How Is Margie?" Day, or HIM Day, for short. National HIM Day, they called it. And Karyn has kept it on her calendar ever since, reminding Margie every May 4 of the importance of National HIM Day.

In the midst of that tumultuous ninth-grade year, a tragedy unfolded involving another classmate and friend of Karyn and Margie's. His name was David.

Margie and David first met when the two shared a homeroom in seventh grade at Curtis. David was of average height for his age, of olive complexion, with dark bangs clipped straight across his forehead, above a big smile. And he enjoyed poking fun at Margie's tomboy qualities, once teasing her with a "that means you" taunt when their homeroom teacher assigned a boys-only task. Two years later, David told his parents what some of his friends already suspected—that he was gay. The response from his parents was to evict him.

That night, David called the Ingebritsens from the Safeway grocery store down the street, and Karyn was the one to pick up the phone. It was midnight. When Karyn's father asked who was on the line, all Karyn needed to say was that it was David, and that he had been kicked out.

"Tell him we're on the way," her father replied, knowing exactly what had happened. After her father's pleas to David's parents failed to budge them, David spent the night with the Ingebritsens, then began moving from house to house, "couch surfing," as Karyn describes it. As word spread about David acknowledging his homosexuality and being alienated from his family, people took sides, at school and in the community. What Karyn and her parents saw and admired in Margie is how, even in her own distress, she emerged as one of David's fiercest protectors.

"Margie may be loyal to her friends, but she changed other people too," Karyn says, reflecting on that period in their lives. "She made a difference in my parents' lives."

Not long after the night that the Ingebritsens took David in, his disclosure led to another wrenching night. Karyn and Margie were Lutherans, but they had friends, including David, who were involved with a Presbyterian youth group, and occasionally Karyn and Margie would attend those events. Shortly after David came out, the group organized a gathering in the nearby town of Lacey to host a Christian writer and artist. From the start, even as the group gathered to do the ride sharing for the trip to Lacey, a dispute broke out as to whether David—having professed that he was a homosexual—should be welcomed and included in the outing. At the hall, in Lacey, with Margie in the audience, David had finally endured enough. Trembling and in tears, he fled the auditorium. Margie ran after him and was able to catch up with him outside, on a baseball diamond. He cried on her shoulder as she tried to console him.

The saga stretched on for years. Although there was at least a partial reconciliation, years later, with his family, the initial brunt of hostility David experienced caused him to leave his school and community and seek refuge in Seattle. He ultimately contracted and died from AIDS in 1988, a year after Margie joined the Air Force. To this day, it is difficult for either Margie or Karyn to talk, without choking up, about what they witnessed in David's alienation and the troubled path toward his early death.

David's story and the depth of Margie's concern at the way he was ostracized only deepened the growing sense of unease in the rich but complex relationship with her parents. In their parenting, Frank and Gloria had instilled the values of fairness and compassion for others, so they were proud to see how their youngest daughter was willing to stand up for her friends. At the same time, Margie's passionate concern and umbrage at the way David was ostracized for disclosing his homosexuality raised uncomfortable questions that the family wasn't willing to discuss openly. Was it okay to be gay? Why was Margie so concerned about David, and why did she so readily include in her circle of friends young people they at least suspected were gay? Was Margie gay? It was, to say the least, a strained conversation because of the conspicuous silences and fear built into it. The silence was awkward, and fear ran in both directions.

Nancy Mellor, a lifelong friend, first met Margie in junior high school. The two of them were standout softball players and continued as teammates through high school, Nancy as a pitcher and Margie as a shortstop. Their parents were on very friendly terms, in part because they were avid fans of their daughters' softball teams.

"There was a period of time when Margie and I were just inseparable. I was either at her house for the weekend, or she was at my house for the weekend," Nancy remembers. She still refers to Margie's parents as "Frank and Glo."

That changed abruptly when rumors of a romantic relationship between one of the team's young coaches, a woman, and Nancy began to make its way through the University Place grapevine. At the time, Margie was a junior at Curtis and Nancy a senior. By then Margie knew, from Nancy, that she was having a relationship with the assistant coach. When Nancy told her, Margie had responded by confiding that she was emotionally involved with a female classmate. Word of the relationship between Nancy and the assistant coach reached Margie's parents. Suddenly, Nancy was not only barred from coming over, but Gloria curtly informed Margie that she had to sever her friendship with Nancy.

Prior to becoming an adult, there was only one time when Margie pushed back against her mother. And this was it.

"If there's any time that Nancy needs my friendship," she told her mother, "it's now."

Still, to avoid further conflict with her parents, Margie kept her continuing contact with Nancy to herself. A line had been drawn, and she knew she couldn't change her parents' minds. If there had been any doubt in Margie's mind before, her mother's directive to avoid Nancy made clear just how explosive the issue would be, if she dared to try to confide in her parents about the questions she was continuing to struggle with about her own sexuality. So she didn't.

For Nancy Mellor, the rupture with the Witt family stung and added to the isolation she was already enduring. Losing Frank and Gloria felt, to her, like losing "my second parents." In retrospect, she thinks the assistant coach may have been a sexual predator. But when she sought out a counselor at the school to talk about the relationship and its consequences, she says he simply told her that everything was "okay" and ended the session. A decade later, as a social worker and HIV/AIDS educator, Nancy would go public about her homosexuality when she launched a project, called Oasis, tailored to the needs of gays and lesbians between the ages of fifteen and twenty-five. The success of the project inspired her to pursue what has become a rewarding career in counseling.

"Oasis was definitely fueled by the fact that I didn't have anybody to talk to when I was in high school," Nancy says. "None of us did."

As for Margie, her defiance of her mother's order to end her friendship with Nancy only complicated the confusion and sadness she was experiencing.

One of the qualities both parents proudly recognized in their daughter was her passion for fairness. Her first hero was Abraham Lincoln, so justice and fair play were topics that came up frequently, especially between Frank (who for years worked as a basketball referee) and Margie when the two were discussing sports.

But it extended well beyond sports, and Margie's interest in David's story and tragedy was at least a signal that she was concerned about fairness for gays and lesbians. It could be seen and interpreted in context with other signals, including another trait that Frank and Gloria admired in Margie: she made friends, easily, and many of those friendships had depth to them. It became clear to them, over time, that her friends included several young men and women who were gays and lesbians. Just why Margie was so concerned and upset about what was happening to David, and then to Nancy, were questions that would be left hanging for several years to come. And this, in turn, was characteristic of the evolving but unspoken dialogue between daughter and parents as the three of them circled warily around the most intimate dimension of Margie's full and true identity. One way to describe it would be "don't ask, don't tell."

Chapter 3

══════════

CROSSING
INTO THE BLUE,
PART I

One droplet in the rich broth of Margie Witt's most excellent childhood was a little game the Witt family played on frequent car trips that took them near the hangars at McChord Air Force Base. Margie was the youngest of the lot, and the contest was mostly for her sake. The object was to see who could be the first to spot a distinctive white-and-gray jetliner with a red cross on its tail.

The elusive aircraft was a modified DC-9, the length of three school buses, with twin engines at the rear. Equipped with a hydraulically oper-ated folding ramp and other adaptations to transport wounded soldiers, it was given a name—the C-9A Florence Nightingale—to commemorate the nineteenth-century social reformer who became the founder of modern nursing. Fewer than two dozen of the C-9As were built for the Air Force, and most were based at Scott Air Force Base in southern Illinois. But the distinctive planes would make regular visits to McChord to deliver and take on patients.

The wonder and intrigue of a flying hospital no doubt fueled Margie's dream, as a young girl, to become a flight nurse one day. Still, it was beyond the reach of her imagination to foresee that by the time she was thirty, she would have spent literally thousands of flight hours aboard C-9As.

Choosing a career would have been a lot easier had there been less to choose from.

As Laura Maes quickly noticed when the two were first graders on the playground, there wasn't a game involving a ball that Margie didn't want to join. As a girl, she wasn't allowed to play organized football, but that didn't stop her from trying on her brother Chris's football jerseys and slipping her feet into his cleats. Her love of sports fed her penchant for connecting with others, and she reveled in the experience of what it was to be part of a team. At Curtis High School she lettered in basketball, volleyball, softball, and tennis. At Pacific Lutheran University she played varsity softball and basketball. Athletics was the most direct way to quell her intrinsic restlessness. She craved physical activity and being outdoors. The idea of sitting inside at a desk for long periods was painful to contemplate. Her main ambition was to become a professional athlete. If she couldn't play, she wanted to coach.

Which isn't to say there weren't pulls in other directions. As the daughter of two teachers, she gave serious consideration to becoming a teacher. Maybe an English teacher who coached sports after school, she thought. Science was another natural direction, given how fully the field trips with her father and his students had captured her imagination.

It was mostly from her mother that Margie gathered inspiration to be a caregiver. Having grown up on a farm in Minnesota, Gloria naturally acquired a knack for self-sufficiency in dealing with minor medical problems, from treating cuts and bruises to weathering the flu. In mothering the Witt children, she always had a thermometer handy, with Phisohex and bandages for wounds, baking soda compresses for stings, alum for mouth sores, and tannic acid from teas to apply to nasty cases of sunburn. In emulating Gloria's caregiving, Margie not only wrapped and taped her own real and imagined injuries, but she also made a patient of Victor, the Witts' Lhasa apso, whom she frequently wrapped in unnecessary bandages.

As with her older siblings, there was no question that she would be going to college. Her electives at Curtis High School were geared to preparing and qualifying her for a collegiate nursing track. There was, to be sure, a rich family history with PLU, and the school's campus in Parkland is only eight miles east of where she had gone to high school. Still, she might have gone elsewhere for college were it not for PLU's nationally recognized school of nursing; but as planned, she breezed onto the campus as an eighteen-year-old freshman in the fall of 1982.

Within days of arriving in Parkland, she was walking with a group of students from her new dormitory to the campus chapel when a resident assistant came up beside her, casually commented on how comfortably she seemed to be adjusting, and asked for a small favor. One of other new students in the group was not doing so well, and would she mind connecting with her?

The struggling freshman was Carla Savalli. An only child of Italian immigrant parents who had settled in Spokane, Carla had applied to PLU after visiting the stately, verdant campus as part of a high school debate competition. But now she was deeply homesick. Margie caught up to her at the chapel, sat next to her, and tossed out a few jokes to initiate a conversation.

The conversations continued, even into the stairwells of Stuen Hall, their three-story residence on the northern side of a narrow greenbelt that meanders through the PLU campus. Both had just moved into rooms on the top floor at Stuen, but neither was bonding well with her roommate. While goofiness may not be a universally attractive quality, it is to Witt and Savalli. Shortly after they had met, the two were in a small group of new students visiting the resident assistant's room. The RA was showing how the bleakness of the unfurnished rooms could be transformed when Carla suddenly gushed, "Oh! It's so warming!" Margie erupted in laughter and henceforth couldn't resist reenacting the exclamation to needle her new friend.

Their friendship grew, and beginning the second semester of their freshman year, the two became roommates on the upper floor at Stuen. Margie was a little nervous at first because the two were so different and still just getting to know each other. What brought them together more than anything was the electricity of their humor. To Margie's delight, she discovered Carla was even funnier than she first realized. The combustions of laughter assuaged their differences and opened up a deep and enduring friendship.

"She saw part of her role in my life to make things easier, to teach me things, and to kind of look after me, in a sense, like a big sister," Carla explains. "And my role was to be sort of a quasi-parent to get her where she needed to go, to deflect and field her parents' phone calls."

It was a peculiar pairing: the sharp-witted and tightly strung young journalism student and the easygoing, sleep-loving athlete with her home-field advantages and array of seemingly natural talents. As an unapologetic jock, Margie typically wore sweatpants and a hooded sweatshirt over a T-shirt to her classes, often not even bothering to tie the laces on her high-top Adidas basketball shoes. Carla unfailingly wore skirts, blouses, and suit jackets. Her drive and talents led her to be named editor of the *Mooring Mast*, the PLU student newspaper. Carla rose at 6 a.m. to shower and prepare for her classes, and when she got to class she would sit in the first row. Margie's objective was to get there in the nick of time, and she would invariably sit in the back.

The ease with which Margie seemed to succeed at everything was not lost on Carla, who saw herself having to work harder to excel. But her envy was leavened with comedy, like being present to witness Margie's daily battles with alarm clocks. She remembers watching her roommate lay her ensemble of casual clothes out on the floor at bedtime, so that she could race from sleep to her first class of the morning in the space of a few minutes.

As with so many of Margie's friends before her, Carla was warmly embraced by the Witt family. There were regular home visits to Frank and Gloria's for downtime and home-cooked meals. The visits offered a glimpse into the family environment that fed what Carla saw as Margie's "profound sense of fairness, and of right and wrong."

As Carla's homesickness evaporated, it was only a matter of time before the two began to impose their will against the conservative and somewhat cloistered PLU culture. Between the two of them, they had wide and diverse circles of friends and were regularly bending and breaking dorm rules at Stuen as they entertained groups of visitors. It was a good thing, Margie realized, to have older friends with money. One of them was a fellow Curtis High School alum who could arrange a whole case of Heineken in her large gym bag and lug it up three floors without rattling the bottles.

They were succeeding at PLU on their own terms and acquiring a touch of notoriety in the process. Privately, there were tensions in their close relationship simply because their personalities were so different. Moreover, they were both still exploring and trying to understand their respective sexual identities. Although the two have never been more than close friends, Carla says she "probably had a horrible crush" on her roommate in their first year living together.

In the winter of their junior year, an argument between the two spun loudly out of control, causing a split. Carla changed dormitories and then moved off campus for her senior year. Given the duo's notoriety and popularity, the end of their long run as roommates was no small news on campus. But the rift in their friendship lasted only a few weeks.

After graduating, Carla launched into her professional journalism career at the *Tacoma News Tribune*. Margie landed what she hoped would be her dream job as an operating room nurse at Tacoma General Hospital, just up the hill from Tacoma's Commencement Bay. For Margie, however, the dream job wasn't. Within a few weeks she was assigned to the 11 a.m. to 8 p.m. shift. It not only cramped her social life, but made it impossible for her to be involved as either a player or coach in organized sports. Even more discouraging was the joylessness of the work environment. It just seemed that most of her fellow nurses—many having done the same jobs for decades—were unhappy, constantly griping about their work lives. She began to have the depressing thought that if she didn't change course, she would die prematurely in the same hospital in which she was born.

The Air Force was Plan B. Given her childhood dream of taking flight as a nurse in an airborne hospital, it likely would have been her first choice, were it not for one closely held fear. She didn't like being yelled at. She dreaded a basic-training experience in which she foresaw face-to-face humiliations as part of the rite of passage. At the same time, though, there were two important women in her life pulling her toward a military career.

One was Kim Krumm, a gifted scholar and student athletic trainer whom Margie met and befriended during her freshman year at PLU, when Kim was a senior. Kim was a leader in the Reserve Officer Training Corps program that PLU shared with the University of Puget Sound. She encouraged Margie to explore the Air Force as a career option and was able to persuade her to attend a formal dinner honoring ROTC graduates. From the Air Force recruiting materials Kim had shared with her, Margie conspicuously tore out two pages, one with a photo of an operating room nurse, the other of a flight nurse.

The final push came from her childhood adventure partner Jill Spangler. Jill had done so well in so many things that she had earned an appointment to the U.S. Military Academy. The two stayed in close touch, and in the spring of 1986 Margie accompanied Jill's parents on a weeklong trip to the East Coast, highlighted by Jill's West Point graduation ceremony. It was only a few months afterward—with Margie languishing in her new job at Tacoma General—that Jill implored her to take what the young Army officer knew would be a transformative step.

"Marg, they would love you," Jill insisted during one of their phone calls. "And you would love them. You don't even have to ask people to follow you, and they follow you."

Accompanied by her parents, Margie would make it official at an Air Force recruiting office near the Tacoma Mall. The timing was just right. To enter the Air Force as an operating room nurse and commissioned officer she needed a state nursing license and six months' experience. As of March 1987, she had secured both.

Carla found herself caught off guard by the news and surprised by Margie's decision.

"I thought, 'Oh my God that's just so big, that's just a huge step,'" Carla recalls.

In Carla-like fashion she was deeply concerned about her ex-roommate's future, while simultaneously processing it with unspoken sarcasm, thinking "Somebody's going to have to stand there and blow reveille right into your ear, or you're going to sleep right through it."

The more Carla thought about it, though, the more the decision began to make sense. She had noticed Margie's admiration for Kim Krumm's leadership in ROTC, and also recognized that Margie's strong desire for independence was balanced with a desire for "a certain amount of structure."

The understanding Margie negotiated with her recruiters—after she learned she couldn't start with an overseas assignment—is that her initial duty station would be somewhere in California. First, though, she would have to fly to Texas. As a medically certified, direct commission officer, she was required to report to Sheppard Air Force Base, where the Air Force indoctrinates its medical officers.

Sheppard is in Wichita Falls, Texas, a small city in the heart of tornado alley. The last leg of her trip, in early spring of 1987, was in a small plane delivering her and a few other new recruits. Pounded by violent, thermal updrafts, the eleven-seat aircraft bucked wildly in the sky above the southern plains. It was as terrifying a flight as she would experience in her entire Air Force career.

It was less harrowing on the ground, though no less memorable. Sheppard is among America's older air bases, and the quarters she shared were in one of the vintage billeting structures. She was jarred awake late one night by a piercing scream. The instant she flipped on the lights she could see a torrent of rainwater pouring through the ceiling directly onto her roommate's bed.

During the day, the orientation included forced marches, drills, and inspections. She had just turned twenty-three, and at least the front of her hairdo bore a resemblance to that of Mike Score, the flamboyantly styled blond vocalist for the English synth-pop band Flock of Seagulls. Her bangs could easily reach to her nose. She tried hair spray to hold them out of her eyes for inspection, but the spray was no match for the unrelenting wind. Standing at attention, her arms forced to her sides, she drew stares and muffled laughter as she tried to use her breath to blow the sheaf of blond hair back into place.

After a couple of weeks at Sheppard, she flew home. This time she packed up for good, heading for Castle Air Force Base in the heart of California's Central Valley. Margie drove, and Carla rode with her as far south as Sacramento before catching a flight back to Tacoma. Moments after Carla's plane became airborne, Margie felt a bolt of panic as she realized she had given Carla her wallet for safekeeping. There was no way she was going to get on the base at Castle without her ID. She had to have Carla paged at the Sea-Tac airport, whereupon Carla quickly arranged to have the wallet flown back to Sacramento on the next available flight.

Castle wasn't exactly what Margie had in mind when she had requested California. She had hoped for a posting more like Travis Air Force Base, just a few miles northeast of San Francisco, or March Air Force Base near Los Angeles, close to where her sister lived. Castle—which closed in 1995—was five miles northwest of Merced, an island of concrete and commerce in a vast, green checkerboard of farm fields. The resident airmen (and women) often referred to it as a "two-hour-town" because of the time it takes to drive to Sacramento, the Bay Area, or Yosemite. She would be an operating room nurse at the base hospital, trying to navigate a new career, a new environment, and a complicated personal life that, among other things, required discretion and secrecy about her sexuality.

As a college freshman, Margie had been sure enough about her preference for women that she confided in Carla about it even before the two became roommates. And, still, as a college senior she had not completely discarded the possibility that she would form a lasting romantic partnership with a man. On her trip back east to attend Jill Spangler's graduation at West Point, she was introduced both to Jill's future husband, Chris, and to a former roommate of Chris's—named Chuck. Chuck was a well-chiseled cadet, handsome and witty. They quickly hit it off.

"I wanted to fall in love with him," she remembers. "He was my knight in shining armor."

And, still, the attraction that a romance requires wasn't there. Her effort to bond with Chuck only reaffirmed that she couldn't fully embrace an intimate relationship with a man, even if he were a knight. The brief experience would finally settle what she had suspected about herself since she was fifteen—that she was a lesbian. Two years later, when Jill and Chris decided to get married, Jill called Margie with the news and included a very touching request. By then, Jill and Chris were both in Germany, serving at different posts. They had chosen to get married in Switzerland but to hold a second ceremony back in Tacoma, where they could be joined before family and friends. Jill's list for the ceremony was very short, and she asked Margie, who was by then stationed at Castle, to be her maid of honor.

Margie accepted without hesitation. But two weeks before the ceremony she had some news of her own to share. Shortly after arriving at Castle, Margie had been invited by a longtime male friend of Carla's—whom Margie had dated in college—to attend a gay pride celebration in San Francisco. She eagerly accepted, and as the festivities led her to a woman's club for a late-night celebration, she met "J," a fun-loving mortician, and began a long-distance relationship with her. It was Margie's first romance since college; and it just seemed safer, to avoid suspicion, to date someone who lived far from the base.

"She calls me and says, 'Hey, I really think I need to tell you something,'" Jill recalls. "I said, 'Okay,' but I'm thinking 'Please don't tell me you can't be in my wedding, I only have two people!' And she said, 'I just wanted to let you know that I'm gay.'"

"So, were you expecting me to tell you not to come?" Jill replied. "Because I'm not going to do that."

On Jill's end, it was an awkward phone call. Yes, it was big news, and yes, as she told Margie, it would take a little time for her to get her head around it. But what mattered much more to Jill was Margie's concern that it *could* matter, that she would even pause to think she might be any less welcome by Jill and her family because she was gay. The deep truth was that the Spanglers had long considered Margie Witt a beloved part of their family. At Jill's stateside wedding in early June of 1988, Margie couldn't have been happier, or more warmly received.

Chapter 4

━━━━━━━━━━━

CROSSING
INTO THE BLUE,
PART II

That Margie could be as honest with the U.S. Air Force as she was with her old friend Jill Spangler was out of the question.

At the time she walked into the recruiting station in a small, inauspicious brick building near the Tacoma Mall in south Tacoma, the general U.S. military practice, dating back more than two centuries, was to purge known homosexuals. This was true even though the contributions of gay men and women to the armed services were well documented and, in large measure, quietly appreciated. Likewise, the premise that homosexual service members are inherently a threat to national security had also been debunked in research commissioned by the military. Although the research had been suppressed, the deep contradictions and absurdities of the expulsion policy were roundly exposed by Randy Shilts in his journalistic tour de force, *Conduct Unbecoming: Gays and Lesbians in the U.S. Military.*

When Second Lieutenant Margaret Witt began her Air Force nursing career assignment at Castle AFB, the military-wide policy had only recently (1981) been standardized. Department of Defense Directive 1332.14 deemed that service members even attempting to engage in a "homosexual act" should—if discovered—be subject to a "mandatory discharge." The policy was not uniformly enforced, in large part because countless known or suspected gay service members were valued by their commanders. Still, there had been approximately one hundred thousand military discharges for homosexuality since the Second World War.

Margie was by no means ignorant of the policy. Neither was it her primary focus. At her own pace and in her own way she was confident she could pursue her Air Force career goals and also find the space and opportunities to have the sexual and romantic companionship she desired. And in that way, she was pretty much your ordinarily closeted gay American in uniform, circa 1987.

Which is not to say there was anything ordinary about her experience adjusting to the Air Force. Just because she was a woman attracted to other women didn't change the fact that she was attractive to men. Her first clue as to how that might play out came almost immediately. Literally within hours after her first visit to the Tacoma recruiting station, she received a phone call. It was a male voice and not a sober one, over the unmistakable sounds of a bar. It was a quarter past midnight. He told her his name, said he had met her at the recruiting office, and wanted to know if she would like to come out for a drink. Quickly realizing he had lifted her phone number off the recruiting forms he had given her to fill out, she was angry.

"*No*, I won't come out and have a drink with you. And don't ever call here again."

The next morning, still shaken, she reported him to the Air Force. A few days later she received a phone call from a man identifying himself as an Air Force judge advocate general (JAG). He asked her to visit him at McChord Air Force Base, not far from the recruiting office. During the interview, the JAG officer told her it was "pretty cut and dried, there's not much I can do to defend this guy." But it wasn't until the end of the interview that he squarely disclosed that he was actually the lawyer appointed to defend her midnight caller. She never learned whether or how the recruiter was disciplined. But neither did she let the creepy misconduct change her course, reasoning that she wouldn't let the actions of one bad apple deter her. A Seattle-based officer specializing in medical officers contacted her to finish the recruiting process and arrange the signing, which her parents attended.

A month later, there she was, alone, in a Motel 6–type temporary billeting room not far from the main runway at Castle Air Force Base. Castle was then home to B-52 bombers, KC-135 tankers, and a few fighter jets, whose engines roared well before the sun came up. There was no need for an alarm clock.

"I remember just sitting there in shock, thinking 'What have I done?'"

In that first year, her saving grace became the two women she worked most closely with, a fellow operating room nurse, and her superior in the operating room, a glamorous and well-traveled officer who, though married to a pilot stationed elsewhere, was more than content with her reputation as being available to other officers, including the generals who were known to send cars for her.

"She was like Hot Lips Hoolihan," Margie remembers, "only a lot more fun." And easy to work with.

That all changed when a new operating room supervisor, a captain who had been recently passed over for promotion to major, arrived at the Castle base hospital. Suddenly, she found herself in a hostile working environment. It extended even to off-hours, because her "on call" assignments—which limited her travel away from the base and required that she refrain from drinking alcohol—increased dramatically. She didn't understand the reason for the hostility. Feeling trapped and frustrated, she eventually sought mediation through the chain of command. During the mediation, the offending supervisor admitted that she reminded him of another young woman officer—at his previous post—who had brought a formal sexual harassment complaint against him. That complaint, he admitted, was why he had been passed over for promotion. Despite his candid explanation for the hostile work environment, the mediation didn't resolve anything.

Her work environment would get even worse. A new general surgeon arrived at the base hospital, and even though he was engaged to be married, he began to make overt sexual advances. When Margie made clear she wasn't interested, the surgeon quickly found ways to retaliate. One of the creepier forms of payback was that the surgeon would situate himself where he could scrub for surgery and watch through a window as she prepped male patients for adult circumcision procedures. The prep procedure invariably caused the patient to get an erection. As this occurred, the surgeon would look at her with a wry smile, to ensure she got the message that he was enjoying her discomfort.

Then came two of the most harrowing experiences of her life.

The first involved the Air Force's Office of Special Investigations.

Although Margie was still new to the Air Force, she already knew OSI agents were active, particularly at stateside Air Force facilities, in investigations to identify and purge gay service members. As Randy Shilts would shortly describe in his *Conduct Unbecoming*, when it came to gathering evidence against gay officers and enlisted personnel, OSI regularly employed highly coercive techniques, even though the Uniform Code of Military Justice forbids interrogation methods devised to pressure service members to incriminate themselves.

One of the things Margie learned she should avoid—in order to lessen the odds she would come under scrutiny as a possible lesbian—were base softball teams. But the OSI came calling anyway.

The strange episode began with a seemingly innocent encounter at the base officers' club, where Margie and other junior officers would gather after work. Among the men and women settling in around a table was a young man, in his late twenties or early thirties, whom she didn't recognize. He told her he was a physician's assistant doing research and mentioned that he had never seen her in the base hospital. He was in civilian clothes, and though he was wearing a wedding ring, he explained that he was no longer married, that his wife had died in a car accident.

The conversation led to one of those moments that lesbians in the military had good reason to dread. The mystery physician's assistant asked her out on a date. Despite being unsettled by his explanation for the wedding ring, Margie reluctantly accepted, mostly because she felt a need to avoid suspicion that she might be gay. He asked her to a movie. In the darkened theater he reached to put his arm around her and promptly spilled Coke all over her shirt and jeans.

"This is oh so not fun," she remembers thinking.

To try to shorten the evening, she had told him she needed to be back at her apartment at ten o'clock, to field a call from her mother. And this was true, because it was Gloria's habit to call after ten, as the long-distance rates dropped at that hour. When he had picked her up for the date, he had invited himself in far enough that Margie's instinct was, in her words, to worry about whether she had "de-dyked" her apartment well enough to hide any signals about her sexual orientation. When he brought her back, after the movie, he again tried to ease his way inside. At that moment, the phone rang. It was her mother, and just in time to provide Margie the excuse to separate, and so abruptly that she nearly closed the door on his hand.

It didn't end there, though. Shortly afterward, she received a note during a meeting at work, telling her to report to the operating room. When she arrived, there he was again, waiting, and asking her to go on another date.

That was too much. She blew up at him, telling him point blank she didn't know who he was and what he was up to. Her outburst drove him away.

Though not for long. A few days later, at the start of her morning shift, she noticed the hospital commander visiting her supervisor's office near the operating room. After the short meeting, her supervisor—the captain who admitted he resented Margie because she reminded him of another nurse who had accused him of sexual harassment—emerged and, in an unsettlingly cheerful manner, told her somebody wanted to meet her, that by order of the commander she should change into civilian clothes and promptly drive to the base exchange parking lot.

She didn't have civilian clothes with her, so she was still in uniform when she pulled into the parking lot shortly after sunrise. The base exchange was not even open yet, and she could feel her naive hope—that this would not be a bad experience—begin to slip away. A blue military sedan circled around the back of her car and parked next to hers.

The driver got out and approached. As he did, she recognized that his passenger was the man who had been pursuing her. She could feel her heart pounding as the driver approached her window.

"Lieutenant Witt?" the man said.

"Yeah," she replied.

"Would you come with us?" he asked.

"This is it," she remembers thinking to herself. "I'm done."

As requested, she got into the backseat, and the pair then displayed cards identifying themselves as OSI investigators. She was reeling inside, and decided to say as little as possible as the car left the parking lot, left the base, and headed to Fresno, seventy miles to the southeast. Once there, they stopped at a diner, and, over breakfast, the two OSI agents offered a story that they were following up on a past incident where a nurse-anesthetist had been arrested for stealing medication and asked if she had observed any suspicious drug activity at work or in socializing with others at the hospital.

"They said they wanted me to be their eyes and ears, basically," she recalls. "It was complete intimidation. It was their way of saying, 'We've got your number.'"

Their parting words to her, back in the parking lot at Castle, were to instruct her not to tell anyone of their presence on the base and to expect that they would be back in touch with her at a later date.

Why she was picked out for such an elaborate and ham-fisted ruse by OSI is a mystery. The waves of fear she experienced in the back of the car on the way to Fresno had been intense. As distressing as it was to think about losing her Air Force career, it was even more frightening to imagine how she would tell her parents.

"How am I going to explain this?" she thought.

To her great relief, she wouldn't have to. As quickly as the OSI came crashing into her life and splattering it with her worst fears, the fake physician's assistant and his partner disappeared. The anxiety remained, along with the same challenges of navigating a demanding and complicated life, not knowing if and when the investigators would return. The advances by the OSI officer posing as a physician's assistant only inflamed the question of whether and how she could resist sexual advances from male officers and enlisted men without feeding rumors, or charges, that she was gay. With annoying regularity, and sometimes with shocking directness, she was going to be hit upon. Sometimes her rebuffs were answered with barbs that could be perceived as a threat, such as the comment of a senior loadmaster who, after she deflated his advances, told her, "I hear you like girls."

The most menacing such incident occurred in 1988, the same year the OSI investigators essentially abducted her for the trip to Fresno. At the time, she had begun seeing a girlfriend who lived at an apartment complex in Merced. As the two would swim and lounge by the pool in the apartment compound's common area, they began to exchange greetings and conversation with a small group of young male officers who were also hanging out at the pool.

Air Force officers are not permitted to fraternize with enlisted men or women, but they can pursue relationships with other officers, as long as they are not in the same chain of command. So there was nothing untoward, per se, when one of the officers, a pilot, eventually invited Margie to his apartment for dinner, offering to initiate her to the delights of Cajun cuisine.

She had not wanted to go. Again, there was the dilemma of how to resist an unwelcome advance without provoking suspicions and muttered accusations about her sexual orientation and private life. The most efficient evasion was to lie, to make up a story about being involved with another guy. But as adept as she had become at guarding her privacy, it was not in her nature to lie, to anyone. As she told her girlfriend at the time, maybe accepting the one dinner date would be enough to quell the pilot's advances. Maybe he would then move on.

It was a harrowing mistake. As the dinner progressed it became increasingly clear he expected sex in exchange for preparing the meal. When she tried to make clear she wouldn't be hopping into bed with him, he physically tried to force himself upon her. Though she managed to resist him and avoid being raped, it was still a traumatic evening, made worse by the officer's anger at being rebuffed. In the days and weeks that followed, the officer and his buddies could be heard shouting homosexual slurs at them across the courtyard, so much so that she and her girlfriend complained to the apartment complex managers about the harassment.

As demoralizing and terrifying as these experiences were, a couple of things kept her going. The first was her determination not to be taken down by the harassment. The other was that she knew Castle was the stepping-stone to an assignment in Europe. She had plenty to keep her busy. In addition to her operating room duties, she was responsible for managing the hospital's sterile supplies, and was chosen to lead a program promoting healthy diets and lifestyles and health screenings for base personnel. To the extent she could get outside the shadow of the harassment she was experiencing, she found she enjoyed being an Air Force officer. She was promoted to first lieutenant in early 1989.

Her childhood friend Jill Spangler had always marveled at Margie's leadership traits. And as Jill had predicted, those qualities would be rewarded in the Air Force.

"She just has a much better way than I do of being able to stand on both sides, of enlisted and officership, and get people to form a unit to do things. She has that gift, and I saw that playing sports."

That gift, as it were, best explains how and why Margie was able to work through and around the harassment she experienced at Castle. It kept her going and fueled the day-to-day connections with people that have always enriched her life. But it was not without complications, and one of the most difficult challenges was learning how to interact with women in ways that were in line with fraternization rules and otherwise beyond suspicion.

One relationship, in particular, would have a deep and lasting effect. It was with a talented young enlisted woman whose name was Tammy, who played with Margie on the women's basketball team at Castle. They met as teammates and, as with other teammates, began to develop a friendship that flowed easily from their basketball camaraderie. But then, for Margie, things began to get too familiar. Tammy worked security at the base's gate. As Margie arrived at Castle on her way to work one day, a couple of other enlisted men who worked at the gate cheerfully handed her a large teddy bear, as a gift from Tammy. Another time, Tammy personally delivered a gift necklace.

For Margie, the nature and openness of Tammy's affection became "a little too obvious," to the point where "she was outing me, even though she never said anything."

Margie reacted by putting up a wall of emotional detachment, purposefully distancing herself. It was awkward. Tammy was funny and guileless, and a good person who made frequent trips to Fresno to take care of her ailing mother. It was on one of those trips, as she was heading down U.S. Highway 99 on what turned out to be her twenty-first birthday, that a drunk driver going the wrong way essentially obliterated the compact Isuzu sport vehicle Tammy was driving, killing her instantly.

Margie received the news from two enlisted women who arrived at her door to deliver it. Her shock was followed by a deep grief and waves of guilt about how she had so deliberately turned away from Tammy. It was at least as likely, she thought, that Tammy saw Margie as an important mentor and had been trying to more deeply connect on that level. Yet Margie's reaction was self-protective, to create distance in order to allay suspicions that the two were lovers. The guilt didn't rinse off easily. Tammy must have been wounded by Margie's sudden coldness toward her, and there was never going to be a chance to explain or resolve that. But what cut even more deeply was Margie's awareness that she had acted out of fear. She promised herself that wouldn't happen again.

"If they're going to come after me," she resolved, "they're going to come after me, and I'm not going to treat anybody any differently, or keep them away just because I think I may be a target."

Chapter 5

||||||||||||||||||

FLIGHTS OF THE
NIGHTINGALES

Gathered along a broad, north-reaching arc of the Rhine River, Wiesbaden, Germany, is home to a quarter million people and famous for its architecture and hot springs. As Margie would come to discover, the city's myriad charms reach back to antiquity. But, for her, Wiesbaden's main attraction in 1990 was that it was an ocean and more than five thousand miles away from Castle Air Force Base. Her long-awaited orders were to report to a regional medical center the Air Force had been operating in Wiesbaden since World War II.

Germany had been on her request list for two years by then. Given the grinding and degrading hostility she had been experiencing, she could have hardly been more relieved.

Before moving on to Europe, though, she would take flight in the opposite direction, to visit Japan. It would be her first trip outside the United States. As fate would have it, it would also offer an unexpected glimpse into her future.

After landing at Tokyo's Narita airport, she found herself sharing a shuttle bus with a group of reservists heading to Yakota Air Base. The reservists were from Tacoma and belonged to an aeromedical evacuation squadron, the same McChord-based unit Margie would join five years later. She had been invited to Yakota by an Air Force flight nurse she had befriended years earlier, when the two met during battlefield nursing training in Texas. Her friend had arranged an unusual orientation tour, allowing Margie to sit in on one of the C-9A Nightingales based at Yakota as the crew picked up and delivered patients along the length of Japan. Once on board, Margie noticed a woman in a flight suit working a preflight checklist from a clipboard. She looked familiar. It was Bethany Ryals, one of the McChord reservists and a former collegiate athlete against whom Margie had competed while she was at PLU. That chance encounter—a reunion between two collegiate athletes who didn't even know each other's names—became the seed of a close friendship.

The Japan trip was an illuminating and fascinating adventure—until Margie became sick with food poisoning. Her symptoms were so severe that arrangements were quickly made to send her home on a C-141 transport plane. It was an aeromedical flight, and, luckily, Bethany Ryals and the other McChord reservists were on board. Margie was so debilitated she could barely get to her feet, and Bethany tended to her throughout the long hours back across the Pacific.

By the time she could make her way to her parents' home in Gig Harbor, Margie had lost nearly twenty pounds. Worse, she had had an allergic reaction to the sulfa drugs used to treat the food poisoning and was covered head to toe with a rash. Still, she was able to keep her departure date for Germany the following week. This time, her traveling companion was Brandy, an unusually cooperative and charismatic cocker spaniel Margie had rescued years earlier while she was a student at PLU.

The reception in Wiesbaden was nothing like the plunge of loneliness that marked her arrival at Castle. She was warmly greeted by Marlys, an old family friend from Tacoma. Marlys was now a psychologist and a senior Department of Defense employee with a home in downtown Wiesbaden. Exhausted from the long trip—she had been grounded in Philadelphia for a day because of mechanical problems with the plane—Margie fell into a deep sleep. In her dreams, she experienced herself speaking in the German she had learned in high school. In the morning, her new supervisor called to press her into reporting for work. As Margie fumbled for words, Marlys snatched the phone from her. With an edge of authority in her otherwise breezy tone of voice, she explained that Lieutenant Witt had just arrived.

"We're going to the fest," Marlys announced, referring to the June street festival under way in downtown Wiesbaden. "Have you ever been to the fest?"

The lieutenant would report for work on Monday, Marlys proclaimed. Carry on.

Everything was better in Germany. Some of the friends she had made at Castle had transferred earlier to Wiesbaden and spoken up for her both as an officer and a teammate. Within hours of showing up she was being feted at the local military club—a merry surplus of Grolsch beer bottles being piled up in front of her—as Brandy (who was easy to sneak into bars and hotels because she didn't bark) nibbled at a plate of nachos and licked at a bowl of beer on the floor beneath a large table.

The Germans were also hospitable. When she learned how few of her young American compatriots had actually ventured into the city, Margie began organizing and leading them on excursions into and around Wiesbaden. One of the things she noticed among her peers at Wiesbaden was an esprit de corps that had largely been missing stateside—a heightened sense that because the officers and enlisted men and women were serving so far from home they were all the more dependent on one another.

Six weeks after Margie reported for duty at the Wiesbaden hospital, Iraqi leader Saddam Hussein's army stormed and occupied Kuwait, setting off the chain of events leading to Operation Desert Storm in early 1991. In late February, coalition forces under the command of U.S. general Norman Schwarzkopf invaded Kuwait and southern Iraq. The battles lasted only one hundred hours, but still resulted in hundreds of coalition casualties, many of whom were airlifted to Wiesbaden for surgery. In those years, Wiesbaden was at least as much in the news for treating noncombatants. Among the patients were hostages from the conflicts in Lebanon, including Terry Anderson, the chief Middle East correspondent for the Associated Press who was brought to the hospital in December 1991 after nearly seven years in captivity.

Her work in the Wiesbaden operating rooms was as rewarding as it was challenging. She was promoted to captain in April of 1991, and—still focusing on her career goal—she traveled to Brooks Air Force Base near San Antonio to receive several weeks of flight nurse training.

In the aftermath of Desert Storm, it was announced that the U.S. presence at the Wiesbaden hospital would be phased out. Margie was eager to stay in Germany, but to do so she would have to secure another assignment. She first looked at a possible transfer to an aeromedical evacuation unit stationed at Rhein-Main Air Base, just a few miles away in Frankfurt. But there were no openings for additional flight nurses at Rhein-Main. Her only route to a flight nurse position was to transfer to Scott Air Force Base in southern Illinois.

She hesitated. The experience at Castle was still haunting her, and she couldn't help but wonder if a new assignment to a stateside base in another rural area would be a step back to a sort of misery she never wanted to experience again. It helped to receive encouragement from Carol, a fellow operating room nurse who had served as a flight nurse before transferring to Wiesbaden.

"You're going to love it at Scott," Carol told Margie.

And that would come to be true. Although Air Force medical personnel are distributed throughout the globe, they are part of a relatively small and well-networked community. As had happened at Wiesbaden, there were already people serving at Scott who knew about Margie Witt and were eager to serve alongside her. Her reception there, in August of 1992, was as warm as she had received upon arriving in Germany two years earlier.

Scott Air Force Base was then the hub of the Air Force's aeromedical transport system for the entire United States, and its C-9As flew daily routes throughout North America. It wasn't unusual for crews to make eight stops in a day on routes to either coast, delivering and taking on new patients along the way. It was just the sort of intense work and close teamwork that Margie enjoyed. Part of what she found so satisfying was that she was now in a part of the Air Force that flew airplanes. She was airborne most days, accumulating over one thousand flight hours (the equivalent of two hundred transcontinental flights) during her four years.

Among the more memorable missions was one that took her and her crew to Edwards Air Force Base in California in late October 1993. Their patients would be arriving from outer space. They were astronauts aboard the space shuttle *Columbia*, which—after two weeks in orbit—would land at Edwards shortly after dawn on the first day of November. Because a main purpose of the mission had been to study the effects of weightlessness on space travelers, the orders for Margie's crew included keeping the returning astronauts off their feet. The astronauts would be transported from the *Columbia* on stretchers and then flown to the Johnson Space Center in Houston. Several family members of the astronauts were also on the flight from Edwards to Houston. Among the *Columbia* astronauts was Shannon Lucid, who already held the record for the most hours in space by any woman. Also boarding the flight, but on foot, was another NASA legend, Commander Robert "Hoot" Gibson, whose distinguished career as an elite aviator included his military service as a "top gun" Navy pilot. Gibson's wife, Dr. Margaret Rhea Seddon, was among the returning astronauts. As evacuation missions go, it was about the best flight imaginable, absorbing stories from astronauts and gathering autographs.

Five months later, Margie was preparing to lead an emergency mission to Chapel Hill, North Carolina, to transport a young woman who had been badly burned. A call came to the plane on the tarmac. Her mission had changed.

Eight hundred miles to the east of Scott, at Pope Air Force Base in Fayetteville, North Carolina, several hundred Army paratroopers from nearby Fort Bragg were going through pre-jump exercises and briefings. They had been gathered in an area near the flight line known as the Green Ramp. Shortly after two in the afternoon, an F-16 fighter jet had collided with the wing of a C-130 transport plane as both were on approach to land, forcing the two fighter pilots to eject. The C-130 would land safely, but after the two F-16 pilots bailed out, their pilotless jet crashed and ricocheted across the tarmac. The plane broke apart, and burning chunks of the aircraft slid into a parked C-141 Starlifter, rupturing its fuel tanks and igniting more than fifty thousand gallons of aviation fuel. A deadly fireball of burning fuel engulfed the Green Ramp and the paratroopers. Some of the troops were killed instantly from flying debris. Rounds of ammunition from the F-16's twenty-millimeter canon were triggered by the intense heat, creating all the conditions of a horrific battlefield. Worse, the flaming aviation fuel had a sticky quality to it that made it extremely difficult to remove from the uniforms and gear the troopers were wearing.

The runways at Pope were closed because of the fiery crash. But as the C-9A Nightingale arrived in the fading light and circled to land at Fayetteville Regional Airport, Margie could see the extent of the disaster from the air, including the remains of the C-141, half of which had been completely incinerated. Once on the ground, she and her crew rushed to the Fort Bragg hospital, where nearly a hundred burn victims had already been taken by helicopter and ambulance. They were struck by how few people they encountered, and how eerily quiet it was, until they went inside the hospital. The beds, including those in the hospital's recovery room, were filled with injured paratroopers, many of whom had suffered horrible burns. The halls were swarming with medical personnel who were tending to the badly injured paratroopers, and service personnel who were delivering supplies and sustenance to the caregivers.

A burn specialist had been dispatched from Brooke Army Medical Center in San Antonio, where the Army's specialized burn unit is located. Like Margie and her crew, the nurse from Brooke had originally been sent for the Chapel Hill patient, only to be diverted to the unfolding disaster at Pope. Aware of this, Margie began searching for the nurse from Brooke and, finding her, learned she and a respiratory technician had been making their way from floor to floor, trying to assess and adjust the care for as many of the severely burned soldiers as they could.

"What do you need us to do?" Margie asked. From there Margie and her team went to work, assisting with intubations, respiratory treatments, and other tasks while doing triage to evaluate which of the soldiers needed to be flown to San Antonio. The number of injured and the ghastly nature of the burns were nearly overwhelming. Severe burns cause dramatic swelling and other life-threatening side effects. Each of the soldiers to be transported required primary and backup respirators, and each had to be cloaked in bright silver thermal blankets to sustain body temperature.

As ambulances ferried the wounded to the airport, additional C-9A Nightingales arrived from Scott. There were three additional planes to transfer the worst of the burned paratroopers. Another plane arrived to retrieve Margie and her crew, because by now they had been working so long that Air Force rules required they be relieved. They could finish loading the patients onto the plane, but another crew from Scott would have to fly the patients to San Antonio. As Margie was finishing preparations for the first plane's departure and briefing the flight nurse who would replace her for the flight to Brooke, she heard a voice behind her. She turned to see a towering figure in a Ranger beret and a row of stars on his uniform.

"I need to see my troops," said Lieutenant General William M. Steele, the commander of the Eighty-Second Airborne Division. She stepped aside as General Steele quietly made his way down the length of the plane. The plane was still shrouded in predawn darkness and silence, except for the sound of the ventilators funneling oxygen into the lungs of the injured paratroopers on board.

All told, two dozen soldiers from the Eighty-Second's 504th and 505th parachute infantry regiments would die from their injuries. Yet, the Green

Ramp tragedy is also remembered for numerous accounts of heroism by soldiers and rescuers. Margie and her team would be among those who received Air Force commendation medals for their life-saving efforts.

In most ways Margie—ever since recovering from the food poisoning she had contracted in Japan—had gone from having the worst times of her life to the best. Becoming a flight nurse was a perfect fit in terms of the work she wanted to do. The flight experience was also a boost to her career in that it would expedite her promotion to major. If the good news was that she had found her niche, the bad news was in the sinking realization that it just wasn't going to last much longer. Her flight nurse designation was, in Air Force parlance, a special duty assignment. It was temporary. With her advancing experience and rank, it was inevitable that her next assignment would be on the ground, in a managerial position. A desk job in an office. Whereas most people might regard this as a perk of seniority, it was, for her, just the sort of sedentary occupation she had always wanted to avoid. If she couldn't prolong her assignment as a flight nurse, she at least wanted to be actively involved with patients.

One way she thought she could control her fate was to become a physical therapist. Yet the best path for this career shift was a narrow one. It was to stay on active duty in the Air Force but gain acceptance into an Army doctoral program that had been created in conjunction with Baylor University in Texas. There were four slots at Army-Baylor for active-duty Air Force personnel. This sounded promising. But then she learned that the Air Force openings had been cut in half, and the two remaining slots were to be exclusively reserved for Air Force Academy graduates. That closed her door to Army-Baylor. Her only remaining choice was to leave active duty, enroll in another graduate physical therapy program, and return to active duty once her degree was in hand. It would also make her already busy life at Scott even busier as she began taking classes on the weekend in order to qualify for a graduate school.

Which is not to say she would abandon her private life.

The intrusion of the OSI agents at Castle six years earlier was jarring and intimidating. But she hadn't let it stop her from pursuing relationships with other women. The Air Force asked quite a lot. She had more than proven to herself and her peers that she could deliver, even in white-knuckle situations like the one she and her crew had flown into at Pope. But she asked a lot of herself, as well, to keep an open heart beneath her uniform, to be present to her patients, her friends, and her partners.

Straight or gay, soldiers and nurses are not caricatures. Military service demands unifying conformity, sacrifice, and risks that include regularly putting one's life on the line. But it was never meant to sever individuals from the intimacies of the heart. Unless, of course, they were gay. Now a decorated and accomplished young officer, Margie Witt was by no means alone in finding that to be an unfair and unrealistic double standard.

By then, the military's own studies (the circulation of which had been tightly controlled) found there were a lot more gay men and lesbians serving in the services than officially acknowledged, and that a higher percentage gravitated toward medical services. Neither of these findings would have surprised Margie, because they squared with her own experience. But the most sensitive part of the suppressed research were the findings that—contrary to the presumption built into the gay expulsion policy—homosexuality was no detriment to the performance of military duties.

One story, in particular, caught her attention shortly after she transferred to Wiesbaden. She began reading about it in *Stars & Stripes*, the military newspaper. It involved Perry Watkins, a gay, African American staff sergeant. Watkins had been raised in Tacoma and was drafted into service there in 1968. He was serving at Fort Lewis—the large Army base adjacent to McChord AFB—when he filed a lawsuit against the Army in 1981.

For Margie, the Perry Watkins story would have drawn her interest simply because of the Tacoma connection. Better still, there were contradictions and elements of comedy in Watkins's case that deeply undermined the legitimacy of the military policy to remove homosexuals from the ranks. To begin with, Watkins was already openly gay at the time he was drafted. He had readily disclosed this truth on multiple occasions, starting when he was inducted at the age of nineteen. Eager to bolster its ranks during the Vietnam era (and suspicious of inductees claiming to be homosexual to escape service), the Army took him anyway. Watkins was then promoted up the ranks as he earned one laudatory performance review after another.

In 1975, while Watkins was serving in South Korea, his commanding officer reluctantly concluded, based on Army regulations, that he had no choice but to initiate discharge proceedings because of Watkins's openly acknowledged homosexuality. By then, Watkins, in his off-duty time, was performing as "Simone," a female impersonator—even at officers' and NCO clubs—and very obviously with the knowledge and approval of his superiors. Significantly, witnesses called before the discharge board by the prosecutor (including the captain who had felt compelled to turn Watkins in) spoke in glowing terms about the quality of his work and his acceptance by his fellow soldiers. The five-member discharge board unanimously voted to retain him.

Still, the issue wouldn't go away. The further Watkins advanced in the Army, the more trip wires he faced, particularly in getting security clearances. After reaching the rank of staff sergeant (and after being allowed to reenlist for the third time), Watkins was told his security clearance was being revoked—again because he was admittedly gay. The Army issued a new regulation in 1981 that removed any ambiguity or exceptions and required all homosexuals to be expelled. Once again, and despite flawless performance ratings, Watkins was sent before a discharge board. This time, with the new regulation on the books, the board saw it had no choice but to expel him.

In response, Watkins sued. The resulting federal litigation went on for nearly a decade, putting both the rationality and constitutionality of the Army's antigay policy to its harshest test to date. In the end, the question of whether the military's expulsion of gay service members was unconstitutional would be left for another day. A federal appeals court in 1989 rendered a narrowly constructed ruling in his favor, finding that Sergeant Watkins had been unfailingly honest with the Army since day one and had performed superbly in every matter assigned to him. Having accepted and promoted him, the Army had no legitimate basis for discharging him. Margie and countless other gay service members were elated that Watkins had prevailed. Yet the court's judgment was so tightly tailored to his unique circumstances as to be of no use to the vast majority of gay service members who, like Margie, would not have been allowed to pursue a military career had they openly declared their homosexuality.

There were many other high-profile cases, including that of Air Force sergeant Leonard Matlovich, a decorated Vietnam veteran. Matlovich appeared, in uniform, on the cover of *Time* magazine in 1975, above the bold cover line—"I Am a Homosexual." As with the Perry Watkins case, though, the legal basis for Matlovich's successful challenge was so narrow that it simply didn't apply to post-Vietnam-era regulations and circumstances.

In the present tense, for Margie, the most inspiring case was also the most chilling. It involved another military officer nurse with roots in the Northwest — Colonel Margarethe "Grethe" Cammermeyer.

If cases like Perry Watkins's illuminated the absurdity of the prejudice embedded in the military's policy, then Grethe Cammermeyer's story exposed its moral bankruptcy. Inspired by Norwegian parents who had bravely resisted the Nazi occupation of Oslo during World War II, Cammermeyer became an Army nurse in 1961. In 1967, both she and her husband — a U.S. Army lieutenant — were sent to Vietnam. There, as a lead neurosurgical nurse serving in field hospitals during the most intense fighting of the war, Cammermeyer earned a Bronze Star. She returned from the war, joined the Army reserves, gave birth to four sons, but then found herself in an increasingly empty and hostile marriage that ended in an excruciatingly bitter divorce in 1980.

Eight years later, at the age of forty-six, and after being recognized as one of the nation's premier military nurses, Colonel Cammermeyer met and fell in love with artist Diane Divelbess, the woman she would eventually marry. Cammermeyer was a full colonel by then and the chief nurse for the Washington National Guard. In 1989 she was a top candidate to become the chief nurse for the Guard nationally, when, to qualify for that promotion, she sought to upgrade her security clearance. Queried about her sexual orientation during the security interview, she readily admitted she was a lesbian. The shattering result of her admission was that the government moved to end her military career, to discharge her under the same zero-tolerance regulation that led to Perry Watkins's expulsion.

To many, including a rising national political star named Bill Clinton, the Grethe Cammermeyer case powerfully illuminated the injustice of the military's antigay policy. At least Clinton could publicly criticize Cammermeyer's discharge without risking being hauled before a tribunal. That wasn't an option for the tens of thousands of U.S. gay service members who would clearly be putting their careers at great jeopardy by speaking out.

Even so, there would be times when Margie felt compelled to speak up within her unit. During one flight, she overheard through her headphones a pilot make a vulgar disparaging remark about male homosexuals and AIDS.

"You obviously don't have a relative who died of AIDS," she said into her microphone. The pilot later left the cockpit to find her in the cabin and apologize.

On another occasion she reached out to help one of her superiors, a captain and fellow nurse at Scott whose brother was very ill with AIDS. To help guide her to answers to the many questions she was asking, Margie went with her to St. Louis, to a gay bookstore, where there was a wide selection of reading material about AIDS and the AIDS epidemic. Margie sensed the captain would be uncomfortable going to the gay bookstore by herself. So she went with her. To and from the bookstore, there was a discreet silence. The captain didn't ask if Margie was gay, nor did Margie disclose that she was gay.

There were other reasons to travel the twenty-five miles from Scott Air Force Base to St. Louis. For example, you could go to a gay nightclub, to meet and dance with other women.

Jennifer Kallen remembers meeting Margie Witt for the first time. She felt a tap on her shoulder and turned around to see a young woman she didn't know who said "My friend wants to dance with you."

"Well," Jennifer abruptly replied, "where's your friend? This isn't high school, you know."

And that would have been the end of it, except as Jennifer got up to leave the club, she was greeted by the messenger's shy friend, Margie Witt.

The two had more in common than they first realized. For starters, Jennifer had also served in the Air Force as a nurse. She had since left the service and was now a civilian pharmacy specialist who worked in hospitals in the St. Louis area. Like Margie, Jennifer had dated men into her late teens before realizing and accepting that she was attracted to women. And like Margie, Jennifer had her own Air Force experience as a lesbian, finding it remarkably uncomplicated, despite the official zero-tolerance policy on homosexual conduct. A difference was that, unlike Margie, Jennifer had been out to her own parents for quite some time.

Says Jennifer: "My first impression was that she was a little shy, because she'd asked someone else to tap me on the shoulder. And I was pleasantly surprised. She was very cute, a good-looking woman. She had a nice smile, a nice disposition, but this was in the period of a minute, maybe a minute and a half."

During that minute, Margie told Jennifer she would like go out some-time, and then gave her a slip of paper with her phone number. Yet, what might have been a warm and romantic first date turned out to be something memorably different. Margie arrived at Jennifer's door carrying a bouquet of flowers. Within moments, however, Jennifer could sense something wasn't right, that Margie appeared to be in emotional duress. Something had come up, Margie told her. In the month or so between their encounter at the dance club and the time they had gotten around to setting a first date, Margie explained, she had begun seeing another woman.

"That was very disappointing to me," Jennifer recalls.

At the same time, though, she was touched by Margie's honesty. That helped, because, as it turned out, Margie still wanted to nurture a friend-ship with Jennifer. Shortly thereafter, the two of them got together again, but this time Margie had her parents with her. Frank and Gloria were in town for a short visit, and Jennifer graciously joined the three of them and showed them around St. Louis.

"They [Frank and Gloria] didn't have any idea, obviously, about what had transpired between Marg and I," Jennifer recalls. "To them, I was just a friend, or someone she had met. And after Marg and I became closer friends, I realized a couple things right way. One was that Marg was not out to anybody within the military, and that she wasn't out to her family."

In addition to being the national hub for the Air Force's medical evac-uation system, Scott was home in those years to a large public affairs de-partment. On one of the few days Margie wasn't flying a mission, members of the public affairs staff began searching for volunteers from among the base's flight nurses and medical technicians. They had been tasked with updating Air Force recruiting materials, and they needed new photographs.

Captain Witt was happy to oblige and pose, in her olive-green flight suit, for several photos captured inside and outside a C-9A Nightingale. In one of the photos—one that would later be used in a *Cross into the Blue* Air Force recruiting brochure—she stands near the tail of the Nightingale, the plane's signature red cross hovering above her left shoulder. Upon her face is the engaging smile that is her own signature. It perfectly captures a moment in time, the realization of a childhood dream. It was a dream with a big secret embedded in it, but a dream come true nonetheless.

Chapter 6

||||||||||||||||||||||

LOVE AND LILAC CITY

Aside from the magnetic appeal of her photogenic smile, the choice to use Margie's image as a face for Air Force recruiting was largely a product of chance. As she knew as well as anyone, there were many other dedicated flight nurses and medical technicians with whom you would be grateful to "cross into the blue" if you were wounded, or sick, and needed to be medically evacuated by air. One, to be sure, would be her buddy Jim Schaffer, the highly experienced Spokane firefighter and paramedic who tended to the "Black Hawk Down" wounded at an overwhelmed clinic in Mogadishu, Somalia, in 1993.

Another would be Ed Hrivnak.

Hrivnak (pronounced "Riv-neck") grew up in Pittsburgh and enlisted in the Air Force at the age of seventeen. As a medic barely out of his teens, he deployed to a field hospital in the Omani desert as part of Operation Desert Storm, the 1990 military mission to liberate Kuwait and battle Iraqi military forces in southern Iraq. Afterward, he joined the Air Force reserves, working primarily as a loadmaster for rescue and relief missions. In the wake of the deadliest act of domestic terrorism in U.S. history—Timothy McVeigh's bombing of the Murrah Federal Building in Oklahoma City in April 1995—Hrivnak dug through the rubble, searching for bodies and survivors. As the search progressed, he volunteered to go to the dangerously unstable top floor of the shredded building to remove large chunks of concrete dangling from strands of rebar, so these "widowmakers" wouldn't fall on others sifting through the debris below.

As a reservist, Hrivnak figured he would use his income as a loadmaster for the 446th to sustain him while enrolled in the same PLU nursing program Margie had graduated from a decade earlier. Shortly after getting his degree in 1996, Hrivnak was contacted by an Air Force flight nurse recruiter. Facing a shortage of flight nurses at the time, the recruiter made him an offer he couldn't pass up. If he would become an Air Force flight nurse, he would be granted an officer's commission, plus the government would pay off his student loans. It was an easy choice.

He began his flight nurse training in 1997, just as the Air Force was making important changes to how it would evacuate wounded soldiers. A new "tactical" approach would involve bringing a retrofitted, long-range aircraft—the C-17 Globemaster—directly into combat zones, where the planes could be quickly loaded and launched toward medical centers thousands of miles away. By then, Hrivnak was a newly commissioned lieutenant and rookie flight nurse who thrived on such challenges. Still, suiting up in body armor to land and load under fire was a mission very different from the "strategic" intercontinental medevac flights for which he had been trained. For those flights, the planes would depart from rear positions, and the preflight routines allowed ample time to perform individual patient assessments.

His lead trainer and mentor for the intense battlefield missions was Margie Witt, now U.S. Air Force Reserve Captain Margaret Witt.

"The patients are coming out very quickly, the engines are running on the plane, and you only have a few minutes on the ground," Hrivnak recalls, "and I'm like 'Well, how the heck am I supposed to do an assessment?' And I remember Margie saying, 'You've got to look in their eyes. Their eyes will tell you what's going on. And the patients who are screaming, if they're well enough to scream, they're in pretty good shape. It's the ones who aren't screaming, who aren't making any noise, that you need to pay extra attention to.'"

Ed Hrivnak, like Jim Schaffer and dozens of other dedicated reservists from all walks of life, would become part of Margie's new Air Force family. In addition to active duty deployments, the 446th reservists would typically gather one weekend a month for Unit Training Assembly (UTA), so-called "drill" weekends, plus a minimum two weeks of active duty per year.

For Margie, leaving the old family—the contingent of active-duty flight nurses and med techs based at Scott—had been wrenching. But events were forcing her hand. Each month as an active-duty flight nurse brought her closer to the day she would inevitably be promoted into a management job on the ground—reassigned to an office. Given the arduous physical demands of being a flight nurse, the transition would have been a welcome career milestone for most of her peers. But for her it was exactly the fate she had long ago promised herself she would do just about anything to avoid.

Still, it seemed like such a crazy thing to do—to leave an active-duty job at which she was thriving in order to rebuild her Air Force career on her own terms. On the day she had chosen to notify her commanding officer of her decision, she was overwhelmed with emotion. She was sobbing and struggling to get the words out as she delivered the news that she would be resigning her commission as an active-duty officer. Her last sequence of flights out through the western states and back aboard a C-9 Nightingale was punctuated with ceremonial tributes to her at each landing, where she was feted with food, gifts, and dousings with pressurized water from hand-held fire extinguishers and fire trucks. Unknown to Margie, her handpicked female crew had stashed champagne in with the medical supplies, but the bottle ruptured in flight during an altitude change, soaking the supplies. The pads, bandages, and sheets then had to be replaced prior to the next takeoff, but by then the whole plane reeked of champagne. Her raucous going-away party back at Scott was at an Applebee's restaurant just off the base. The gift that drew the most laughter was a box of condoms to "prepare" her for a return to campus. Most everybody was in on the joke. "I must have turned fifty shades of red," she recalls.

She signed out at the base the morning of December 15, 1995, drove through St. Louis, and then toward Oklahoma on Interstate 44, her belongings packed into her white, 1991 Honda Prelude. To avoid winter storms in the Rockies, she took a circuitous route toward the southwest, planning her overnight stops at military billeting sites along the way. She drove through Tulsa, then the Texas panhandle, endured a snowstorm in New Mexico, then crossed the desert to Southern California for a brief visit with her sister. From there she turned northward, driving the length of the Pacific Coast to her parents' home in Gig Harbor for Christmas.

Just as there had been culture shock coming into the Air Force, now there was culture shock in reentering civilian life so she could become qualified to later re-join the service as a physical therapist. As a flight nurse she was largely undaunted, even after the Pope tragedy, by the challenges she might face on any given day. Now she was aware of how unsettled she felt, not just at being out of uniform, but being out of her carefully scripted routes and routines, separated from her challenging and collegial work environment, and disconnected from the Air Force system that delivered paychecks and handled her health-care needs.

It didn't help matters that the coursework requirements just to gain entry to a graduate-level physical therapy program seemed insanely arduous. Even though she held a nursing degree and was in fact an active nurse, she was required to complete several undergraduate courses, and receive nothing less than A's. Thus, on New Year's Day 1996, she was back on the road, driving on icy highways through Washington's Cascade Mountains. The last of the classes she needed were at Eastern Washington University in Cheney, a rural campus bordered by dune-like hills covered in snow and wheat stubble. This is where she spent the rest of the winter, as an older undergraduate student.

In some ways, it felt like she had been abducted.

One of the required classes was a biology course of the sort she would have breezed through at PLU a decade earlier. Oh, how times had changed: to now find herself among seemingly carefree, teenage undergrads moon-walking toward their futures and fumbling with their earbuds. And it was she—"for the first time in my life"—who planted herself in the front row of the class, utterly determined to get an A.

The silver lining in this new chapter of her life was that she knew she would be joining the 446th in the spring. It would reconnect her with work that fulfilled her and bring her home to the very place she first imagined herself working aboard a flying hospital. After so many years struggling against the Air Force's paradoxical regulations, she could now—as a re-servist—actually remain a flight nurse and stay attached to the same unit for as long she wanted. In her mind, though, her stint in the reserves would be fairly short, because her plan was to apply for an active-duty assignment as a physical therapist, as soon as she got her degree.

The question of where she would live, as a civilian, was answered when EWU accepted her application to its graduate program. She would not be going back to the EWU main campus in Cheney, though. As part of the school's effort to enhance its presence in Spokane, the state's second-largest city, the EWU physical therapy classes convened in the lower floors of the city's Paulsen Building. The elegant office tower with a glazed terra-cotta exterior was built during Spokane's gilded age, and is located only a couple of blocks from where the "Lilac City" had hosted a World's Fair in 1974. It was there, in the fall of 1996, that Margie met Tiffany Jenson.

The two easily became friends and study partners, working and visiting over coffee on their ways to and from classes. As their comfort with each other grew, Margie confided that she was gay. Still, it simply didn't occur to Margie that the quiet, shy, smart blond with a decidedly feminine voice would become romantically interested in her. That revelation came about in a most playful way, as the two were scrimmaging against one another, preparing for Spokane's signature Hoopfest basketball tournament the following summer.

Margie lowered her shoulders and feigned a quick drive to the basket before hitting the brakes with a sudden jab step.

"Oh, I could have had you!" she exclaimed with a laugh.

"You could have had me a long time ago," Tiff quickly replied.

Margie promptly dribbled the ball off her foot and felt a blush rise on her face.

"Did you just say what I think you said?" she asked.

Their relationship blossomed from there. After both received their degrees and completed internships on the west side of the state, they returned to Spokane and began living together.

By mere coincidence, one of their neighbors was Jan Gemberling, a lawyer and one of Spokane's most ardent civil rights advocates. Jan soon began exchanging hellos with the pair during her crack-of-dawn walks with her dog. She not only accepted the new gay couple in the neighborhood but was eager to befriend them, and their dogs. Their bond as neighbors was sealed after a Mickey Mouse antenna puppet was stolen from Tiff's car. A day or two later, a ransom letter appeared with a tiny black felt ear attached to it, demanding cafe lattes and cookies, or else. It was clearly a gag hatched in Tiff's new workplace. The abduction occurred just as Margie and Tiff were about to leave for Hawaii. As they packed for their vacation, the pair playfully decided to lawyer up and ask Jan to represent them in ransom negotiations while they were away. Ultimately, the cookies and coffee were delivered, and the Mickey Mouse antenna ball was returned to its owner's vehicle.

"So, we got off on just a very pleasant, funny relationship," Jan recalls.

"They brought me back a box of chocolate-covered macadamia nuts from Hawaii, and after that I went and watched *West Wing* with them every Wednesday night."

Before meeting Tiff, Margie had planned to get her degree and return to active duty as soon as possible. But she couldn't return to active duty without moving again. Tiff made clear she didn't want to leave Spokane. Margie's response was to change her plans. As her buddy Jim Schaffer had found, commuting to their 446th assignments from Spokane was manageable. She would stay in Spokane, find a civilian job as a physical therapist, and remain in the Air Force reserves so that she could continue building a life with her new partner. There was another obvious plus to staying in Spokane. By then, Margie's feisty college roommate, Carla Savalli, had returned to her hometown to work as an editor for the *Spokesman-Review*, the city's daily newspaper. The two had sustained and strengthened their friendship over the years, but now, living in the same zip code, they were all the closer. Carla and her partner at the time, Laura, were both fond of Tiff, and the four socialized regularly.

"There were things that I enjoyed about every one of the people Margie had been with, but they weren't quite what I wanted for Margie. And that's exactly how she felt about the people that I was with," Carla recalls. "When I met Tiffany, I thought, 'Okay.' For a while, you know, the four of us got along really well. And I don't know how to explain what happened, except that the closer Laura and Tiffany became as friends, the more I kind of got sucked into that. Because now I've got my friend, but I've got my partner too. And my partner seems to think Tiffany is a good person."

By most measures and appearances, it seemed like a normal life. Except it wasn't a normal life. One way in which Margie was reminded of this came as she dealt with the legal paperwork to take title to their new house. The forms that would become public records were rife with required disclosures that, to say the least, pointed to a close relationship between her and Tiff. One of the legal documents that arrived in the mail even listed the two of them as husband and wife, because that's just how the form was designed. While filling out and filing such records might be a nuisance to an ordinary couple—whether heterosexual or gay—the very existence of the forms was disquieting if you happened to be a gay or lesbian in the U.S.

military. To be sure, Margie had by then made an accommodation for the inherent stress of pursuing an Air Force career in spite of the government's long-standing practice of removing known homosexuals from the ranks. She had not forgotten the terrifying experience at Castle Air Force Base a decade earlier. Yet neither had she allowed the fear of being outed and discharged keep her awake at night. Still, she was keenly aware that here she was creating a new paper trail that could conceivably be used by OSI investigators to end her Air Force career.

Another way in which life was not normal was that Tiff, like Margie, was not out to her parents—each was known to the other's families as a close friend and roommate. The distance between that and the full truth could create odd and wincing experiences, such as one that occurred on a day when Margie and Tiff went to visit Tiff's mother at her home in north Spokane's Five Mile neighborhood. The three were at the kitchen table when Tiff's mom remarked to her daughter that she wanted her grandchild sooner rather than later. She then began trying to interest Tiff in meeting a young man she had gotten to know during visits to the gym at the company where they worked. The discussion left Margie feeling both bewildered and humiliated. By this time, there was already tension between her and Tiff over Tiff's expressed desire to co-parent a child through in vitro fertilization. How could this be happening, Margie wondered, when neither set of parents knew (or if they did know, acknowledge) that the two were lesbians?

There were also fissures developing in their relationship that had little, if anything, to do with their sexuality, the discussion over whether to have a child, and the secrecy surrounding both.

The most ominous trend was Tiff's hardening attitude toward some of Margie's closest friends. When she and Tiff first became attracted to each other as study partners, it seemed that one of the things Tiff found intriguing about Margie was that she was a weekend warrior. Yet within a year after they had become a couple, Margie began to sense and experience a chill in Tiff's attitude toward the companionship and bonhomie Margie enjoyed with both men and women she served with in the 446th. By 2000, it had gotten to the point where Tiff would hang up on Margie's Air Force comrades if she fielded a call from one of them before Margie could get to the phone.

All the while, and true to form, Margie was building new friendships, many through her physical therapy work with special-needs students. In the summer of 2001, she landed a job at District 81, Spokane's citywide school district. She would work in pediatric physical therapy under the supervision of Nancy Royse, whom Margie had met while working on her advanced degree at EWU. It was through Nancy that Margie had gotten her introduction, in a clinical setting, to working with special-needs children. The two women knew each other well, and Nancy was thrilled to welcome Margie with her diverse skills to the tightly knit team of therapists and orthopedic assistants.

One of the new members on Nancy's District 81 team was Laurie Mc-Chesney, a wife and mother of three. Laurie had been encouraged to apply for an instructional assistant position by a staff member she had met and gotten to know through church. What Nancy and others soon noticed about Laurie was that she learned quickly and seemed to have a special ability to engage even the most difficult kids. There was also, though, a discernible sadness. The start of Laurie's new job coincided with the death of her father, and as she returned from a bereavement leave, it was obvious she was still working through a deep sense of loss.

It was at this time that Laurie, like most of the District 81 staff, was introduced to Margie Witt. There was something about Margie that Nancy Royse had discerned years earlier, something she viewed as Margie's larger-than-life personality. Her professional presence and level of engagement were unmistakable. But so were her sense of humor and commitment to joy.

It may have been only a day or two after Margie joined the District 81 team that large boxes arrived at their office in east central Spokane. Inside the boxes were the unassembled parts to oversize tricycles that the therapists would use with special-needs kids. And now it was the new girl, the gregarious Air Force major with the can-do spirit, who was taking charge of putting the trikes together.

"I had to triage it and organize it," Margie explains.

Then, of course, the tricycles had to be tested. And before she knew it, Laurie McChesney was laughing hysterically right along with everyone else. Margie had hopped into the seat of one of the big-wheeled trikes and started riding through the hallways, joking and hollering. Then came the tricycle races in the hall.

"We had to make sure they worked," Nancy Royce deadpans. "We wouldn't want to deliver a defective product."

September and the start of the 2001 school year were only days away. So, too, was a historic tragedy, one that would make it all the harder for Margie Witt and her comrades in the 446th to live in two worlds at once.

Chapter 7

⸻

HALLOWEEN

Like Margie Witt and countless other Americans who live west of the Rocky Mountains, Ed Hrivnak was still in bed when the World Trade Center came under attack on September 11, 2001. And, as Margie was with Gloria, it was only a few minutes after the first plane slammed into the North Tower that he was on the phone with his mother. She had called to wake him, and then struggled for words to explain why. But the urgency in her voice was unmistakable.

"Turn on the news," he finally understood her to say. "Turn on CNN."

Waking up alongside him in Spanaway, Washington, was his wife Jennifer, who was also a flight nurse with the 446th. The couple turned on a television in time to see the second plane explode into the South Tower, ending any speculation about what was happening.

"At that point, I knew we were at war," he says. "And I told Jennifer, 'We've got to pack our mobility kits.'"

Three days later, President George W. Bush stood atop the rubble at Ground Zero in Lower Manhattan. As he spoke into a bullhorn, his free arm was draped around the neck of a sixty-nine-year-old firefighter, Bob Beckwith, who had come out of retirement to help with the recovery efforts. Greeted with applause and chants of "USA! USA!" the president tried to address the other helmeted workers surrounding him, and when some called out that they couldn't hear him, the president used the moment to send a message.

"I can hear you!" he shouted into the bullhorn. "The rest of the world hears you! And the people who knocked these buildings down will hear all of us soon!"

But the deployments that Ed Hrivnak, Margie Witt, and others in the 446th were expecting didn't come soon. President Bush decided the Central Intelligence Agency, working with the Northern Alliance (militias of ethnic factions hostile to the Taliban regime in Afghanistan) would take the lead in overthrowing the Taliban and pursuing Osama bin Laden's al-Qaeda terrorist network in and beyond Afghanistan. At least in the early stage of what became known as Operation Enduring Freedom, the U.S.-led coalition relied heavily on air strikes and select use of relatively small and specialized combat units. Coalition casualties were relatively light.

The specter of a broader war and far greater casualties began to emerge in 2002 as the Bush administration shifted its focus toward Saddam Hussein and Iraq. Top administration officials, led by Vice President Dick Cheney, tried to make a case for an Iraqi connection to the 9/11 attacks. They also pushed what turned out to be erroneous claims that Iraq had active, clandestine programs to manufacture nuclear and chemical weapons of mass destruction.

The public and congressional debates over whether a war with Iraq was justifiable revealed a nation far less unified than it had been in the immediate aftermath of 9/11. Twenty-three U.S. senators, including Washington's Patty Murray, voted against an October 2002 resolution giving the president authority to take military action against Iraq.

Of more immediate consequence was the depth of international opposition. Several key U.S. allies who had sent troops for the Afghanistan operation—including France and Germany—declined to participate in an invasion of Iraq. The United States proceeded in its preparations without them.

In the run-up to the war, it was at least thinkable, at times, that the expected invasion would be deferred. In her journal, Margie wrote about mentally preparing herself for the expected casualties as she arrived for duty in Oman shortly after New Year's. She had noted how the sense of urgency in their encampment began to dissipate as the United States tried, and largely failed, to gain traction in the United Nations for military action. Then came U.S. secretary of state Colin Powell's speech to the UN Security Council in early February, in which he all but committed the United States to taking military action, even in the face of UN opposition. Suddenly, the invasion of Iraq once again seemed imminent.

"We are building here faster than anyone can imagine," she wrote from Oman on February 26. "I had no idea the government could move this fast."

So much of Margie's training and experience had geared her for flying toward the trouble. Now she was having difficulty reconciling those instincts with her new orders. No doubt it was time for her and Jim Schaffer to leave for the states, as both had been seriously injured in separate accidents during their tour of duty. And still, she wrote, "going home at a time when literally thousands of soldiers are being brought into the theater is not easy. I found myself not wanting to share with anyone that I was going home."

As she and Jim were ending their deployment, many of their 446th colleagues were just getting their orders to ship out. Ed Hrivnak received his just four days before Margie and Jim were scheduled to return from Oman.

"I know there is a lot of concern about the validity of this war," he wrote in a message to friends and family on March 11. "I don't care to discuss it. I do ask that you support those of us who serve this country and defend it."

His orders were to join a crew of six other reservists to fly long-range missions from Europe to pick up badly wounded U.S. soldiers in Kuwait and transport them to medical centers in Germany and Spain. For what turned out to be the first five months of the war, the long flights would be all the longer because even the medevac aircraft were barred from Turkish airspace on their ways to and from the war zone. Initially, Turkey—a normally reliable NATO ally that controls critical airspace between U.S. bases in Europe and Iraq—refused to let U.S. military aircraft fly over its territory.

Through the lens of his experience in the reserves, it was a situation that Jim Schaffer had worried about for years. The U.S. military had taken so few casualties during the first Gulf War (1990–1991) that the two top causes for evacuations out of theater were sports injuries and injuries sustained in noncombat vehicle accidents. This, in turn, changed the shape of the military's medical response in future missions, shifting more responsibilities onto reserve units like the 446th. Schaffer had seen this in his own assignments—within weeks after returning injured from Somalia, he had to push back against a new active-duty assignment that would have sent him to Rwanda.

"That's how bad it was," he says. "We were short, and with this [the imminent Iraq invasion in 2003] it was obvious we would be going."

At the time Ed Hrivnak was called for active duty in late February 2003, he was an experienced trauma care nurse. But his civilian experience was only of so much use for what he and his crew would now have to take on. It was, he says, one thing to be in a civilian emergency room dealing with the aftermath of a car wreck or a single gunshot wound. But it was quite another "to deal with thirty-six patients who have amputations, traumatic injuries, blast injuries, shrapnel injuries, and seeing bodies torn to a degree I'd never seen before. It was overwhelming."

Hrivnak and his crew found themselves working shifts longer than twenty-four hours, flying in 1960s-vintage C-141 Starlifters, all of which were deteriorating and some of which were even leaking hydraulic fluid onto the patients. He was also separated from Jennifer, who deployed to Oman and then to Pakistan, while he was based in Europe.

As frustrated as he and his team were by the dilapidated airplanes and difficult working conditions, Hrivnak was also being exposed on the long flights from Kuwait and Iraq to something else that was deeply affecting him: stories from the wounded soldiers. In addition to the blood, sweat, sand, and other foul material clinging to his flight suit, there were pieces of tape attaching patient notes. After using the notes to inform his care for the soldiers, he would consult them in writing e-mail dispatches to describe what he was seeing and experiencing. His motivation for the long e-mails, he says, was his anger at news accounts about the war that didn't, or couldn't, account for the carnage he was witnessing.

The stories brought him a much bigger audience than he expected, as people on his e-mail list began to pass them on electronically to their friends. A month after the war started, he opened a letter from his mom and was stunned to find with it a tightly folded newspaper article, with his byline. It was from the *Tacoma News Tribune*'s April 21, 2003, edition. "Medic Writes of Nursing Bodies, Spirits of Wounded," the headline read. It was one of his journal entries. His first-person accounts would later appear in the *New Yorker* and become a part of Operation Homecoming, an award-winning, multimedia anthology about the war. Hrivnak wound up having a lot to say not only about what it is like to care for America's wounded, but about war in general. When the time was right, he would also have a lot to say about Margie Witt.

Given Margie's deep ambivalence about having to depart the Middle East just as the Iraq War was about to begin, perhaps it was fitting that the first try didn't take. When the senior Department of Defense official sitting behind her and Jim Schaffer started having seizures, it took only a few minutes to realize how limited their choices were. By then, both she and Jim were on their knees on the cabin floor, doing all they could to stabilize their patient as the World Airways MD-11 made a U-turn and headed to an emergency landing in Bahrain.

The second try at leaving the Arabian Peninsula for their long flights home had been mercifully uneventful. A fresh Bloody Mary helped calm her nerves. It also helped that she didn't have to explain to Jim how much she was dreading what awaited her back home.

Jim already knew. The close friendship they had formed even before their deployment had grown even closer at their base in Oman as he had helped Margie collect herself after enduring the excruciating late-night, long-distance phone calls with Tiff.

It wasn't just that Margie was no closer to wanting to have a child; she was also losing hope that she and Tiff could reverse the unraveling of trust that now infected the impasse.

In 2002, months before she deployed to Oman, Margie had approached JP Wirth, an aeromedical technician and one of her closest friends in the 446th, to see if he would be willing to be the sperm donor. If Tiff's pregnancy was going to happen, she figured, then one way for her to join her heart and spirit to the child would be for the sperm donor to be someone she knew well and admired.

Initially, Tiff not only gave her approval to Margie's proposal but participated in conveying the request to JP. After reflecting on it and discussing it with the two of them, JP agreed. He submitted to the extensive medical tests—including numerous lab visits to make sperm samples—with Margie agreeing to pick up the cost. He also worked up a contract to define his involvement and expectations, not as a parenting partner but as a future male role model for the child to be. Not long afterward, though, Margie was puzzled to find new sperm donor profiles lying in plain sight on the desktop of a computer she and Tiff shared. At first, Tiff offered no explanation. But after several weeks she told Margie that JP would be too involved for her comfort. She now insisted the donor be anonymous. For Margie, it was another dispiriting signal that Tiff was isolating her and trying to control her, that she was more committed to having a baby on her own terms than she was committed to their relationship. The rebuff to JP was also a rebuff to her, and was part of the distress and heartache she had carried with her on the deployment to Oman.

Groggy and emotionally drained, Margie and Jim Schaffer finally made it back to Washington State, landing at Sea-Tac on the last day of February 2003. Although they were now half a world away from the escalating conflict, they remained on active duty. Both were required to report to McChord, where the first order of business was to complete after-action reports that would be used to brief their comrades. Among other things, this meant Margie and Tiff's reunion would be in Tacoma, as the struggling couple agreed that Tiffany would drive from Spokane for a weekend visit.

Margie's inner turmoil was reflected in a journal entry written as if it were a letter to Tiff, though one that would never be sent.

"It seems as I write more, I become more angry about this. Not the right kind of energy if I was at all interested at this time. I don't want to be angry at you—I love you with all my heart and want what makes you happy—I always have. I am angry because I feel I don't matter in this except for my convenience. I feel used and yet useless. I am not choosing something else. I am voicing what I would prefer—a life without children—you prefer with—what now? I feel it would be a huge mistake for me to go along and be miserable and locked in in the future, or leave you and the baby after the fact. Sometimes I wonder if you WANT to lock me in—then I think you truly believe I would love being a parent."

The question of where they would stay in Tacoma became the next blister in their relationship. Over the years, with practice, Margie and her parents had worked with respectful finesse and silence around the issue of her clear preference for women partners. This extended to welcoming Tiff as Margie's "roommate" and accepting as "practical" the two of them sharing the downstairs room in the Witts' spacious Gig Harbor home. Frank and Gloria were obviously eager to see and spend time with their daughter upon Margie's return from Oman. The unspoken expectation was that Margie would come home and that if Tiff were in town she would simply join them at Gig Harbor.

But not this time. Perhaps anticipating an argument over the parenting impasse, Tiff insisted that Margie find a hotel room instead. She also insisted upon Margie's full attention for the weekend; no slipping off to Gig

Harbor. That left Margie to come up with an explanation for her parents as to why she wouldn't be staying with them. The tension and awkwardness of the situation only deepened her frustration.

"I just thought, that's it," she recalls. Her exasperation fed her resolve to give a final and direct answer to Tiff. The answer would be no. She was not okay with her and Tiff having a baby together.

By then, Margie and Jim had checked into a Shilo Inn just off Interstate 5 in south Tacoma. Aware of her distress, he proposed an outing to get something to eat. They would go to a nearby Hooters, eat spicy chicken wings, and share a pitcher of beer.

Hooters?

"It was food," he would explain. "I wasn't making a point or anything."

Back at the Shilo, Jim also supplied a bottle of Absolut vodka and a cigar for each of them. To distract Margie from her dread of Tiff's impending visit, Jim was working with everything he had. It was, however, a non-smoking hotel. The smoke had to go somewhere, and their solution was to open the back window in Jim's room and set the lit cigars on a small shelf of masonry just outside the sliding glass. That worked well until it didn't, and the lit cigar tumbled into the foliage below.

Under the circumstances, it provided merciful comic relief. At least for Margie:

"Here's this fire captain, okay? And the cigar falls off the window ledge, down a couple stories, into all these leaves. And it's just about dark, so we're scrambling out of the room, down the stairs, around the building, trying to sneak by all the windows, looking for his cigar."

The cigar had actually fallen into a hedge of juniper bushes. Schaffer is allergic to junipers, so while a firefighter-induced blaze was averted, he still came away with welts.

The inevitable reunion with Tiff the following weekend was every bit as painful as Margie imagined it would be. The conversation quickly flared into an argument. Margie's answer on the baby issue inevitably slid to the larger question of whether they would remain together as a couple.

The answer to that question seemed, also, to be no. At least from Margie's perspective, the two agreed they would end their romantic relationship. They would begin moving toward an eventual separation, so that Tiff could find another partner who would welcome having a baby with her.

Yet there were no hard deadlines as such, and both accepted, for the time being, that they would continue living together. They also decided they would have one last vacation together, and that Margie would fund it out of the extra pay that came with her seven months of active duty. In her mind, it was a way of acknowledging the disruption and distance caused by her active-duty assignment to Oman. At the end of July, when Margie's active-duty assignment would end, the two would go to Honolulu.

With those agreements seemingly worked out, the reunion at the Shilo Inn by the freeway was over. Tiff drove back to Spokane with the dogs. Margie sat on the bed at the motel and sobbed. She was three weeks away from her thirty-ninth birthday, and her six-year relationship with Tiff was, by far, the longest of her life. Tiff's preoccupation with having a baby had left her no room to breathe. But the frustration flowed in both directions, and it had, by then, devoured virtually all the romance and trust between them.

The weeklong vacation at Waikiki Beach in Honolulu was tense, offering fresh evidence of a fractured relationship that went well beyond the parenting impasse. As much as Margie wanted to avoid a major blowup, things boiled over when Tiff objected to Margie's suggestion that they meet up with her good friend Julia Scott, who would be in Honolulu after arriving on a medevac flight at nearby Hickam AFB.

When the estranged couple returned to Spokane together the two would, once again, share the same home. It was a surreal arrangement, and one that created more confusion and a reprise of the questions about their future together. Adding to Margie's distress was an increasing tension with Carla Savalli, as her best friend sided with Tiff in the parenting saga. Distracted by work pressures (she had, by then, become the newspaper's city editor) and troubles in her own personal life, Carla's attitude toward Margie's struggles with Tiff was that it was time for Margie to settle down and become a parent. The irony in this unwelcome turn was that for years Margie and Carla had been very open with each other about their aversion to having children, and often joked about it.

"Yet, at the time she was faced with this," says Carla, "I tried to talk her into it, which is really weird, because I, of all people, should have understood what it's like to know in your core that this is just not going to be a role for you."

Tiff made no effort to hide that she was moving forward, searching anew for a sperm donor. During a walk after work one day, she told Margie she needed her help. In addition to the medical tests and screenings for actual sperm donors, the policy of the clinic she was using required a blood sample from the birth mother's partner. Tiff was asking Margie to present herself as that partner, and give the blood sample. The request shocked her. Not only did it seem an absurd requirement, but it was a request for Margie to participate in something she had already made clear she wanted nothing to do with. No, she said, she wouldn't do it.

Yet, as was the pattern in their relationship, Margie acquiesced the following week after Tiff told her that she couldn't proceed without the signature. Margie went to the clinic and gave the blood draw. She viewed it as a parting "gift" to her longtime partner, yet it only amplified her anxieties about what was coming next.

Given the frostiness in her recent conversations with Carla, Margie turned instead to the counselor she and Tiff had been seeing in the months before her deployment to Oman. Whether it was her parents, the Air Force, or her partner, her first instinct was to try to make everybody happy. And now that instinct, coupled with her aversion to conflict, was further complicating matters with Tiff. Especially after their painful reunion in Tacoma, and the joyless vacation in Hawaii, it was all the more clear the two didn't have a future together. They had already agreed that Margie would compensate for Tiff's payments on the home, although the exact terms of the buyout had yet to be finalized. Even so, they continued to share the home and foster the perception they were continuing to be a couple. The two were sliding into a different phase of the same quandary Margie had resolved, months earlier, to bring to a close. But it wasn't closing.

There was at least one thing she could do to take her mind off her personal turmoil. She could go to work. At McChord, she was continuing to thrive at the 446th, so much so that she would soon be assigned a key leadership role as head of standards and evaluation for the unit. But the best part of her homecoming was her return to work at the school district in Spokane, where the physical therapy team, under her supervisor Nancy Royse, was like a second family.

Among her most valued new work friends was Laurie McChesney. A Southern California native who had moved to Spokane as a young, Catholic housewife in the mid-1980s, Laurie had been hired in 2000 to assist physical therapists in their work with the district's special-needs students. She was married to Pat McChesney, a Spokane accountant and investor. The couple had three children, the youngest of whom, Sam, was still living at home and about to enter middle school. Their family also included an older daughter from one of Pat's two earlier marriages.

Laurie had no sooner begun work at the district when her father passed away. She took bereavement leave to travel to San Diego for the funeral and to comfort her mother. In part because she and her father had strengthened an already close relationship in the year before he died, his loss struck her hard, and the sadness she had carried home with her was noticeable and concerning to those in the closely knit physical therapy team.

Her sadness was deeper than the grief of losing her father. Shortly after returning from California, Laurie had a long, soul-baring conversation with Debbie Duvoisin, one of her oldest and closest friends.

"When she was talking to me, I could see there was a pain, and her marriage wasn't good," Debbie recalls. "She wasn't happy, and she didn't know where to get happy."

When Margie joined the district staff in August 2001, she had noticed how quiet and subdued Laurie seemed. She remembers asking about her, and learning from fellow staff members about the struggles in Laurie's life. She also began to notice Laurie's intelligence and sense of humor. The two tended to sit together during staff meetings, and when Margie found a need, or just a ripe opening, to inject a little humor, she would find herself delighting in Laurie's comebacks. "Who is this?" she found herself thinking. "You're funny."

Then came Margie's active-duty deployment to the Middle East in early 2003.

"All of us missed her desperately because Margie was who she was—she's just one of those larger-than-life people," Nancy Royse recalls. "When she's not there, you notice. But Laurie really missed her more than anybody."

Margie's neighbor, Jan Gemberling, remembers meeting both Laurie and her husband at a casual Wednesday evening gathering at Margie and Tiff's place where they all watched *West Wing*, and Pat helped Margie set up a new computer.

"And so Laurie was somebody she'd met at work," Jan recalls, "and I think initially the whole sense was that Laurie was straight and she was going to be a good friend."

That was Margie's expectation, as well, though at one point she did confide to one of her trusted acquaintances that Laurie was the kind of person she wanted to be with. Laurie, for her part, was experiencing just how happy she was in Margie's presence, and how that joy and the sound of her own laughter were giving her glimpses of the person she wanted to become.

Laurie was all the more eager to renew and build upon their friendship when Margie finally returned to Spokane in late summer. Midway through September she took the bold step of inviting Margie to take a yoga class with her on Monday nights, half expecting that she would decline. But Margie accepted, and the yoga outings became the highlights of Laurie's week. She would pick Margie up on the way, and afterward the two would go drink beer at a bustling pub in the city's Browne's Addition neighborhood.

There was, though, a small problem with the yoga experience. The two were so giddy together that the instructor would have to shush them to try to maintain ascetic decorum. At one point the instructor had to separate them, and so Laurie got up and moved to the opposite side of the large room. The next yoga position involved a handstand against the wall, and as Laurie was upside down, lifting herself into place, she heard somebody across the room crash to the floor. "Then I heard the sound of legs trying to get back up on the wall. And I knew it was her. She sounded like a great big bug." And, of course, nothing could stop the giggling after that.

The other shoe dropped in late October.

It was just days after Margie had taken most of a week to participate in an Air Force training mission to New Zealand. It helped that Tiff was, for a change, not only accepting that Margie would be off doing Air Force work for a week, but had actually encouraged her to go. That was a good thing. But in Margie's view, even positive experiences with Tiff were adding to her stress, because the irreconcilable difference remained. The two had reached an agreement in joint counseling that there would be no big surprises between them, that they would keep each other notified of events and decisions that would affect the other. Still, with Tiff continuing to move toward the pregnancy she wanted, it was only a matter of time before they would have to separate.

By now, Margie and Laurie were close enough that Margie was sharing the agony of her unraveling relationship with Tiff. When she returned from the mission to New Zealand, she also arranged to meet with her counselor. The appointment was on October 30. Looking toward the day when Tiff would become pregnant, Margie told the counselor that she knew Tiff would be thrilled. But she also knew what her own response would be. She would be neither joyful, nor supportive, and there would be no way for her to conceal it. As painful as it would be to revisit this irreconcilable difference yet again, she just knew it had to be done. She had to give voice to it.

The next day was Halloween. Margie arrived home first, and as the darkness quickly settled, she busied herself preparing for trick-or-treaters. She secured the excitable dachshunds in the kitchen behind a kiddy gate. She then went to set out the tea-light candles in paper bags that would illuminate the front walkway. She was doing this with the hardening realization that what she now had to tell Tiff couldn't wait. To steady her nerves she began drinking vodka. Vodka on the rocks.

Suddenly enough, there was Tiff, in the doorway. And before Margie knew it she was talking, talking to Tiff about her new friend Laurie, then listening to Tiff say, in response, that it was a good thing that Margie had a new friend to support her. And then Margie told Tiff she had something important tell her. If Tiff was really committed to the pregnancy she was planning, Margie said, it only made sense for Tiff to be with a partner who could support her and share in her joy. She continued, to try to explain further the deep ambivalence she was feeling.

"I'm already pregnant, Marg," Tiff interjected. Tiff was still standing just inside the doorway, still wearing her coat.

It was as though Margie had been struck in the solar plexus. All but speechless, she grabbed for her car keys and began walking out the door. She drove a short distance and started making phone calls. The first person she was able to reach was Carla, and her request to Carla was for her and her partner to take Tiff in—the days where she could share the same living space with Tiff were over. It was a short conversation, and Carla readily agreed to the request. The next person Margie was able to reach was Laurie.

She happened to be only a few blocks away at a family gathering at her cousin's home. She excused herself, saying a friend was in crisis and needed her help. It was dark by the time Margie arrived, and Laurie met her in the driveway. Margie moved to the passenger seat, and Laurie drove west to a historic mansion and art center on a hillside overlooking the city. Tears poured from Margie's eyes as all the pent-up frustrations, and lost love, came gushing out at once. She also felt betrayal as she realized that the reason Tiff had been almost eager for her to fly off to New Zealand a few weeks earlier was that Tiff planned to be inseminated and, contrary to their earlier "no surprises" agreement, had not spoken a word about it. One thing she knew for certain was that she wasn't going home that night. She was done with Tiff. Finis.

Adjacent to the McChesneys' home on a patch of the Glenrose Prairie just south of town was a barn that had been remodeled to include a bedroom in the loft. Laurie invited Margie to stay the night there. In the course of the divorce proceedings to come, there would be a number of uncontested facts. One of those facts would be that the two of them spent that night together, in the bedroom at the barn.

Chapter 8

|||||||||||||||||||||

THE SCARLET LETTER

When they awoke in each other's arms, still in the dark, it was November. Mercifully, it was the end of the week, and neither had to jump into jeans and race off to work. The nearest road with any traffic or noise to speak of was more than a mile away. No leaf blowers, no snowblowers, no sirens. Just the dull clop of hooves from the horses quartered downstairs in the barn. And, still, to step out of bed and out of the loft was to step into a whole new minefield of complications.

Laurie had reacted instinctively when she received Margie's phone call the evening before. She could hear the deep distress in Margie's voice. She had also known for a while that, to her, Margie was more than a friend, that in the joys of the companionship they had been sharing she was experiencing a genuine, binding love. It was a calming realization, because in that joy she was finding a pathway to a much fuller existence. Two years earlier, her friend Debbie Duvoisin was troubled to find Laurie in tears, not even knowing where to search for happiness. This was no longer true. As time would tell, a lot of people, most especially her husband, would have objections to the new course in her life. But that couldn't put so much as a dent in the truth. Not even a scratch, really.

Lying next to her, Margie was still trying to absorb and make sense of the emotional tempest that had blown through her life just twelve hours earlier. The Halloween vodka on the rocks as she waited for Tiff was supposed to buffer roughly equal amounts of pain and anxiety. The pain was grief and confusion about losing a partner to a cause she neither shared nor understood.

Now it was Saturday morning, the day after. And the woman lying next to her was Laurie. The trust between them as friends had evolved for well over a year, and ever more so with Margie's return in August. It was only in September that Margie told Laurie she was gay, and she did so without harboring a clue that Laurie was interested in women. Still, her candor with Laurie was indicative of a growing bond from which both drew sustenance. Even in their earliest footsteps into intimacy, Margie could feel a deep serenity and trust in Laurie's embrace. She was, at the same time, also feeling emotionally overwhelmed, both by the crushing news from Tiff and by just how crazy it seemed that she and Laurie, literally overnight, had begun to explore a much deeper relationship, one that had so recently seemed unthinkable.

Even if her world hadn't veered sharply into chaos, the days ahead were still going to be a challenge. A year earlier, while working in a school auditorium with special-needs students, Margie had caught a glimpse of a young, autistic boy heading toward the edge of an elevated stage. She spun quickly as she moved to catch the child, but the sudden pivot had torn the cartilage in her left knee. The procedure to repair the knee first required that bits of her own cartilage be removed and cultivated in the laboratory. The cultivated cartilage would then be surgically implanted in the damaged joint, and the date for that operation was scheduled for November 4, only three days away. Afterward, she would need to be in a wheelchair and use crutches for weeks to come. And now, after what was surely the final straw with Tiff, she would be alone in her house.

She now had less than seventy-two hours to get a lot done. Added to the list was the urgent task of finding a lawyer and getting documents together so the financial terms of the separation with Tiff could be finalized. In the midst of this she got a phone call from her good friend and neighbor Jan Gemberling. Jan had just returned to town at the end of a long European vacation. Could Margie come get her at the Spokane airport and give her a lift home?

Of course. Off she went.

The two exchanged warm greetings and stowed Jan's luggage in the trunk of the car. In the course of conversation during the twenty-minute drive home, Jan asked about Margie.

"My world is upside down," Margie said. Jan listened with a look of incredulity as Margie, struggling to control her emotions, walked her through what had happened. Jan took it all in, absorbing Margie's distress, but not to the point where it suppressed her sense of humor.

"I can't go away anymore, can I?" Jan deadpanned.

It was a blessing that Jan returned when she did.

When Laurie told Pat about the depth of her feelings for Margie, he didn't take it well. His moods swung wildly, and during one of his outbursts he insisted Laurie return home from a friend's house. When she arrived, he led her into their bedroom, produced a handgun and, holding it to his head, demanded to know whether she wanted him to kill himself. Their youngest son, Sam, was in next room. It was all she could do to steady herself and try to defuse his anger. The next day, when Pat was gone, she removed the pistol's magazine and hid it under a mattress. His rages continued, and at one point, again in the bedroom, she could only respond by pretending to be broken, by curling up in a ball and sobbing. Looking back on it, she says, it was "mind-boggling that I had put myself there." Throughout the remainder of the fall and into winter, the couple continued to live in the same large house on Glenrose Prairie, albeit in separate parts of the home.

At the time, only fourteen-year-old Sam was still living with them. But shortly before Christmas, after their daughter Abby and oldest son Dan had come home for the holidays, Pat insisted on a meeting where they would each in turn speak about how they felt about Laurie's relationship with Margie. To make sure Abby and Laurie didn't leave, he confiscated their car keys. Laurie was the last to speak, and, as resolutely as she could, she told of her feelings for Margie. As wrenching as the meeting was, it seemed to calm matters for a few days. But shortly after New Year's, Pat once again angrily confronted Laurie about her continuing contact with Margie. A few days later, as Laurie arrived in her gray Toyota Camry to pick Sam up at his middle school, she was served with divorce papers, right there on the curb. It all portended a custody battle over Sam, and what turned out to be a years-long and unsuccessful effort by Pat to shield his assets.

"There was no question in my mind that Pat was going to use Laurie's relationship with Margie, and that he was going to do everything he could," Jan remembers. "I've seen ugly divorces, but it was clear this was going to be really, really ugly."

At Jan's recommendation, Laurie retained Mary Schultz, a highly regarded Spokane lawyer known for her unflinching approach to aggressive litigation.

From her end, Margie was trying to be as supportive as she could, given the immobilization required after her knee surgery. Her recovery took a turn for the worse when, still on crutches, she fell going up a short flight of stairs at Jan's house. As she reflexively reached to break her fall, she caught her left hand on the side of one of the wooden steps and tore a tendon in her thumb. Now it was going to be even harder for her to care for herself. Laurie, for her part, was already feeling bad that she had been unable to spend more time tending to Margie, given her own family turmoil and the new siege of the divorce filing. She urged Margie to ask Gloria to come over from Gig Harbor to help, as Gloria was eager to do.

There were, however, good reasons why Margie was hesitant to ask her mother's help. To be sure, Gloria and Frank had been quietly deferential and hospitable to Margie and Tiff during their visits to Tacoma and Gig Harbor over the years. But these had been casual visits, with respectful silences and boundaries of discretion. Now, in January 2004, Margie's situation in Spokane was quite different, and much more volatile. She had few other options, though. After already injuring herself just trying to move around, she realized she really needed her mother's assistance.

It didn't go well. Once Gloria arrived and moved into the house, she couldn't help but observe how deeply Margie and Laurie were already involved in each other's lives. Laurie was a friend from work, Margie explained, and needed her help because she was in the throes of a family crisis and divorce. That brought more questions from Gloria. She learned Laurie was the mother of three children, and that her older son had a history of behavioral problems. One evening Laurie and Jan came over to use one of Margie's computers to draft statements and responses from Laurie for the divorce proceedings. It would have been hard not to notice the stress in the room as the two wrestled with the assault of paperwork and muttered aloud about Pat's scorched-earth tactics. Gloria asked Margie if she was the reason for Laurie's divorce.

"He would like to think so," Margie replied.

Gloria's discomfort intensified, and she couldn't hide it. After Laurie and Jan left, she told Margie she didn't want Laurie coming by the house anymore. That only escalated the tension between Margie and her mother. In most ways, the cushions of silence around Margie's relationships with women had served both of them well for years. But not this time. A few days later, it came to a head. Margie stepped out on her porch to make a phone call, and Gloria mistakenly surmised she had fled the house to go see Laurie. She became distraught. When Margie came back inside, Gloria was in tears, half pleading and half asking why Margie would choose to be involved with Laurie.

Though Gloria was in distress, Margie needed to deliver a firm message about who she was and what she was unwilling to forfeit. She chose nine words.

"No one has ever loved me like Laurie does."

In Laurie's social circle—especially the part connected to her church and the Catholic middle school Sam attended—whispers about Laurie's lesbian relationship became rampant as Pat contacted people seeking statements and declarations to bring into the divorce proceedings. As word spread, Laurie was effectively wearing a scarlet letter, experiencing face-to-face humiliations.

"Most definitely she had been shunned," says Debbie Duvoisin, who was raised Catholic in the upper South Hill Catholic community from which Laurie was now feeling ostracized.

Animosity was coming at Laurie from all directions, including from Carla, who didn't hide her irritation when she came to visit the hospital just before Margie's knee surgery and found Laurie was already there. But her worst day came in a courtroom, on a frozen Monday in mid-January. In the battle over custody for Sam, Pat's lawyer submitted that their son would be ostracized from his peers as more of their mothers learned that Laurie was involved in a lesbian relationship. The moms would then forbid their sons and daughters to associate with him. The court commissioner concurred. He awarded temporary custody to Pat and ordered Laurie to leave the home on Glenrose Prairie.

The commissioner's ruling, delivered in open court, left Laurie struggling to catch her breath. She had already been counseled not to make any verbal outbursts in the courtroom, but as she got up to leave, she came face to face with Pat.

"I knew I couldn't say anything, but I looked into his eyes in a way I never had."

Jan followed Laurie outside, down a sidewalk bordered by shin-deep snow, and caught up to her on a street corner. Jan held her, and Laurie wept onto her shoulder. "I still have a hard time driving past that intersection," Laurie says.

"That was horrifying," Jan remembers about the custody decision and the immediate effect it had on Laurie. "By that time, the law was absolutely clear that gender preference could not be a factor in making these decisions."

Indeed, in two weeks the legal tables had turned. The commissioner's ruling was swiftly appealed to a superior court judge, who promptly reversed both the custody order and the order removing Laurie from the home. The judge also issued a new order evicting Pat.

All the while, as Laurie was fighting to keep custody of her son, she was struggling in her heart to stay connected with her twenty-year-old daughter, Abby, a student at Carroll College, a Catholic, liberal arts school in Helena, Montana. The oldest of the three children, Abby naturally took to her role as being the "glue" among the siblings and her parents, as she worked in various ways to keep the family connected. In the tension-filled family gathering just before Christmas, Abby says, "it was very quickly about sides," and she felt pressure from her father to side with him in trying to persuade Laurie to end her relationship with Margie. In Abby's view, her father had framed the issue as "Do you want the family to be together or not?"

"He is a very persuasive person, and I was mad about it," she explains. She sided with her father, and as the family was meeting to discuss the issue, Abby weighed in and openly questioned Laurie's continuing communication with Margie. Laurie held her ground, which didn't sit well with Abby, and for weeks afterward there was a chill in their relationship.

When Abby returned to school after the break for the holidays, she thought the stress of the situation in Spokane was at least partly to blame for her having missed several periods in succession. By the time medical tests confirmed she was pregnant, it was May. There was no question as to whom she would call. Laurie and Margie were sitting on the front lawn at the farm on Glenrose when the phone rang. Within an hour, Laurie was in the car heading for Helena, leaving Margie to care for Sam.

Word that Abby was pregnant unloosed another round of family turmoil. Abby decided that when she delivered the baby, she would put the child up for adoption, and do so in a way that she would know the adoptive mother and at least be able to sustain a connection to her child. Pat tried to push her toward a different plan, one that would involve him and his new girlfriend raising the child. As an alternative, Abby said, Pat suggested the child be adopted by Pat's own father and his father's second wife. Abby was appalled and quickly wound up arguing about it with her father's girlfriend. The difference in the reaction of her two parents steered her back toward Laurie and, in time, toward Margie.

All told, it was a brutal and emotionally exhausting winter. And, yet, just when it seemed things couldn't get any worse, spring arrived, and life actually did stop getting worse. With Pat being ordered to leave the premises, Abby joined Sam and Laurie at the farm on Glenrose Prairie. Even though Abby was pregnant, it became one of the better summers of her life. Her emotional bond with her mother was restored, and she found herself deeply enjoying the visits from the clusters of friends, old and new, who arrived to lend support to her mom and Margie.

"And that's when I made my reconciliation with Margie," Abby adds. "She's part of the deal, and it felt better in my heart. It was the light."

Chapter 9

MEETING MAJOR TOREM

By the time Margie turned forty, on the second day of spring in 2004, it seemed as though she had tumbled into a life that was beginning to feel complete. She was finally able to walk without crutches after the two major knee surgeries. Her thumb had healed. Better still, the wrenching, emotional ordeals she and Laurie and Abby and Sam had endured the previous fall and winter were receding and being replaced with a quality of happiness she couldn't have imagined a year earlier. There was a swimming pool behind Laurie's house up on Glenrose Prairie. As the long days of summer arrived, the pool became their oasis.

In late July, a brief heat wave arrived, just as Margie was heading off to her monthly, weekend reserve duty. Over at McChord, west of the mountains, it was twenty degrees cooler, and beneath clear skies it seemed as though you could reach out across the flight line and touch the ice-covered dome of Mount Rainier. Given her precious childhood memories of Rainier, it was like looking up at her second home. It was postcard perfect.

She was almost too busy to notice. In addition to her continuing regular duties as a flight nurse, she was also a lead trainer and performance evaluator for the 446th. Her glowing performance reviews highlighted her communication and coordination skills; the most recent evaluation noted that she was regularly "sought out by peers and numerous Critical Care team members" because of her "unprecedented" knowledge in the field of aeromedical evacuation.

After seven years at the 446th, she had become a fixture in the unit's leadership.

"It's like Margie's always been a part of us," says Julia Scott, a veteran flight nurse who joined the reserve squadron at McChord in 1985. "It's hard to explain."

A key measure of Margie's value to the 446th was that she was chief of standards and evaluations (Stan/Eval) for the two-hundred-plus-member squadron, responsible for closely monitoring the unit's readiness. In July 2004 this was an especially important job, because the squadron was preparing for a major inspection. There was so much to get done that Margie was planning to stay over two additional days. She was up to her elbows in preparations, surrounded by several members of her staff, when the 446th's commander, Colonel Mary Walker, appeared in the office doorway. It was mid-morning, Sunday, July 25.

"Major Witt, will you come with me?" she heard Colonel Walker ask.

"Yes, ma'am," came her quick reply.

Though it was unusual for Colonel Walker to ask to see her, she thought little of it as the two started walking down the long, narrow hallway toward the commander's conference room.

"I'm walking with her, and she isn't saying anything," Margie recalls. "So I just ask her, 'What's this about?'"

"Somebody wants to talk to you," the commander replied.

"Well, what's this about?" Margie repeated, and then, half in jest, "You're kinda making me nervous."

Colonel Walker explained there was an inquiry under way involving someone in the unit, and investigators were going about getting statements from people.

Margie was aware that another member of the squadron was having problems. Maybe it was about him, she thought. But if it was, she really knew nothing directly and wouldn't have much to say.

When they reached the conference room, Colonel Walker opened the door and steered Margie through. Reaching his hand out to her was a man about her age, trim, and wearing a standard blue uniform.

"Major Witt?" he asked, as he stood to introduce himself. As she accepted his handshake, she couldn't help but notice Colonel Walker closing the door from the outside, leaving just the two of them in the room.

Something in the abrupt handoff from Colonel Walker to the man in the blue uniform didn't feel right to her. As she took a chair across the table from him, she could feel her heart starting to race.

"Okay," she was thinking, trying to steady herself, "this isn't about me, this isn't about me." But it wasn't really working. Within seconds, her anxiety was close to what she was feeling when she was a young second lieutenant at Castle AFB, sixteen years earlier, as she was put in the back-seat of the car by the two OSI investigators, who then drove her to Fresno.

It is more likely than not that when the man in blue reached for Margie's hand he also formally introduced himself. His name was Major Adam Torem, an active-duty JAG investigator attached to the Sixty-Second Air Transport Wing at McChord. On account of the stress involved, Margie's memories of the meeting are jagged, like the pieces of a shattered vase. The first thing she can remember him saying is:

"What is your relationship with Tiffany Jenson?"

After the nonchalance that Colonel Walker had affected on the stroll down the hall, his question landed like a sucker punch. It quickly answered the questions about why he was there, and who was being investigated. Six weeks earlier, a two-page letter had been sent by e-mail to General John Jumper, the Air Force chief of staff. In the first three paragraphs, the message asserted that Margie was a lesbian, that she was involved in a romantic relationship with Laurie McChesney, and that the romantic relationship with Laurie followed Margie's breakup with her "six year lesbian partner, Tiffany Jenson."

The tone of the letter was venomous throughout, but its author saved the worst for last. Not only was the author willing to provide more information, he assured General Jumper, but Tiffany Jenson was also willing to provide additional information, including information about one of Margie's earlier relationships with another woman.

Major Torem would have noticed the shock on her face as she struggled for a breath. There was an edge of anger in her voice when she replied to his question about Tiff.

"She was my roommate," she replied.

She continued listening in stunned silence until she heard him name Pat McChesney as her accuser.

"He's crazy," she interjected. "He's nuts."

By now she perfectly understood the gravity of the situation he was presenting her with, and he reacted to her distress.

"Major," she remembers him saying, "I want you to think like an Air Force officer. You've been an Air Force officer a long time. I want you to act as an Air Force officer."

His message also underscored just how serious her circumstances were. She began to tremble.

Picking up where he had left off, he added more information. He said he had already decided that Pat McChesney's statement wouldn't be used to press adultery charges because his credibility was suspect. But, he added, Tiffany Jenson had given a statement, and she was considered credible.

The implication was clear. As Major Torem would shortly confirm, the Air Force was pursuing her dismissal for homosexual conduct.

Inside she was processing Torem's advice, and telling herself not to say anything. But she couldn't help herself.

"I haven't done anything wrong," she insisted. She repeated the statement, for emphasis.

In Major Torem's investigative report recommending the Air Force initiate discharge proceedings against Margie, he described the meeting this way: "Although Maj Witt did not provide any formal sworn statements, verbal or written, on 25 Jul 04, I was able to make various observations about her reaction to the allegations against her. From the outset, Maj Witt appeared shocked by the suggestion that she had committed homosexual acts. When she learned that Mr. Pat McChesney was the source of the complaint against her, she stated 'he's a lunatic!' Upon learning that Ms. Jenson had confirmed the allegations, Maj Witt become more emotionally upset, turning tearful and red-faced. Expressing frustration, she rhetorically asked 'why?' several times and inquired as to whether Ms. Jenson was upset with her for some reason. Maj Witt characterized Ms. Jenson as a 'former roommate' and nothing more. During the explanation of her rights under and the processes set out in AFI 36-3209, Major Witt was tearful and variously repeated 'I didn't do anything wrong' and 'I can't believe this' several times each. At the end of the 45 minutes we spent during the interview in the 446 AES conference room, Maj Witt asked permission to leave the building and not return to her duty station until later that afternoon, after she had a chance to recompose herself. I secured this permission on her behalf and allowed her to depart the area. 446 AES/CCF confirmed Maj Witt's return to duty later that same afternoon."

From where she sat across the table, Margie remembers trying to limit her responses to single words or short phrases. When Major Torem explained her choices to her, she remembers him sliding a form across the table. He said she could sign the statement admitting her relationship with Tiffany Jenson and that would be that; she would be discharged in two weeks.

She pushed the paper back to his side of the table.

He offered it again, and then asked if she wanted to visit with a chaplain.

"No," she answered. "Are we done?"

Yes, Torem replied. She remembers him telling her that she was free to take a break and compose herself but also informing her, on behalf of Colonel Walker, that she was expected to attend the squadron's leadership meeting that afternoon. It would be in the same room.

Chapter 10

▬▬▬▬▬▬

WHEN LAWYERS
ARE A GIRL'S
BEST FRIENDS

As Margie got up to leave her life-shattering encounter with Major Adam Torem, she was concerned her legs might buckle beneath her. When she realized she was still able to move, she walked briskly out of the room, out of the building, and into the parking lot.

The depth of betrayal was incomprehensible. While she had, for years, considered ways she could be ensnared by the military's antigay policy, she had never imagined something like this. The JAG officer's earlier meeting with Tiffany—at which Tiffany corroborated Pat McChesney's report to the Air Force that the two had a long-standing lesbian relationship—had taken place on July 14, at a Spokane Starbucks, just ten days after Tiff had given birth. This was a nightmare, just a wailing shitstorm of anguish radiating from Margie's core to every extremity. Yet, Torem's advice—to carefully consider her choices and to put her experience as an Air Force officer to use—had registered. She still had a ways to go to steady herself, but she began working the problem, with her cell phone.

She called Jan Gemberling in Spokane.

"I picked up the phone and there's somebody crying," Jan recalls. "It probably took me a minute to figure out it was Margie. And she was just overwhelmed."

The question Margie was asking over and over was: "What do I do?"

In those first moments all Jan could think to do, given the distress Margie was so obviously experiencing, was to offer emotional support. And then she tried to help her sort through some logistics, to try to protect herself and others who might get caught up in the investigation. The first step was for Margie to get off the base and try to catch her breath, which she did by driving to a friend's house fifteen minutes away. She then began making calls to gay Air Force colleagues with whom she was in regular contact. Her message to each of them was to protect themselves by not trying to contact her, especially via e-mail, so as to lessen the risk that they too would come under investigation. There was a lot of other work to do that could only be done back in Spokane, but she knew she would be in no shape to make that long drive. Fortunately, one of her best and most trusted friends from the 446th, JP Wirth, was available and more than willing to make the drive if she could pick him up in Seattle.

Before long, it was time to return to the base, for the mandatory 3 p.m. meeting in the same room where, hours earlier, she had endured one of the worst experiences of her life. Now, with the other members of the 446th's leadership team gathered in the room, she would try to control her emotions and fight back tears. It was all the more strange because Colonel Walker remained poker-faced throughout, even cheerfully reminding the others in the room how important Margie's role would be in finishing preparations for the crucial inspection. The weirdness of being told how vital she was to her unit, just hours after being offered an expedient discharge from the Air Force, did nothing to loosen the knot in her stomach. If only she could have left her body in the chair and plunged her battered spirit into Shadow Lake.

When the meeting ended, Colonel Walker exited the room by a back door connecting to her office. Margie left through the main door but then walked around the corner to the front side of the colonel's office. She knocked, entered, and curtly informed her commander that she would not be staying over Monday and Tuesday as she had originally planned. Her next stop was in Gig Harbor, to Frank and Gloria's, where she had to pack up her things and tell her confused and concerned parents that her plans had changed, that she was headed back to Spokane. It was early evening by the time she got to Seattle to rendezvous with JP, hand him the keys, and head east on Interstate 90 for Spokane.

The urgency of Margie's situation was very clear to Jan.

"It hit me fast," she recalls. "Before Margie got back to town, I'd shifted from emotional support—which is not really my strong point, normally—to 'I am a lawyer, and I know some lawyers.' And I thought early on, this is a big legal case. This is a Don't Ask, Don't Tell case that can be fought and can be won. Because I could see that Margie was an ideal plaintiff."

How it could be won she wasn't exactly sure. By mid-2004, approximately ten thousand U.S. service men and women had been expelled by the military since Don't Ask, Don't Tell had taken effect a decade earlier. Although a few had successfully challenged their expulsions under previous policies, no one had prevailed in a case challenging his or her dismissal under DADT.

What Jan could say, from her own experience as a lawyer, is that if you were going to litigate against the military and the U.S. government, you couldn't hope to find a better client. And Jan was thinking not just of Margie, but Laurie as well.

"They'd already established their grit, dealing with the divorce," she said. "These were not throw-in-the towel people. These were smart people. These were dream clients."

Maybe there were a few dozen people in Spokane who knew about the case of Master Sergeant Perry Watkins, the openly gay Tacoma soldier who, fifteen years earlier, had successfully challenged his discharge from the U.S. Army. There was, though, one person in Spokane who had actually worked on the *Watkins* case. That person was Jan Gemberling.

The lead attorney on the *Watkins* case was Jim Lobsenz, a former King County deputy prosecutor. He had only recently joined the Seattle firm of Edwards & Barbieri when Jan, fresh out of Stanford with her law degree, came to work there in 1984. By then, Lobsenz was in his third year as Watkins's volunteer attorney, working in conjunction with the ACLU of Washington State. Like Lobsenz, Jan had a passion for civil rights cases, and it wasn't long before she was coming in on weekends to help him with *Watkins v. U.S. Army* and other pro bono cases.

"That's what I went to law school for," she says. "It was all great stuff."

Although they had worked together at Edwards & Barbieri for only a few months, Jan had followed Lobsenz's career. She knew he was still an active trial attorney with a continuing interest in civil rights cases. To be sure, Margie's situation was quite different from Perry Watkins's, and the military's antigay policy had since been hardened and recast in a new statute. All Jan knew for certain is that Margie Witt would be a great client. And if there was a new or emerging constitutional vulnerability in the ways

Don't Ask, Don't Tell was being used to purge the military of gay service members, Jan was confident Jim Lobsenz had been thinking about it.

"Jim knows the law. Good lawyers are reading a lot of cases and staying on top of what's new. And this was clearly within the ambit of things he would be aware of."

When she dialed his number on Monday morning, July 26, she was pretty sure he would remember her, and take the phone call.

He did.

There was a new twist, or at least a recent one. It was a U.S. Supreme Court decision, *Lawrence v. Texas*, that had come down a year earlier, in June 2003. The majority opinion, written by Justice Anthony Kennedy, drew an unusual amount of attention for a couple of reasons. The first is that, with *Lawrence*, the Supreme Court had reversed itself by overturning a 1986 decision, *Bowers v. Hardwick*, which had upheld the right of states to criminalize homosexual sex. Second, the opinion in *Lawrence* was eloquent where it spoke to the rights that gay men and women should enjoy without fear of government prosecution.

"It suffices for us to acknowledge that adults may choose to enter upon this relationship in the confines of their homes and their own private lives and still retain their dignity as free persons," Justice Kennedy wrote. "When sexuality finds overt expression in intimate conduct with another person, the conduct can be but one element in a personal bond that is more enduring. The liberty protected by the Constitution allows homosexual persons the right to make this choice."

Still, just because the Supreme Court had ruled that states and the federal government couldn't criminalize gay sex among consenting adults, it didn't mean that other laws and policies that clearly discriminated against gay men and women could no longer be enforced. Indeed, as Margie had just learned, the U.S. government had every intention of removing her from the Air Force because another woman had been willing to come forward to say the two had been sexually intimate.

On the other hand, the majority's reasoning in *Lawrence* was frightening, at least to those who still regarded homosexuality as an apostasy. In a blistering and prophetic dissent, Justice Antonin Scalia lashed out at Justice Kennedy's majority opinion, writing that by overturning *Bowers* the court majority was inviting a "massive overturning of the current social order."

Jim Lobsenz was intrigued by the *Lawrence* decision for much the same reason that Justice Scalia was hopping mad about it. While the immediate effect of the decision was to decriminalize gay sex, the court's reasoning—as Scalia pointed out—implicitly challenged the legal footing of other laws and policies that discriminated against homosexuals. The reach of the decision was as yet unclear. But a reliable way to bring clarity was to bring a lawsuit.

After they had spoken for several minutes during their phone conversation that Monday morning, Jan remembers Jim saying he might be interested in a challenge to Don't Ask, Don't Tell.

"The reason why I'd be interested is because of *Lawrence v. Texas*," Jan remembers him saying. "There is an angle, and nobody's done it yet."

"It really hinges on the client," he told her. "I can't decide anything until I talk to her."

That was good enough for Jan. She was elated.

"He was the closest thing to the perfect lawyer, and they [Margie and Laurie] were the closest thing to a perfect client. I really, really wanted Jim to do it, for both their sakes."

Chapter 11

━━━━━━━━━━━━

SILVER WINGS

JP Wirth was not at McChord for the 446th's busy drill weekend in late July. Having just returned from a long deployment to Ramstein Air Base in Germany—where his med-tech duties included long flights to retrieve soldiers wounded in Afghanistan—he was on leave, at home in Seattle, when Margie reached him by phone.

As with Jan Gemberling just minutes earlier, it was instantly clear to him that Margie was in distress. His natural instincts, coupled with his medical experience, were to work through the emotional shock and find the underlying wounds. Among his first concerns was whether she had been physically injured. No, he learned, the trauma was all emotional, all connected to what she had absorbed in the ambush she was led into by Colonel Walker.

"I'm going to be the brain right now," he remembers thinking, and that meant trying to take stock of what had to happen in the next hours and days, and set a course.

She needed to get home to Spokane but was in no condition to make the long drive by herself. With JP's guidance she would take it one step at a time. She would leave the base, pack up her belongings in Gig Harbor, and then make the forty-minute drive north to Seattle. JP would then take the wheel and drive them east to Spokane.

Laurie was sitting on the grass at Glenrose Prairie, enjoying a nearly perfect summer afternoon, in puffs of dry, piney breezes, when Margie called with the news. There would come a point when Laurie's tears would flow, but not at the immediate shock of the news. The first thing she remembers noticing is that her hands were shaking.

JP and Margie were on the road, but they were still hours away. Fortunately, Abby was home, and after Laurie shared the news with her, it was clear they both needed to do something to occupy them. What they had on hand was an artsy cardboard cylinder with a lid on it—it was big enough to hold a dachshund—that one of them had picked up at a craft store. They quickly decided they would fashion it into a care package for Margie, so they went to work with scissors, cutting out photographs and phrases from *National Geographic* and other magazines to decorate the exterior.

"There were some real serious world concerns going on in these phrases and pictures," she recalls. "And we thought, 'This is a world concern, we have to wrap our heads around this.'"

In the meantime, JP was driving east, with the amber wash of sunlight finally beginning to ebb as they crossed the Columbia River and then angled northward into the high desert south of Grand Coulee. He remembers that she kept asking why Tiff had outed her to the Air Force, and then wondering aloud how she was going to tell her parents if and when she was removed from the Air Force. She was worried about how devastated Frank and Gloria might be.

Gradually, with JP's quiet encouragement, she began to steady herself and regain a sense of resolve. The breakup with Tiff, months earlier, had sent her into a similar spiral, though this one was more intense. Now she was all the more determined that it wasn't going to be the end of her, nor the end of her life in the Air Force. With Laurie she had already found an unexpected new dimension to her life, one she shared with somebody who loved her unconditionally and who understood her better than anyone had before. That was a life worth fighting for, and she was going to get up the next day and do just that.

Seven years earlier, it was their common tastes in food that drew JP and Margie together as friends and created space for their quicksilver humor. Another common trait that JP noticed is that both were very task oriented. And that is how they worked together in the following days, moving from one step to another. Assuming she was now subject to surveillance, they closed the blinds at her house and replaced the cordless phones with corded equipment that would decrease the chances of electronic intercepts. Then all her personally sensitive materials—books, recordings, photos, memorabilia, journals—anything that could conceivably be gathered by federal investigators and used against her—was boxed up and hauled down the street for storage at Jan Gemberling's house.

The early connection with Jim Lobsenz lifted Margie's spirits, especially when she learned from Jan that he had been Perry Watkins's lawyer. In fact, literature on Perry's case was among the material they had packed up and moved to Jan's house. In their first phone conversation, Lobsenz said he needed to review her service files. She and JP promptly drove down the hill to Costco, purchased a fax machine, and then began the task of feeding it more than four hundred pages of her records.

In his 1993 book *Conduct Unbecoming*, Randy Shilts noted that Perry Watkins likened Lobsenz's distinguished demeanor to Gregory Peck's portrayal of lawyer Atticus Finch in *To Kill a Mockingbird*. Lobsenz was only twenty-eight years old when he became Watkins's attorney. Part of what intrigued Watkins about Lobsenz, Shilts reported, was that Jim is a Quaker, and Watkins (who died from AIDS in 1996) was well aware of how vital the Quakers were to the abolition of slavery. Were it not for his prominent role in taking (and winning) cases challenging the military's gay ban, Lobsenz would be best known as a fierce opponent of capital punishment and for his pro bono representation of death row inmates in Washington State.

More likely than not, Lobsenz would not have become Margie Witt's lawyer had he not become Watkins's lawyer twenty-three years earlier. His interest in representing Watkins was at least partly inspired by an experience he had as an undergrad at Stanford. After having drawn a lousy number in the Stanford student housing lottery, Lobsenz recruited three classmates to share an old trailer with him. One of his new roommates was "Kerrigan," whom he had met as a prep school student at the Phillips Academy in Andover, Massachusetts. The two remained college roommates for years, and after Lobsenz was accepted into the University of California law school at nearby Berkeley, the two decided they would share a large apartment in the fall. Over summer break, Lobsenz received a letter from Kerrigan, informing him that his friend now realized he was gay, that he would no longer hide that part of his identity, and that if this were a problem it would be okay if Jim decided to live elsewhere.

Lobsenz was taken aback—not because Kerrigan was gay, but because of the loaded suggestion that it might matter. So far as he knew, Kerrigan was the first gay person he had ever known, but the idea that it would alter their friendship was deeply upsetting. As his irritation subsided, Lobsenz reflected on the letter and what it implied about Kerrigan's struggles to be accepted as a gay man.

Lobsenz was in his third year working as a deputy prosecutor in Seattle when he learned about Sergeant Perry Watkins. By then Lobsenz had begun serving, in a volunteer capacity, on the legal committee for the Washington State ACLU. Watkins had sought the ACLU's help on the private recommendation of a Fort Lewis officer who was familiar with the organization's civil rights work. The ACLU agreed to represent him, but then had difficulty finding a volunteer attorney to take the case.

"So, I say, 'Okay, I'll do it,'" Lobsenz recalls. "Which is kind of nuts, since I didn't have any experience at all in civil litigation. I'm not saying that I sat down and said 'Kerrigan would really want me to do this case,' but I would never have done the *Watkins* case if all those things hadn't happened in my life, with having Kerrigan as a roommate and finding out about his life. By the time Margie's case came along I'd thought about it for years and years and years, and there was like nothing to decide or think through."

Air Force records show that Lobsenz first contacted Major Torem within forty-eight hours of Torem informing Margie of the accusations against her.

The streams of faxes that Margie and JP were sending off to Seattle were arriving in the sky-scraping offices of Carney Badley Spellman, one of the state's largest law firms, where Lobsenz has been a principal partner since 1989. There were things that Margie Witt and Perry Watkins had in common. They were both from Tacoma, they were both in the military, they were both popular with their colleagues and valued by their superiors. They were both gay.

The main difference was not that she was a white female and he a black male. It was that he was fearlessly open about his sexual orientation, and she was conspicuously discreet about hers. There was a short stretch of time where it seemed, in the eyes of the law, that this difference might not matter. It came during the seventh year of the legal battle against the Army, when Watkins, Lobsenz, and the ACLU appeared to have grasped a historic civil rights victory.

"Homosexual Ban in Army Rejected by Appeals Court," read the headline in the *New York Times* on February 11, 1988. A three-judge panel of the federal Ninth Circuit Court of Appeals had ruled, 2–1, that the policy the Army invoked to expel Sergeant Watkins violated the Constitution's guarantees of equal protection because it discriminated against homosexuals and wasn't necessary to promote a compelling government interest.

The ruling clearly would have provided constitutional protection to all gay service members—if it had stood. Yet, as the *Times* story indicated, it would be difficult, on appeal, to square the appeals panel's finding in *Watkins* with the U.S. Supreme Court's recent ruling in *Bowers v. Hardwick*, the 1986 decision upholding the constitutionality of the Georgia antisodomy law.

As expected, the government's lawyers moved swiftly to have the case reargued to the full complement of Ninth Circuit judges. The appeal was accepted, and the resulting en banc court ruling revoked the earlier decision. The Army still lost, but this time it lost its battle against Sergeant Watkins in a way that allowed the military to keep its antigay policy in place. In a 7–4 opinion issued on May 3, 1989, the full Ninth Circuit held that federal courts didn't need to "reach the constitutional issues raised" in the panel's earlier ruling. Instead, the new decision focused on the basic unfairness of Perry Watkins's particular circumstances—that he had always been open with the Army about his homosexuality, that the Army had drafted him anyway, allowed him to reenlist, continued to promote him, and allowed him to work toward his pension. Then the Army changed the rules and moved to discharge him.

Just like that, the earlier historic decision trumpeting equal protection was gone, replaced by a ruling rooted in the common law doctrine of "equitable estoppel."

Lobsenz, a father to young daughters at the time, would explain it this way:

"If I say to my daughter, you know, eat all the carrots on your plate. If you eat all the carrots, you can have some dessert. So she relies on my express assurance that if she eats the carrots, she can have dessert. And she eats the carrots, then says 'Okay, I'm ready for dessert.' And then if I say, 'Ha, ha! Fooled you! No dessert.' That's unfair. She has detrimentally relied on my promise, and now for me to break the promise is in violation of the principles of equity—basic, fundamental fairness. She gets to say 'You are estopped, you are prohibited from changing your mind now, now that I've done what you've said.'"

The George H. W. Bush administration appealed even this narrowly framed decision. But in late 1990, the U.S. Supreme Court declined to hear the appeal, thus upholding the Ninth Circuit's ruling in Watkins's favor. That was good for Watkins, because Lobsenz was then able to negotiate a settlement including back pay and a full pension. But, in strict legal terms, it had no ramifications that would help other gay service members.

"Where are you going to find the case of another guy who told them at his draft physical that he was gay, and then they kept him for fifteen years?" Lobsenz explained. "There are no such other people. His case, as a precedent, was not useful to 99.99999 percent of all gay people in the armed forces."

Still, there was something else Lobsenz noticed, and one can easily find it in the Ninth Circuit's en banc decision, written by Judge Harry Pregerson. There wasn't a shred of evidence in the record that Watkins, as an openly serving gay soldier, was a detriment to his unit. To the contrary, the judges who ruled on his case seemed to delight in reciting the official commendations and trial testimony about how valuable his contributions were and how well regarded he was by his compatriots.

The case came before several federal trial and appellate judges over the years, Lobsenz noted, "and even Reagan appointees were beginning to say, 'This policy isn't very rational, is it?'"

Despite such questions, the policy lived on, even as other high-profile cases emerged, adding fuel to a political movement to bring an end to it.

In the Pentagon and in Congress, the rationale for the policy began to shift. Up through World War II and into the period of the Cold War, "sexual perversion" and other terms of moral condemnation were used to justify the expulsion of homosexuals from the military. But as time went on, proponents of the gay ban began to make a different case: that military esprit de corps would suffer if straight soldiers knew they were living and fighting in close quarters with gay service members. It was this less polarizing argument that coalesced in the 1994 directive issued as part of Don't Ask, Don't Tell.

"As a general rule," the policy stated, "homosexuality is incompatible with military service because it interferes with factors critical to combat effectiveness, including unit morale, unit cohesion and individual privacy."

As the initial shock of her outing and the Air Force's announced intention to expel her began to wear off, Margie would mock the proposition that she was a detriment to unit morale and cohesion in the 446th.

"Really?" she would ask. "That's the one you're going pull out? Because, you know, I'm the one who leads karaoke."

Laughing about it was a way of coping with the pain. The bland legal declaration that just because she was gay she was a detriment to her unit was deeply offensive to her. Of course, there were thousands of service members before her who felt the same way, and who had already been dismissed under the DADT policy without recourse.

Long before Don't Ask, Don't Tell, Lobsenz had argued on behalf of Perry Watkins that the military policy of expelling gay service members violated constitutional rights. The "gay soldiers hurt morale" argument was directly rebutted by Watkins's military experience. There was also a conspicuous analogy to the military's initial resistance to racial integration. Lobsenz hammered away at the fact that even in the years following World War II, scores of military leaders still insisted that unit morale and cohesion would suffer if white soldiers were forced to serve in the same units as blacks.

"They were *all wrong!*" Lobsenz all but shouts as he relives the arguments.

The wording of the 1994 Don't Ask, Don't Tell policy was adopted when the raw moral condemnation of homosexuality—embedded in the Supreme Court's 1986 *Bowers* decision—was still on the books, legitimizing laws in Georgia and other states that codified homosexual coupling as a crime. But then came *Lawrence v. Texas* in 2003, revoking *Bowers* altogether.

"Once Lawrence comes down," Lobsenz recalls, "it's like the light goes on in my mind."

In part because of Justice Scalia's pyrophoric dissent—warning that the *Lawrence* decision "effectively decrees the end of all morals legislation"—there was plenty of discussion in legal and political circles about the opinion's broader implications. What *did* it mean if homosexuality could no longer be considered a crime?

Instinctively, Lobsenz began thinking about whether *Lawrence* could be interpreted to rein in the power the government was wielding through Don't Ask, Don't Tell to root out and expel gay service members. With Major Margaret Witt, he now had the perfect client with whom to find out.

Within a week of being informed that she was being investigated for discharge for engaging in homosexual conduct, Margie met Jim Lobsenz for the first time at his office on the fifty-eighth floor of the Seattle Municipal

Tower. By the end of the meeting, it was clear to him that Jan Gemberling was right, and that Margie had the resolve to see the case through. Given Margie's knowledge of the Perry Watkins case, he didn't have to tell her that it would be neither easy, nor quick. But he reminded her anyway.

In the decorated care capsule Laurie and Abby worked up for Margie on July 25 were boxes of tea but also a little bit of booze. There was no masking the bare-knuckled revenge at play in Pat and Tiff's outing of Margie, and words of consolation couldn't begin to deflect the nightmare the two had delivered by going to the Air Force. Yet this very nasty turn of events was happening to people who were already well on the way to creating a new family anchored in a deep, resilient relationship.

"They have a lot more in common than their senses of humor," observes Jan Gemberling. "I think Laurie had been horribly repressed during her marriage. She had never been allowed to be who she was. It was like a flower unfolding. She just acquired skills and accomplishments and learned how to manage so many different things. I mean, to be emotionally supportive to Margie and to be nurturing to her children. She was given an opportunity to be who she really was, an opportunity she'd never really had before."

The powerful storm that continued to engulf them had, consequently, a celestial eye at its center. In the weeks before July 25, Margie, Laurie, Abby, and Sam were experiencing a sublime summer, and even after the devastating news from Major Torem, they just kept right on flourishing.

"It was the most beautiful transitional season of my life, in every way I could imagine," Laurie recalls. "For lack of a better word, I had blossomed, and everybody around me had too. And we were living and breathing it every day. And it *was* terrifying, but it was nothing that I even considered letting go of, any part of it. There was huge happiness."

In spite of what had happened at McChord, and the whirlpool of emotions it had unloosed, Margie hadn't lost sight of the people in her life to whom she was committed. It was clear to her that the top priorities that summer were Abby and Sam. Especially Abby, as she neared her delivery date.

That day came on August 10. Laurie was with Abby early that morning when she went into labor. In the birthing room there were only two others, a midwife and a hospital nurse.

"I'd never experienced birth from that angle," Laurie says, recalling how she cut the umbilical cord. The nurse cleaned the infant and then turned to her, called her "Grandma," and asked if she would like to hold the child. It had been an exhausting night for both Abby and Laurie, and Abby soon fell asleep, as the sunrise unfolded.

"And I had a cup of coffee," Laurie remembers. "I don't know where it came from; maybe the nurse brought it. The window was behind me, and the sunlight was just shining right on me. I could feel the warmth of the sun, and I had the coffee, and I had this baby, and she just smelled better than a puppy, just like a baby. And then to just watch my own baby sleeping. I was so proud of her."

Thirteen years earlier, Margie's brother Chris had flown to San Antonio to be part of a graduation ceremony at the School of Aerospace Medicine, during which family members could pin the silver wings to the uniforms of the newly certified flight nurses. On the morning of August 10, 2004, after the newborn infant had been gracefully and respectfully transferred to the adoptive mother who would raise her, Margie arrived to see Abby, with whom she had so richly bonded over the summer. During the visit, she handed her the silver wings, for keeps.

"Abby would call me her hero. And I would say 'No, you're the hero. You've done something far braver than I.'"

Chapter 12

▬▬▬▬▬▬▬

"MAJOR WITT IS GAY"

For twenty-five years Margie had struggled daily to reconcile two of the truest things about herself.

First and foremost was her deep love and loyalty to her parents; not just the love tied to dependence, but the kind of love that you stand up for, as she did that day as a first grader when she got into trouble for insisting on including her mother's story in a writing assignment about what fathers do.

The unwelcome realization that she might be a lesbian began to arrive as she reached her mid-teens. It turned out to be a suspicion her parents shared, but not as a topic of conversation with her.

"We felt we were waiting for her," Gloria says. "There was no way we were going to bring anything up, because it never . . . I should say that we always, you know, accepted the kids she was with, and it just rolled, rolled along."

The communication was, at best, indirect, but on Margie's end it formed a message nonetheless.

"I felt like I wasn't who they wanted me to be."

There were reasons for that, observes Margie's older sister, Virginia, and many of them were rooted in misinformation and generational attitudes about homosexuality.

"As my parents, they feared for her life going forward if everybody knew, because it would make everything harder," Virginia says. "Back then it was harder to fit in, or be accepted, or go to church, or get a job if people knew you were gay. They were terrified that if you were gay that it must also mean that you're a pedophile."

And part of her parents' fear, Virginia surmised, was that their parenting—via genetics or the environment they had created—might be implicated as a factor.

"I knew they would always love her, no matter what," she says. "But I also knew that it was going to be hard for them because they would feel . . . they would feel as though they had some blame in this."

Beginning in her late teens, and without telling her parents, Margie began seeing a succession of counselors to help her cope with the depression she was experiencing.

"I was trying to deal with how to be myself, how to live my life as me, and make everybody else happy too."

At age twenty-three, even before she was essentially abducted by the two OSI officers, it became vitally important to keep the Air Force happy as well. And the Air Force made it more than clear that it didn't want to hear from her that she was gay. Adding the Air Force regulation against homosexuality to the equation only intensified her inner conflict and raised the stakes.

"I really had nothing else to be down about, but it was always this heartache. It always had a hold on me. All those years I just wanted to wake up and not have to think about it, about being different, about who I would befriend and whether I could trust them. Who wanted to befriend me? And could I let them in? That gets really tiring."

Being outed to the Air Force in July 2004 had been traumatic, yet it also meant the inner turmoil of holding her secret would be coming to an end. A decision to fight the Air Force was a decision that would inevitably lead to her parents learning—right along with the rest of her world—that she was gay.

She would swiftly take the first step. Now that she knew an Air Force JAG had been to Spokane and that the investigation of her private life would be ongoing, she wanted to make sure her civilian employers heard it first from her. After telling her supervisor, Nancy Royse, she arranged a meeting with Nancy's superiors at the school district's headquarters. She was nervous, but the pair of District 81 officials responded as sympathetically as Nancy had, and instantly became unwavering supporters as well. When the district's physical therapy staff had its first gathering in preparation for the coming school year, Margie and Laurie arrived to find their colleagues dressed in military attire, some even with face camouflage, holding a banner that read: "We're all in this together."

Laurie had begun notifying a few of her closest friends months earlier once she learned, weeks before the divorce filing, that Pat had sought out members of their church community and disclosed Laurie's relationship with Margie. Debbie Duvoisin was one of four women Laurie had bonded with nearly twenty years earlier when they were all mothers with young children attending the same South Hill day care. As she began to experience social backlash, Laurie arranged to meet one on one with each of her friends, to disclose and explain what had happened in her life, and to give them the opportunity to gracefully end their friendship with her if they were uncomfortable. None of them did.

"What we saw," says Debbie, "is that there was this trial by fire, and this strength, such a fierce, passionate strength that I'd never observed in her before. There just wasn't any question that this wasn't the right path, and it was, for us, 'whatever we can do.'"

For Margie and Carla—best friends for over twenty years—events had dragged them to a new low point.

Margie's breakup with Tiff the previous fall had not gone over so well with Carla. And then came the confusing and testy encounter in the hospital, as Margie was being prepped for knee surgery, where Carla arrived and bristled when she found Laurie already at Margie's bedside.

"I walked in like I owned the joint and pissed all over every hydrant I could find," Carla recalls. "Because it's like 'I don't know who you are, but let me tell you who I am. I am her friend.'"

It was in response to Margie's plea that Carla and her partner had taken Tiff in after their wrenching breakup on Halloween. Now, nearly a year later, Carla still found herself torn. Margie insisted Tiff had cooperated with Pat McChesney in outing her to the Air Force, but Carla was also hearing Tiff deny the accusations.

"That was one of the hardest parts for me," Margie says. "Not having my very best and closest friend. Not having her believe me."

In late fall 2004, however, Margie was provided a copy of Major Torem's report, including a very detailed account of the interview at the Spokane Starbucks in which, according to the report, Tiff disclosed "Margaret was my second lesbian lover" and that the pair had been involved in an intimate relationship for over six years. To which, according to Torem, Tiff added: "Margaret was always fearful of the Air Force discovering our relationship."

Torem e-mailed a copy of his interview summary to Tiff for her review, and the records also show she replied, on September 9, correcting only a minor detail about the couple's home ownership.

And that's what it took to convince Carla: Margie, in Carla's words, going through the evidence "like a prosecuting attorney," explaining in vivid detail what Tiff had shared with Torem.

"I think she thought, 'What is wrong with my best friend here?'" says Carla. "She just couldn't figure it out. So she was talking me through this . . . because I just think she was bound and determined to get me to see what I couldn't see. And I just listened to the whole thing, and I was stunned. I was just stunned."

At that point, Carla says, she and her partner severed their friendship with Tiff.

"It was like, 'Wow, where was I?'" Carla says. "I was really stunned by the magnitude of the whole thing."

With one of the nation's best civil rights lawyers now working on Margie's behalf, she and Laurie fully expected the "whole thing" would see the light of day. It was, after all, the truth, their truth, and they both believed their truth was better than the Air Force's tale that Margie was a liability to her squadron and, by extension, a detriment to national security.

The question of how Margie could afford Jim Lobsenz and a cloud-parting Seattle law firm like Carney Badley Spellman was easy enough to answer. She couldn't. And she didn't have to. As Lobsenz had with Perry Watkins, he intended to represent her in his capacity as a volunteer lawyer for the ACLU of Washington. He and the firm would donate his time. Lobsenz was confident the ACLU would agree to pick up the expenses, in exchange for collecting any legal fees the court might order the government to pay in the event Margie prevailed.

As was the case with Perry Watkins, the ACLU of Washington, like other nonprofit law firms, has a standard evaluation process, typically including an intake interview with the person seeking representation. A key step in that process is a request to the legal committee to weigh in on whether to take the case.

That was not quite how it worked for Margie, though. Shortly after her trip to Seattle to meet Lobsenz, Jim went directly to Kathleen Taylor, the ACLU affiliate's executive director.

"We'd love to have that case," she told him.

Taylor well remembers the conversation, and chuckles when asked about her response.

"Are you saying that I made the decision instead of letting the legal department make the decision? Probably so."

For Taylor, a nonlawyer who was an aide to Idaho's legendary U.S. senator Frank Church early in her career, it was all about the story. A veteran, decorated female flight nurse, with an otherwise impeccable record of service to her country, was being pushed out of the military just short of the years needed to qualify for her pension. She was being discharged not because she had violated the "don't tell" part of the supposed Don't Ask, Don't Tell compact. She was being driven out because someone seeking revenge had gone to the Air Force to report that she was a homosexual. How was that fair?

Taylor had known Lobsenz for over twenty years and was, in fact, the ACLU of Washington's top executive when he had stepped forward to take the *Watkins* case. She knew that he and the legal committee would discuss and evaluate the legal theories involved, but plainly concedes this didn't factor into her decision to bring Margaret Witt on as a client.

"I want to take cases because the unfairness shouldn't have happened. And I'll leave it to the lawyers to figure out what the best legal argument is to make."

In a sense, Lobsenz then backfilled Taylor's decision, and on October 29, 2004, he delivered a standard case memo seeking authorization from the chapter's legal committee. "Suit on Behalf of Military Officer Challenging 'Don't Ask, Don't Tell' Policy in Light of *Lawrence v. Texas*" read the subject line.

To help protect her identity as an active Air Force reservist, Margie was referred to in the memo as "Major John Doe." Lobsenz made clear his expectation that the case would at least reach the Ninth Circuit Court of Appeals.

Presumably, he wrote, *Lawrence v. Texas* had, on its face, rendered the military's criminal prohibition against consensual gay sex unconstitutional. The question was how much further *Lawrence* went, in terms of expanding the privacy rights of homosexuals, including homosexuals serving in the military.

The federal Court of Appeals for the Armed Forces, Lobsenz noted, had "recently ducked this issue" in a case involving a gay Air Force sergeant decided only two months earlier. Notably, it was not a case challenging Don't Ask, Don't Tell. Rather, the sergeant had been tried and convicted under the Uniform Code of Military Justice for having sex with a subordinate. The sergeant's lawyers had cited the *Lawrence* decision in his defense. But the appeals court ruled that, in his case, "the protected liberty interest recognized in *Lawrence*" simply didn't apply. The charge was not that he had engaged in homosexual sex, but that he had had sexual contact with a subordinate. The fact that the sergeant was gay simply didn't matter.

But that left what was, at the very least, a smoldering legal question. The appeals court wasn't saying that the "protected liberty interest recognized in *Lawrence*" didn't apply to gays in the military. It was just saying it didn't apply in this particular case. But what about other actions against gay service members, like the hundreds of discharges every year under Don't Ask, Don't Tell? What, if anything, did the "protected liberty interest recognized in *Lawrence*" mean in those cases? That was the question that this case, Margie Witt's case, could be used to answer.

Lobsenz's memo was succinct about the chances of prevailing in the Air Force process: "The administrative board has no discretion to decide not to discharge." It would merely be a military show trial. The only path to halting Margie's discharge would be to win in federal court. His strategy recommendation was to wait until the administrative discharge proceeding was set to convene and then file the lawsuit.

In the meantime, Margie would be living out a twilight zone existence, at least with respect to her Air Force service. On drill weekends at McChord, she would still show up at the 446th offices and continue to direct her large staff in preparation for the squadron's upcoming major inspection. She was under orders not to disclose to others in the unit that she was under investigation.

On Saturday, November 4, she was working away at McChord when, this time, Lieutenant Colonel Janette Moore-Harbert—who regularly filled in for Colonel Walker—appeared in the same office doorway as Walker had on July 25. Margie froze and gently shook her head.

"No," she said quietly.

"Come on," Moore-Harbert replied, and the two made the long walk down the hall to the commander's conference room. Once there, Moore-Harbert informed her the Air Force would soon be initiating separation proceedings against her.

"This is the hardest thing I've ever had to do in my military career," she heard the senior officer say as they both fought back tears. "I need you to pack your things and leave the base."

The memo Margie received five days later confirmed what Moore-Harbert had told her. She was henceforth prohibited from engaging in "pay or point activity" pending resolution of the separation proceedings. That meant she couldn't do any work for which she would be compensated and for which she would normally receive points toward promotion or earn retirement benefits. The latter sanction was especially harsh, as she was only a year short of the twenty years she needed to earn a full retirement pension.

If this was her last day in the Air Force, her last day with the 446th, it was nothing at all like her departure from active duty back in 1995, when she was celebrated with cheers, hugs, gifts, and playful soakings at each landing of the C-9 Nightingale before returning one last time to Scott Air Force Base.

Being ordered to leave McChord would leave a psychological scar. At the time, it left her numb. She would tell only JP and Jim Schaffer, and Jim had to be told because he was her ride from Spokane to McChord for the drill weekends. Her greatest fear was that her parents would find out. It would have been hard to enough to tell them, straight up, that she was gay. But to wrap that revelation inside the dreadful news that the Air Force was moving to discharge her for being gay was just too daunting a prospect. She wasn't ready, and because she wasn't ready she acted as though nothing had changed. She and Jim would still drive to and from Spokane together, and she would still spend the evenings with her folks in Gig Harbor. But instead of commuting to McChord on those weekend mornings, Margie would go elsewhere, including frequents visits with her old friend Laura Maes.

This went on for over a year. Back home, in Spokane, she struggled to move on with her life. The reason to fight was there, and, most days, so was the will. But there were just so many days, and she had to find the energy and resolve to make it through each one.

"It was hard to get up, and then when I got up I realized what was happening, again, and again, like *Groundhog Day*."

There would be times when she would have a breakdown. When that happened she would call Jan Gemberling, and she and Laurie would go over to Jan's place and sit in Jan's kitchen, where Jan would listen to it all and then remind her that the legal battle was going to take a long time and urge her to compartmentalize it.

"Jan was really the one who covered those immediate moments," Laurie says. "And she was always there."

All the while, Margie was expecting a certified letter from the Air Force, officially notifying her that the administrative discharge proceedings against her had begun. She knew she would have to sign for this dreaded letter when it arrived. Because it would likely take her breath away and cause her knees to wobble, she wanted to receive and sign for it on her front porch, not at the window of the local post office where there would be postal employees and customers, and the red, white, and blue paraphernalia of a government that was treating her as though she were a cancer. On most days, she would try to leave her work at the school district in time to get to her house early enough in the afternoon so she could be there when the mail arrived. When the weather was nice, she would sit on her front porch swing, waiting for the mailman.

The weeks of waiting for the letter were both grueling and surreal. Shortly after her encounter with Major Torem, Margie was notified that an "area defense counsel," a captain, had been assigned to be her advocate within the Air Force discharge process. A year later, with no discernible movement toward a hearing, the captain called with what seemed to be very good news. A major at the Air Force Reserve Command at Robins Air Force Base in Georgia had determined that inasmuch as the discharge action against her was triggered by vengeance, it was going to be dismissed. She told Margie she should contact the 446th to review how and when she could return to the unit. When Margie called the 446th, she was quickly informed that this was news to the 446th—that as far as the 446th was concerned, she was still subject to the discharge proceeding that Major Torem had initiated with his recommendation. A week later her Air Force counsel called back to report that the major at Robins had been overruled, that the discharge proceedings would be going forward, and that she should be getting her letter before long. There was one more thing. The captain said she was leaving her post and that another Air Force lawyer would be assigned to Margie's case. This was in September 2005. Weeks passed.

"It was just driving me nuts, that I was hearing nothing," Margie remembers. "And I was in limbo. Is the discharge happening, or is it not. Did they just lose me?"

The formal notification letter was key. Lobsenz and the legal team would use it as the trigger to file the federal lawsuit to try to block the discharge from taking effect.

Finally, she began to make calls. The first was to the number given her by the captain who had first been appointed as her Air Force counsel. The call went through to voice mail and wasn't returned. On the second try, the call also went to voice mail, but this time the recorded message was a man's voice. That call wasn't returned either. On the third try, in late January 2006, the captain assigned to be her new Air Force counsel answered the phone. Margie introduced herself and explained she had been told that he was now assigned to her case.

"He didn't recognize my name at all," she recalls. "He said, 'just a minute,' and then I actually heard him open his file drawer. Then he says 'Oh here . . .' and then I hear 'Oh shit!'" A few moments later, after trying to calm himself, he told her he needed to "take a look at this" and that she should be hearing something shortly.

Finally, in early March 2006, the postman arrived with the letter that had been sent from the Air Force Reserve Command's personnel division. As the handsome young postal deliveryman made his way down the walkway, Margie spotted him and went outside to greet him.

"I have something for you to sign for," the postman said breezily, with a smile.

"I figured you might," she replied.

"I hope it's good news," he said.

"It's not," she replied flatly.

Even as he was handing it to her she could recognize from the Air Force insignia that this was the long-awaited notice of discharge proceedings. As she reached for the pen he was offering her, she noticed her hand was shaking. She was trembling all the more as she took the envelope, tore it open, and began reading the letter. Without another word she began walking down the block, heading for Jan Gemberling's kitchen table. Laurie caught up to her and walked by her side, all the while reminding her to breathe.

"By this memorandum," the letter began, "discharge action is being initiated against you for homosexual conduct."

The letter required an acknowledgment of receipt within twenty-four hours, provided a summary of her rights, including a right to an Air Force–appointed counsel, or a civilian lawyer of her choice, to represent her at a discharge board hearing that would be held at Robins Air Force Base, one hundred miles south of Atlanta. She could choose the discharge board hearing, or she could tender her resignation by filling out a resignation form that had been attached to the memo. If she chose the hearing, she would be reimbursed for travel, but there would be no per diem.

"Your failure to make an election will result in the convening of a discharge board to hear your case," the letter concluded. "You will be notified of the time and place the board will be convened. You should consult with your counsel prior to making an election."

The letter was signed by Lieutenant Colonel Deborah S. Divich, the deputy chief in the Air Force Reserve Command's personnel division, headquartered at Robins AFB.

The arrival of the letter lit the fuse on *Witt v. Air Force*. As planned, Lobsenz and the ACLU began putting the finishing touches on the lawsuit they would file at the federal district court in Tacoma.

The ACLU would take the lead in introducing the case, and the plaintiff, to the media and the public. The media piece was not an afterthought. As much as the ACLU is known for the lawsuits it brings, its broader mission is to win in the court of public opinion as well. Kathleen Taylor and her staff knew the story would resonate, and they wanted to break the news with a Seattle press conference, where Margie and her story would be the focus of attention.

"We showed her a draft copy of the press release that referred to her as a lesbian," Taylor recalls. "And she was surprised by that. And she said, 'My god, I've got to tell my parents!'"

The prospect of Frank and Gloria turning on KOMO-TV or picking up the *Tacoma News Tribune* and reading that their gay daughter was now suing the Air Force was mortifying. She had to tell them, and soon; and despite her sister's assurances that they could handle it, Margie wasn't sure how it would go. Certainly, she had not forgotten how upset her mother had been when she made her impassioned stand for Laurie two years earlier.

But it had to be done, and this time Margie turned to another old friend, Jennifer Kallen, the former Air Force medical technician whom she had shyly and somewhat hilariously tried to pick up in a St. Louis bar thirteen years earlier. Jen had since moved to Seattle and was now working as a surgery scheduler for a medical group. To help relieve some of the stress Margie was enduring, Jen picked her up at the Sea-Tac airport and navigated Seattle's hectic traffic to make sure she got to her first meeting with Jim Lobsenz on time.

Now, Jen would help steel her nerves and, if necessary, drive the getaway car. Margie arrived in Seattle on a Friday, five days before she would be introduced to the media at the ACLU press conference. Jen cheerfully greeted her and took her to lunch. Joining them was Nicki McGraw, a fellow partner with Jim Lobsenz at Carney Badley Spellman who specialized in employment law. Nicki, who is also gay, understood, as did Jen, just how much was on the line for Margie as she was girding herself to tell her parents about all of who she was, and what now lay ahead for her.

"They knew how difficult the discussion would be," says Margie. "It was what I most feared in my life."

After lunch, the two women presented Margie with a bottle of scotch as they parted for the afternoon.

The next morning, Jen drove as they headed south down Interstate 5, through Tacoma and then westward over the Tacoma Narrows bridge to Gig Harbor. If the meeting with Frank and Gloria went badly, Margie's plan was to bolt out of the house and have Jen whisk her away. Her fears were unwarranted. Neither of her parents was surprised to hear her say she was attracted to women, and that she was in love with Laurie. They both listened, and then she noticed, after she told them the Air Force had removed her from her unit and was planning to discharge her, that her father was getting mad. But he wasn't getting mad at her.

"You're going to fight them, aren't you?" he asked.

No words would capture the release she felt, to have told her parents the raw truth about herself, and to have them completely accept her. And then she had to tell them, yes, she was going to fight the Air Force. That would mean it was going to be in the news. And it would be in the news for a while.

There was a gentle silence as she allowed that to sink in.

"Now, um," Gloria finally spoke. "I'm not necessarily going to have to do what Ellen's mom did. Do I?"

It was such a funny thing to ask. By "Ellen," Gloria was referring to talk show host Ellen DeGeneres, whose adorable mom, Betty, regularly speaks publicly in support of her gay, celebrity daughter.

"Then she wanted me to invite friends over," Margie recalls, "and it was just like this *huuuuuge* weight was lifted off me. I had my family. And they had me, completely, for the first time. I couldn't ask for anything more in my life than that."

Margie went out to the car to tell Jen, who then walked in the door to be embraced by Frank, who, wiping away tears, thanked her for being there for his daughter. At Gloria's insistence they would celebrate with a dinner, seafood from their favorite market along the waterfront.

Then, soon enough, it was Wednesday, April 12, the day of the ACLU press conference in Seattle. In the wings, as the press filed into the room for the announcement, the paradox at the heart of Margie's story played itself out in a last-minute skit between Margie and Aaron Caplan, the ACLU-Washington staff attorney. The word "lesbian" was already on the press release. How, Caplan asked, would she like him to introduce her?

"Alien," she joked. "Nurse? Lutheran? How about Norwegian?"

She wasn't trying to make Caplan's job harder. She was just reflexively making the point that she wanted to make to the Air Force and everybody else. All those years in the Air Force, serving her country, tending to the wounded, training and mentoring the med techs and the flight nurses who by now had flown thousands of missions to bring home troops badly wounded in Iraq and Afghanistan. Pick a label. What did it matter? And why should it matter most that she also happened to be a lesbian? And the answer, of course, is that this was the part of her that the U.S. government considered unacceptable.

"Major Witt is gay," Caplan finally announced aloud to the press.

"I still can't remember if I actually dropped to my knees or if I just thought I did."

Suddenly she was out to the world, and walking out into the glare of camera lights, nervous but smiling broadly. She was wearing the same style green, Air Force flight suit with the flag and other patches on the shoulders that she had worn thirteen years earlier. Back then she was a face for "Cross into the Blue," a confidently smiling flight nurse on a poster for Air Force recruiting. Now she was a wire service photo, a fresh new face for civil rights, her name alone on a lawsuit filed in the U.S. District Court for the Western District of Washington. *Major Margaret Witt v. Department of the Air Force; et al.*

Chapter 13

〰〰〰〰〰〰〰

A SOJOURN TO LANGLEY

Shortly after one o'clock, Margie rose to her feet as a trim man with an athletic physique came into view through a doorway on her left. It was the last day of June 2006.

Federal district court judge Ronald Leighton, as per his daily routine, had just returned from a midday workout. As he reached and settled into the high-backed chair behind his bench he was briskly cordial. The fifty-five-year-old judge greeted "Major Witt" and her two attorneys by name, and then complimented all the lawyers—including a pair of Justice Department attorneys and an Air Force trial lawyer—on their opening briefs in the case.

On her side of the aisle were Jim Lobsenz and ACLU staff attorney Aaron Caplan. They were in Tacoma—barely a mile from the hospital where Margie was born—inside Union Station, the city's landmark federal courthouse. To reach Judge Leighton's courtroom, you first have to walk through the elegantly remodeled former train station, featuring a vaulted, central rotunda beneath a ninety-foot-high copper dome. If you had to wait as long as Margie had for your day in court, you would be hard-pressed to find a more exalting venue.

Before being confirmed to the federal bench four years earlier, Ronald Leighton had been a highly regarded Tacoma trial attorney. An active Republican in a state largely controlled by Democrats, Leighton had initially been appointed in 1992 by President George H. W. Bush, only to see his nomination languish in a partisan standoff in the U.S. Senate. A decade later, with the persistence of Republican U.S. senator Slade Gorton, he was nominated a second time, and this time he cleared the Senate. Becoming a judge hadn't been an easy decision for Leighton. He had thrived on the intellectual challenges of being a litigator, and even though he was now holding court, he still thought of himself as a trial lawyer. On this day, it took only a couple of minutes for him to communicate how eager he was to dive into the case and to highlight the issue that had so clearly gotten his attention.

"Excellent presentations of the law on this subject," he said, referring to the pre-hearing briefs. "However, given the manner in which the *Lawrence* decision is written, even outstanding briefs cannot make the decision any easier. This will be an interactive process today, as we wind our way through some rather thorny constitutional issues."

In the complaint Lobsenz and the ACLU filed on Margie's behalf, they were seeking a restraining order to prevent the Air Force from discharging her. They were also seeking a ruling that her expulsion under Don't Ask, Don't Tell would violate her constitutional rights. As Lobsenz anticipated, the pivotal questions—which Judge Leighton was already deeply engaged in—were whether, and to what extent, the 2003 *Lawrence* decision had expanded due process rights for gay service members generally, and for Major Margaret Witt in particular.

In *Lawrence*, the Supreme Court was clear that not even the military could continue to criminally prosecute gay people for having intimate sexual relations. The court majority not only overturned the high court's 1986 ruling in *Bowers v. Hardwick*, but it resurrected and affirmed Justice John Paul Stevens's dissent in *Bowers*. In that dissent, Justice Stevens asserted that intimacy among gay partners was "a form of 'liberty' protected by the Due Process Clause," and that the protected liberty should extend to married and unmarried couples alike.

"When sexuality finds overt expression in intimate conduct with another person," Justice Anthony Kennedy wrote for the court majority in *Lawrence*, "the conduct can be but one element in a personal bond that is more enduring. The liberty protected by the Constitution allows homosexual persons the right to make this choice."

To many legal observers, including Jim Lobsenz, Justice Kennedy and the court were giving voice, in *Lawrence*, to a fundamental right that went well beyond decriminalizing gay sex. If so, that would make it extremely difficult—even for the military—to legally justify actions and policies that discriminate against homosexuals. If Judge Leighton concurred with this broad interpretation of *Lawrence*, he could simply do as Lobsenz was requesting—issue a restraining order prohibiting the Air Force from discharging his client under Don't Ask, Don't Tell.

With his opening remarks, Leighton was signaling to both sides that he would be moving cautiously. He didn't argue with Lobsenz so much as pace him to the hurdles both knew were there, including the arguments the Justice Department lawyers would surely make when it was their turn. The dialogue between Leighton and Lobsenz, while layered in legal complexities, was remarkably lean, lucid, and respectful.

For example, as they had in the *Watkins* case, Lobsenz and the ACLU briefed and brought forward multiple legal theories on why they should win the case for reinstatement. Of course, the best possible outcome would be to win with a precedent-setting court ruling that would end a discriminatory policy and benefit countless others. But a lawyer's first duty is to his or her client, and it would obviously be better for the client to win on a narrowly construed issue of law than to lose on a broad constitutional claim.

In the *Witt* case this strategy involved bringing a procedural due process claim as a companion to the far-reaching substantive due process issue framed by the Supreme Court's recent decision in *Lawrence*. Their argument was that the Air Force violated Margie's constitutional right to due process by failing to give her timely access to a hearing on the accusations against her. After all, she had been barred from serving with the 446th in November 2004 and didn't receive notice that she could opt for a hearing until March 2006.

However, it would soon become clear that Judge Leighton recognized the importance of the substantive due process issue, in light of *Lawrence*, and that he wanted to give it his utmost attention. He and Lobsenz handled the two different due process claims with lawyerly efficiency:

Judge Leighton: You're on.

Lobsenz: Thank you, Your Honor. I want to say at the outset, Your Honor, that although I have a planned order, way in which I will address things, if that doesn't seem right to you, just let me know, and I can go to any point, any topic you wish.

Judge Leighton: Good. I have a habit of interrupting. Let me pose a question at the outset because we have the procedural due process issue here. Is there anybody who is advocating that a hearing, an administrative hearing should be ordered? Clearly, you're not. Your argument would be the time has already passed and—

Witt family photo, 1967

Margie, age four

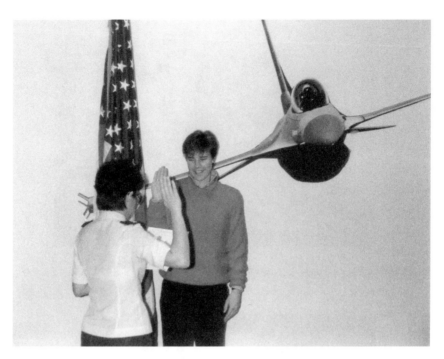

Receiving officer's commission into the Air Force, Tacoma, 1987

Enjoying a homecoming dowsing with pink champagne after first
check ride as an Air Force flight nurse, 1992

A Good Life
Choice...
The Air Force
Nurse Corps

Choices we make in life determine
which roads we'll travel. Many choose
the easy way that is routine or
uninspired—while others choose to Cross
Into The Blue on a path that takes them to
new challenges and opportunities.

If you choose to Cross Into The Blue,
you can experience what it takes to
make a real difference in your career,
professionalism, self-esteem and lifestyle.

One of four photos of Margie that the Air Force used in recruiting
brochures and pamphlets from 1993 to 2008, even after discharge
proceedings had been initiated against her under Don't Ask, Don't Tell

Aboard a C-9 Nightingale mission out
of Scott AFB, Illinois, 1993

above Oman, 2003, with Stacey Julian and Anna Friscia

right Aboard a mission in southwest Asia with Senior Master Sergeant Jim Schaffer, 2003

On the flight deck
of a C-130 during
Operation Enduring
Freedom, 2003

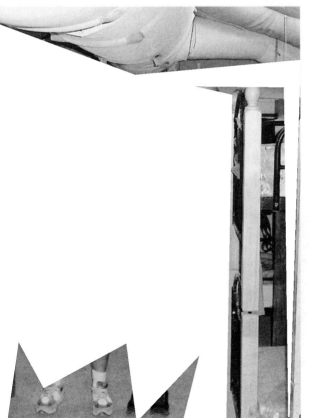

Finding refuge in
the boys' tent the night
before leaving Qatar,
February 2003

With sister Virginia and brother Chris, Christmas 2003

Gloria and Frank Witt at Sunrise Point,
Mount Rainier, 2006

Laurie and Margie, 2008 (photo by Mychal Richardson)

In Tacoma on the eve of the trial in *Witt v. Air Force*, September 2009. *From left*: Jim Schaffer, Margie, Laurie, Carla Savalli, former U.S. Army medic Sergeant Darren Manzella, former Navy lieutenant Jenny Kopfstein, retired Navy Chief Petty Officer Lee Quillian, Air Force lieutenant colonel Victor Fehrenbach.

Laurie and Margie emerging from the courtroom, just minutes after U.S. District Court judge Ronald Leighton's historic ruling, September 24, 2010

Amid the raucous celebration that followed Judge Leighton's ruling on September 24, 2010, Margie found Frank for a quiet father-daughter moment back at the hotel.

Margie with her triumphant ACLU of Washington legal team in 2010: Jim Lobsenz, Sher Kung, Margie, Sarah Dunne, and Nina Jenkins

Grethe Cammermeyer and Margie in the Interior Department auditorium where President Barack Obama signed the bill to repeal Don't Ask, Don't Tell on December 22, 2010

With Colonel Grethe Cammermeyer and Lieutenant Colonel Victor Fehrenbach at the 2011 Servicemembers Legal Defense Network national dinner in Washington, DC

Laurie and Margie celebrating the Don't Ask, Don't Tell repeal with Jim
Lobsenz and Sarah Dunne at the 2011 SLDN national dinner

Jacob Evans Towne, an
openly gay high school
student from Deary, Idaho,
came more than a hundred
miles to meet Margie when
she was the grand marshal
at the June 2011 Pride
Parade in Spokane.

Margie and Grethe at the retirement
ceremony for Margie and Victor
Fehrenbach at the Air Force Memorial
in Washington, DC, October 11, 2011.
Grethe officiated at the ceremony. Photo
by Anthony Loverde

Margie with Laurie and her children, Abby and Sam,
at the retirement ceremony for Margie and Victor Fehrenbach,
October 1, 2011. Photo by Anthony Loverde

All smiles, with Laurie at the Air Force Memorial,
as Margie's journey in uniform comes to a close.
Photo by Anthony Loverde

A thank you kiss for Laurie. Photo by Anthony Loverde

Margie and Laurie after receiving their marriage license
at the Spokane County Courthouse the morning
of December 6, 2012. Photo by Tim Connor

Attorney Jim Lobsenz presiding over Margie and Laurie's Spokane wedding in December 2012. Photo by Tim Connor

Wedding photo, December 15, 2012. Photo by Nate Gowdy

At Fairchild Air Force Base the day Laurie was officially recognized as a "military spouse," September 3, 2011. Photo by Tim Connor

Lobsenz: We have requested one, but it is our position that the time has already passed such that it is a constitutional violation at this point. If the court were to disagree on that, we would want to go ahead and have our opportunity to have that hearing. We have requested specific witnesses for it. We obviously hope we won't get there.

Judge Leighton: What's the government's position on that issue?

Department of Justice attorney Peter Phipps: Your Honor, our position is that there has been no denial of hearing. Before Major Witt is discharged, she will have a discharge hearing. That has been scheduled. There has been—

Judge Leighton: That has been scheduled?

Phipps: Not to a definite date, but the procedure under which that will be scheduled is scheduled. It's scheduled in a process of first in / first out, generally. She's in the first in / first out. It's not a perfect first in / first out process, however, because certain enlistments that are about to end move to the top of the list. But she is in that. We don't have a definite date for that, but it is a first in / first out.

Judge Leighton: Okay.

Phipps: It's at Robins Air Force Base in Georgia.

Judge Leighton: Thank you. That was by way of, I guess, suggesting that I'm probably more focused on the substantive due process questions at this point. I don't want to ignore your argument on procedural due process, but the *Lawrence/Marcum/Cook* [*Marcum* and *Cook* were other cases challenging DADT in light of the Supreme Court's decision in *Lawrence*] analysis is probably of greater interest to me at this point. And if you could, maybe, move that to the front of the—

Lobsenz: Okay. I can do that, certainly, Your Honor.

Judge Leighton: —of the train.

Lobsenz: May I make one comment first?

Judge Leighton: Sure.

Lobsenz: Because I thought this might appeal to you. I think as sort of an intellectual matter, lawyers, judges, we're riveted on one thing. What is *Lawrence* about? All those big, big, big issues. But traditionally, the judicial branch tends to refrain from making a broad, sweeping constitutional ruling involving a coordinate branch of government if it can be avoided and the case can be decided on a narrower ground.

Judge Leighton: Right.

Lobsenz: For that reason — I won't, if you direct me to go elsewhere — but for that reason it occurred to me that you might wish to start with an analysis of the narrowest ground possible because if Major Witt is entitled to win on that ground, and I submit she is, then you could decide that Major Witt wins on that ground, and if the government wants to appeal, the Ninth Circuit can figure everything else out.

Judge Leighton: Well, apropos to your comment, I pulled out something from one of my old folders that says that — it was written by somebody smarter than I — a judge must have a disciplined modesty about his role. I think that's sage advice. However, yesterday I would have said, let's start with procedural due process.

Lobsenz: Okay.

Judge Leighton: What I'm afraid of is getting bogged down in the procedural due process —

Lobsenz: Okay.

Judge Leighton: —and spending our time inequitably at the expense of the substantive due process, which I think is the broader issue. And when we explore that, then I think we can come back to the substantive part of the procedural due process issue and focus on your narrowest of issues.

Lobsenz: Then I will start with the *Lawrence* substantive due process claim.

With that Lobsenz turned to the central issue — his argument for why the Air Force was violating Major Witt's constitutionally protected liberty interest as the Supreme Court had staked it out in the *Lawrence* decision. In his meticulous preparation, Lobsenz had come with what amounted to a Plan A and a Plan B within the substantive due process realm of the *Witt* case. If Judge Leighton didn't think *Lawrence* rendered Don't Ask, Don't Tell unconstitutional on its face, there was also a basis in the *Lawrence* decision for requiring the military to actually demonstrate that the presence of a particular gay soldier, or sailor, or flight nurse was undermining unit morale and cohesion.

Both options were delivered with ease and clarity. As Lobsenz's dialogue with the judge progressed more deeply into the weeds of case law, it was almost as though the two were finishing each other's thoughts.

"I will get an opinion out as soon as possible," Leighton said near the end of the session. "Obviously, this is a significant issue. Certainly, Major Witt, it is a significant issue to you, but it also has implications that are far greater, and it has been a subject of much debate in chambers."

Sitting next to Aaron Caplan at the plaintiff's table, it was hard for Margie to know how well Lobsenz's arguments were landing with the judge. The legal and procedural issues were complicated. At the level of her daily life, in terms of her direct experience and sense of fairness, the issues didn't seem very complicated at all.

But part of what she took away from the hearing was a clear sense of Judge Leighton's decency, in the way he had met her eyes and spoken to her.

That was about all she could absorb that day. What few in the courtroom knew was that she was there under duress, her heart and mind reeling from a jolting tragedy.

Laurie's oldest son, Dan, was living in Coeur d'Alene, Idaho, that summer, where he was working as a cook and learning to become a chef. Late on the evening of June 26, he was at a bar after work when he overheard disparaging remarks about two young women he knew. An argument ensued, and as Dan left the bar, the young man with whom he had argued attacked him, sending him to the pavement and badly fracturing his skull. In a desperate effort to save his life he had been transported by air ambulance to Harborview Medical Center in Seattle. His brain was badly damaged.

The police were trying to reach Laurie the next morning, but their calls were ringing a phone on Glenrose Prairie, while she was away teaching a summer school class elsewhere. But they were able to reach Pat McChesney, and he, in turn, had gone to pick up Sam at a track-and-field camp nearby. Margie was at a new home that she and Laurie were moving into near Manito Park when Sam arrived. He was distraught and emotionally overwhelmed at learning what had happened to his older brother. Margie worked to calm him down in the kitchen and, in time, convinced him that he needed to meet with Laurie before he and his father left to try to catch a flight to Seattle. She was then able to reach Laurie on her cell phone and share the awful news about Dan. It was Tuesday morning. The hearing before Judge Leighton was scheduled for Friday. She had only a few minutes to make several things happen, and in the midst of it all she somehow remembered to grab the uniform she would wear in court. Laurie arrived and shared a tearful conversation with Sam. Then it was time to get to Seattle as quickly as they could.

In the shock of a mother's worst nightmare, Laurie needed to busy herself, so she drove as Margie made phone calls, trying to learn about Dan's condition and make arrangements for a place they could stay near Harborview. A friend put her in touch with a Seattle couple, one of whom was a nurse anesthetist who worked at Harborview. After Margie was able to connect with her at the hospital, the nurse not only provided updates on Dan but insisted that Margie, Laurie, and Sam stay at the couple's home in West Seattle.

The next ten days—encompassing Margie's court hearing, and the family vigil at Dan's intensive-care bed at Harborview—would push them to their limits. It would also lay bare everything at stake in their lives.

Margie had put off telling her parents that she, Laurie, and Sam were coming to Seattle. Although being embraced by Frank and Gloria back in April had meant the world to her, she was aware that the sting of her mother's rejection of Laurie two years earlier was still being felt. There would have to be a reconciliation, but with Dan clinging to life at Harborview intensive care, this did not seem at all like the right time. Daily phone calls are like vitamins in the Witt family, however, and by Friday afternoon a weekend family barbecue at Gig Harbor, including Margie's sister Virginia and her family, had been arranged.

Laurie came. As she walked through the door, she was about to meet Frank for the first time. That part was easy, as he walked over and wrapped his arms around her.

Gloria was out back, sitting by herself at a table. It was a warm afternoon, and she was wearing a large hat to shield herself from the sun.

"By that time," Laurie recalls, "I had been through so much, especially with Dan, that I just walked over and sat right next to her. I was thinking, 'this woman has nothing on me.'"

It was the right move. Gloria was ready to open her heart, to accept her, and console Laurie in her grief for her critically injured son. Laurie and her children became part of the Witt family that afternoon. Gloria's embrace was also, for Margie, the realization of a decades-long dream, to be fully accepted by her parents for all of who she was, and for all of whom she loved.

The vigil at Harborview continued. Dan was going to survive, though he would remain in a coma for two months. Another week passed. Out of concern for their well-being, a senior nurse persuaded Laurie and Sam to take a break from their vigil and spend a day away from Dan's bedside. With Margie, they would drive a half hour north of Seattle and catch the Mukilteo ferry to Whidbey Island, one of the larger green jewels among the densely forested islands of northern Puget Sound.

Waiting for them at a spacious home overlooking Saratoga Passage, near the town of Langley, were Grethe Cammermeyer and her longtime partner, artist Diane Divelbess.

As had Sergeant Perry Watkins, Grethe won her battle against the Army after several setbacks and years of litigation. In 1995, a year after she was vindicated and reinstated by a federal judge, actress Glenn Close had played her in a made-for-TV movie based on the autobiography *Serving in Silence*. Grethe Cammermeyer was a hero to thousands, including countless silently serving gays and lesbians like Margaret Witt.

In May of 1997, Margie had had a brief opportunity to introduce herself to Cammermeyer in a reception line in Spokane, where Grethe had been the featured speaker at a luncheon in support of a campaign to safeguard the civil rights of LGBT Washingtonians. Years later, as it became clear that Margie was in for a prolonged legal battle against the Air Force, she sent messages requesting an opportunity to meet with Grethe to talk about her case. Grethe replied in early July, while Margie, Laurie, and Sam were in Seattle, shuttling to and from Harborview. Of course she would see them.

In Margie's world, a meeting with Grethe Cammermeyer was about like having a conversation with one of the faces carved into Mount Rushmore. The soft-spoken, retired colonel and still-active care provider is a tall, angular woman whose broad shoulders accentuate the depth of her persona.

"I wanted to know what to do," Margie says. "I wanted direction and a different kind of direction than my legal team could offer. Because Grethe had been on the other side of it and had given her whole life to the cause. I wanted to hear it from her perspective. And I also wanted some insight as to what was going to happen to me."

Grethe and Diane graciously welcomed the visitors, who by then were, in Margie's words, "exhausted, worn out, lost, glassy-eyed numb people."

Says Grethe: "The fact that Margie and Laurie could even concentrate on this military matter with the acuity and intensity of what was going on with Dan was just, you know . . ." She finished the sentence with a gentle shake of her head.

"How can you juggle this much tragedy at the same time?"

It was going to be necessary, Grethe realized, to have separate conversations with Laurie and Margie, to speak directly to what each of them was facing.

Grethe had earned her Bronze Star as an intensive care nurse in Vietnam, where she had been assigned to the Twenty-Fourth Evacuation Hospital at Long Binh. During the height of the conflict, she was tasked with being the head nurse in the hospital's neurosurgical unit. The experience is vividly described in her memoir.

"The hopelessness that floods over the soldier with an inoperable cervical spinal wound can be overwhelming for both patient and the staff," she wrote. "The childlike condition of a patient with brain damage causes profound spiritual and emotional stress for everyone. All of this work, this care, requires that you use heart and head in equal proportions."

After coming home from Vietnam, Grethe gave birth to four sons. And, now, sitting alone with Laurie on the deck outside her home overlooking the blue waters of Saratoga Passage, she tried to comfort her, while being completely honest about what lay ahead.

Says Laurie: "She said, 'Think about what your son was before this accident; he's never coming back. He's gone. The only way you'll survive this is to think of this as a birth. This is your new son. And any advances he makes, no matter how small, are a blessing. It's something you can cherish and be happy about. But if you think of it in terms of what he was, it will always be a heartache. But this is your new son.' And that kept me going."

When the time came to speak with Margie, the two took a long walk into the nearby village of Langley with its breathtaking views of Mount Baker and the north Cascades rising beyond the seascape. An annual summer arts and music festival, the Choochokam, was under way, and Grethe thought it would lift Margie's spirits.

As she listened to Margie, Grethe was reminded of her own vulnerability, from the time in her life, sixteen years earlier, when she felt a need to reach out to Captain Carolyn "Dusty" Pruitt. Pruitt was a California pastor and reservist whom the Army discharged after she told a newspaper reporter she was gay. For Pruitt, it had taken four years to prevail and win reinstatement. Grethe wanted to know if she would do it all over again, given the invasions of her privacy and the constant stress of the legal proceedings.

"Absolutely, I would do it again," is what Grethe remembers Dusty Pruitt telling her. She would offer the same answer, now, to Margie, about the importance of seeing it through.

The conversation was harder than Margie expected, as she tried to share her anxieties about the time it would take and the loss of connection and purpose she was already experiencing.

"She finally just stopped as we were walking through Langley," says Margie. "And she said, 'What do you want from me?' And I said, 'I don't know what to do. I'm supposed to be with my unit, this is my purpose.' And she just stopped me, right there, and said very firmly, 'Major, your mission has changed.'"

There was no mistake about what Grethe meant, and how she meant it. Her words landed like a splash of ice water on Margie's face. For two years she had been preoccupied with rejoining the 446th for all the purposefulness and camaraderie she had been missing.

Her new mission was clear: to bring down Don't Ask, Don't Tell

.

Chapter 14

ııııııııııııııı

THE WILDERNESS

If Grethe's advice to Margie had a certain edge and ring to it, it was because she had, in her own time, met the Army and the U.S. government at the brink.

By telling the truth about her sexual orientation during her security interview in 1989, she had triggered a landslide of bricks from above.

"I did not realize," she wrote in her memoir, "that by saying to Agent Troutman, 'I am a lesbian,' I would lose my career in a country that espoused equality for all. And I didn't know that by being forced to speak out, first privately, then publicly, I would find the most important mission of my life."

She had gone public in August 1991, giving a long telephone interview to Randy Shilts for an article in the *San Francisco Chronicle*. Given her rank, her list of achievements, and her award for valor in Vietnam, the story traveled well. She became a cause célèbre, especially in the Pacific Northwest, and it wasn't long before she came to the attention of a rising political star, Arkansas governor Bill Clinton. As Clinton was running for president in 1992, he used Grethe's life story to build public support for his pledge to end the military's ban on gay service members. The pledge helped him capture a growing wave of Democratic Party activists, especially on the West Coast. At age forty-six, he became the third-youngest president in U.S. history.

Then came the cloud of locusts. Clinton's vow to end the policy triggered an extraordinary cultural and political backlash, fueled by well-organized fundamentalist Christian organizations like the Family Research Council and the Traditional Values Coalition. Even worse, the Pentagon was in revolt. The Joint Chiefs of Staff, led by its chairman, General Colin Powell, were so vehemently opposed to lifting the ban that, according to *Newsweek*, they threatened to resign en masse.

Congressional supporters of the military's ban on homosexuals also took steps to block any move by the new president. One of Clinton's fiercest opponents on the issue was another leading Democrat, Senator Sam Nunn of Georgia, who chaired the powerful Senate Armed Services Committee. In March 1993, Senator Nunn and his committee opened a round of hearings. Grethe was the lone, lesbian service member invited to testify, and by then the die was cast. There would be no end to the ban on gay service members. Instead, the government would repackage the policy. The military would no longer ask recruits about their sexual orientation. Service members would henceforth be expelled only "when their homosexuality is manifested by objective criteria—homosexual acts, homosexual statements, or homosexual marriage."

The "Don't Ask, Don't Tell" shorthand for the modified policy was coined by a sociologist, Charles Moskos, who was closely connected to Senator Nunn. In practice, though, "Don't Ask, Don't Tell" was highly misleading, as there would be countless cases—Margie's among them—where the military didn't ask, the service member didn't tell, and the expulsion happened anyway.

A humbled Bill Clinton announced his support for the new policy in July 1993, defending it as "an honorable compromise." Two months later, the U.S. Senate voted overwhelmingly to codify DADT, giving it—for the first time in U.S. history—the full weight of federal law.

The political implosion in 1993 was so breathtaking that some of Clinton's earliest backers in the gay community wound up chaining themselves to the White House fence in protest. The debacle was an especially bitter experience for Grethe, given how her hopes had soared when Clinton lifted her up as a shining example of why the ban needed to be lifted.

"This new law was a travesty," she wrote in her memoir.

Grethe's discharge hearings had been especially wrenching, beginning on a day that marked the thirtieth anniversary of her being commissioned into the Army. When it was time for the verdict, the presiding officer began the announcement with this sentence: "I truly believe you are one of the great Americans, Margarethe." After adding several accolades and quoting from glowing testimonials offered by those who had worked with Grethe, the board president explained that because Colonel Cammermeyer had admitted to being a homosexual, she was in violation of Army regulation AR 135-175. She would thus be severed from the National Guard in June of 1992. Several years later, in retirement, the board president, Colonel Patsy Thompson, revealed that she herself had been a closeted lesbian for thirty years.

Grethe's vindication would come in the courts. On June 1, 1994, U.S. district court judge Thomas Zilly, a Reagan appointee, concluded the government had violated her constitutional rights to substantive due process and equal protection. His twelve-thousand-word decision was a scathing condemnation of the military's antigay policy in general and its application to the decorated colonel in particular. He ordered the Army to reinstate her and refused to delay the reinstatement pending the government's appeal.

"Viewing all the evidence in the light most favorable to the Government, the Court must conclude that the rationales offered by the Government to justify its exclusion of homosexual service-members are grounded solely in prejudice," he wrote, adding: "A cardinal principle of equal protection law is that the federal government cannot discriminate against a class in order to give effect to the prejudice of others. The government has discriminated against Colonel Cammermeyer solely on the basis of her status as a homosexual and has failed to demonstrate a rational basis for doing so."

Judge Zilly's ruling didn't just puncture the old policy used to justify Grethe's discharge. The government's lawyers had upped the ante by presenting the then-new congressional findings supporting Don't Ask, Don't Tell to retroactively justify her expulsion. In doing so, the government exposed Don't Ask, Don't Tell to Judge Zilly's scrutiny. He shredded it, pointing out that even the government's key witnesses had effectively admitted in their depositions that "the government's objection to homosexual service is based solely on the fears and prejudices of heterosexual service members."

When the government appealed Judge Zilly's ruling to the Ninth Circuit Court of Appeals, Grethe's legal team used the opportunity to argue that DADT should be struck down based upon the full record in Judge Zilly's courtroom. Instead, the appeals court ruled that consideration of DADT was a moot point, given that Colonel Cammermeyer had been reinstated and the Army had rescinded the pre-DADT regulation under which she had been wrongly discharged. The effect of the appeals court ruling was to up-hold Judge Zilly's reinstatement order without reaching the constitutional questions surrounding the new law and policy. In that sense, it was a near miss. Grethe's legal challenge had come very close to collapsing the legal foundation beneath the policy through which the government continued to discharge hundreds of service men and women each year.

The years-long struggle had tested Grethe's resilience and broadened her perspective. She had become a civil rights icon, but she had also ab-sorbed the emotional brunt of being treated as if she were a threat to the nation for whom she had devoted and risked her life. The experience pulled her to deep reflection, but also left her restless with the knowledge that the military—girded with new statutory authority that Judge Zilly had essentially scoffed at—was continuing to dismiss gay service members en masse. When Margie Witt came to see her on Whidbey Island, Grethe recognized she was welcoming a compatriot to the cause, someone who had the tenacity to pick up the baton and mount a serious legal challenge to Don't Ask, Don't Tell, someone who might be able to help bring an end to an injustice that continued to undermine the integrity of the military and the moral authority of the government as a whole.

"She was doing all the legwork, and I don't think she realized, because none of us do, what the emotional toll is and what you end up giving up in the process. You have to stay focused on why it is that you're doing something. That's why I thought it was important to tell her that it becomes more than just about you."

For her part, Margie can't talk about the importance of Grethe's mes-sage without choking up. Before the visit she was as determined as ever but "floundering" for direction and focus. Grethe's firm command set her on a course through the wilderness that lay ahead. No matter what Judge Leighton decided, either the government would appeal, or she and her lawyers would. That much was certain.

The ruling from Judge Leighton came on July 26, just two weeks after Margie and Laurie's sojourn to Langley. He accepted the government's arguments for why her case should be dismissed, but not with enthusiasm.

"This Court is not unsympathetic to the situation in which Major Witt currently finds herself. Within the military context, she did not draw at-tention to her sexual orientation, and her colleagues value her contribution to their unit and apparently want her back. She has served her country faithfully and with distinction. It is tempting to accept plaintiff's urging to apply DADT narrowly within the context of Margaret Witt's individual circumstances. This the Court cannot do."

His personal sympathies for Margie were deeper than she knew. His own father, after serving in the Army Air Forces as a ball turret gunner in bombers during World War II, had became a teacher and migrant-education director in Stanislaw County, California. Both the judge's parents were devout Christians, but it was a Christianity of acceptance.

What he couldn't get past was what he saw and others saw as an unfilled gap in Justice Kennedy's opinion in *Lawrence v. Texas*. Everybody agreed the *Witt* case had to be examined in light of the constitutional due process ramifications of the *Lawrence* opinion.

But what were those ramifications?

If *Lawrence* could be read as creating a fundamental liberty interest for homosexuals—tantamount to the liberty interests protecting people on the bases of race and religion—then a government action or policy discriminating against homosexuals would be subject to "strict scrutiny" by the courts. "Strict scrutiny" would force the government to prove that a discriminatory practice was both narrowly tailored and absolutely necessary to fulfill a compelling government interest.

This was Jim Lobsenz's lead argument—that in light of the *Lawrence* decision, the practice of routinely expelling gay men and women from the military violated their constitutional rights to substantive due process. There was little question that if Don't Ask, Don't Tell were subject to "strict scrutiny"—as Lobsenz, the ACLU, and several other civil rights advocates argued it now should be—then DADT would be ruled unconstitutional.

Just as Lobsenz began his oral argument by offering Judge Leighton an expedient path to reinstating Margie Witt, the Justice Department's Peter Phipps began his by proposing an equally swift off-ramp for the judge to dismiss her case altogether.

"Major Witt is a reservist," Phipps said. Unlike active-duty service members who had challenged Don't Ask, Don't Tell, he asserted, Margie couldn't show that she was being deprived of a constitutionally protected interest, because, as a reserve officer, "she sits at the pleasure of the executive branch."

"So by virtue of her being a reservist," Phipps continued, "we don't even trigger the first instance due process protection. If the court's looking for a narrow ground to decide this case on, that's the narrow ground to decide it on. We don't even have a due process protection."

As to the central constitutional question before the court—whether the *Lawrence* decision created new substantive due process protections for gay service members, Phipps argued that it hadn't. The standard of judicial review in DADT cases before *Lawrence* was rational basis review. And the *Lawrence* decision, he insisted, hadn't changed that.

"I think it's really important to pay close attention to what the *Lawrence* majority did," Phipps said in his June 30 oral argument. "They applied rational basis review by finding there was not a legitimate state interest in play. There was not one articulated. In contrast, here, 'Don't Ask, Don't Tell' has been repeatedly upheld as having sustained rational basis review due to the interest in unit cohesion, good morale, reduction of sexual tension. It has been upheld as rational basis. Those are legitimate, if not compelling, government ends, and that they are rationally related to the service—and the policy is rationally related to the service."

On this pivotal issue, Judge Leighton agreed with Phipps. The "thorny" constitutional issues the judge referenced at the outset of oral arguments really boiled down to determining the correct level of judicial scrutiny to apply.

In his July 26 decision, Judge Leighton wrote that he did not see, in *Lawrence*, "a clear statement that the [Supreme] Court was changing the level of scrutiny directed to laws regulating private, consensual same sex intimacy." Thus, he continued, "This Court concludes that *Lawrence* is based on rational basis review; the same level of scrutiny applied by the Ninth Circuit Court of Appeals in upholding the constitutionality of DADT prior to *Lawrence*."

The way he read *Lawrence*, Leighton explained in a subsequent interview, "Justice Kennedy would walk up to the cliff and he wouldn't take the step, he wouldn't take the leap of faith."

What he meant is that while Justice Kennedy's opinion for the court was replete with eloquent statements conferring to homosexuals "the full right"—under the due process clause of the Constitution's Fourteenth Amendment—to engage in consensual sexual relations, nowhere had Kennedy's opinion actually declared that government actions interfering or impinging upon that right should henceforth be subject to heightened judicial scrutiny by the courts. Moreover, the opinion in *Lawrence* was altogether silent on what level of judicial scrutiny (rational basis review, intermediate scrutiny, or strict scrutiny) should now be applied by the lower courts. Again, in legal parlance, "rational basis review" gives the government the benefit of every doubt, while at the other end of the scale, "strict scrutiny" would place a heavy burden on the government to prove that any discriminatory effect of a policy would be minor, unintentional, and justified by a compelling governmental purpose. The "leap of faith" to which Judge Leighton was referring would have been language in Justice Kennedy's ruling that the Supreme Court was at least renouncing rational basis review in cases involving government-sanctioned discrimination against homosexuals. He could find no such language.

"So it seemed to me that it was an open question," Leighton explained. "What my job is as a trial judge, as a fact finder, is to apply the existing law, and so I did what I did."

Leighton was not alone in his view. Running parallel to Margie's lawsuit against the Air Force was *Cook v. Rumsfeld*, another post-*Lawrence* challenge to Don't Ask, Don't Tell, brought by a dozen former military service members — six men and six women — who were expelled for being homosexual. The case came before Judge George A. O'Toole in the U.S. District Court of Massachusetts.

Before Judge O'Toole, lawyers for the *Cook* plaintiffs also contended that *Lawrence* had created a fundamental liberty interest for homosexuals that now required "strict scrutiny" review. Judge O'Toole didn't accept it. "Though the matter is not free from doubt because of the ambiguity of the *Lawrence* opinion," he wrote, he could not find a "fundamental" liberty interest warranting a higher level of judicial scrutiny.

Judge O'Toole rendered his order dismissing the *Cook* lawsuit on April 24, 2006. Judge Leighton had read it by the time he presided over oral arguments in the *Witt* case in June. It did not escape Leighton's notice that his counterpart in Massachusetts had been appointed by President Clinton. Thus, by the fall of 2006, two district court judges — one a Bush appointee and another a Clinton appointee — had looked at two nearly identical actions challenging DADT in light of *Lawrence* and reached the same conclusion. If *Lawrence* didn't make a dent in rational basis review, then both challenges to Don't Ask, Don't Tell had to fail, just as every previous legal challenge to DADT had failed.

For Margie and Laurie, the news of Judge Leighton's decision was disappointing but nothing they weren't, by then, conditioned to absorb.

"There is no crying in baseball," Lobsenz would say, borrowing a line from Tom Hanks in the movie *A League of Their Own*. It was his way of reminding Margie of the vicissitudes of litigation. It was a nine-inning game, and he and Jan Gemberling had stressed that from the beginning. Regardless of which side prevailed in Judge Leighton's district court, there would be an appeal filed with the Ninth Circuit Court of Appeals, which is where the case was now headed. The expectation was that the appeal could take months, and even if Margie prevailed, it was plausible that it would be sent back to the district court.

In the fuller sweep of their lives it was a long march through an emotionally hostile terrain, and both Margie and Laurie were increasingly aware of what that entailed, and how to help each other.

Says Margie: "You have to figure out where your energy is going to go at different periods of time, and if you take that negative step backward, you're kind of wasting energy if you let yourself get sad, or angry, or fall apart. Because then you have to gather yourself up again, and it takes more energy to get back on these different tracks. We had to keep moving and be really conscious of what energy we were putting out because it had to be positive with Dan, it had to be positive with Sam, like it had to be positive with Abby when she had the baby."

"Margie's an air evacuation nurse," Laurie adds. "She was trained for trauma, and I think that was the glue for her, to get through it."

Dan had survived, but as Grethe understood and had spoken to Laurie about, his lasting injuries were severe. He still required tubes to breathe and receive nutrition. In August, he was moved from the hospital in Seattle to a north Spokane care facility. Laurie would drive the nine miles to be at Dan's bedside each morning at 6:30, to spend time with him before she drove another seven miles to work.

"I would just sit with him and sing with him, that ukulele song, *Over the Rainbow*. It still brings me to tears, because that's what I would hum to him constantly. Being in a coma and coming out of a coma are pretty much the same thing."

Laurie's longtime friend Debbie Duvoisin was never far away.

"You never know what you're made of until you're tested. It wasn't just their strength and the courage. You could see how much Laurie and Margie supported each other, and how they were mindful that this was a serious relationship, right from the very beginning. They knew it, and they also knew it was going to take some time. They just had to take care of one thing at a time; they couldn't take on the whole battle at once."

In late September it was time for Margie to pack her uniform and catch a plane for Atlanta. Jan Gemberling would meet her there, as would Jim Lobsenz, the three of them arriving the same evening on separate flights. Twenty-six years earlier, Jim had represented Perry Watkins at his discharge hearing in Fort Lewis. Now he would appear, on Margie's behalf, at her discharge hearing at Robins Air Force Base, the home of the Air Force Reserve Command, in Warner Robins, Georgia.

Under Don't Ask, Don't Tell—as with the earlier military policy that required Sergeant Watkins and Colonel Cammermeyer to be removed from the Army—the discharge hearings were little more than show trials. There was no way they were going to win this, Jim reminded Margie. The best they could hope for was to use the two-day "charade" to build a record with the hope that further down the line the facts they introduced would make a difference in a civilian court.

After Margie, Jim, and Jan connected in the Atlanta airport, they rented a car and started driving south, through what seemed like an endless tunnel of loblolly pines and billboards. In addition to his legal prowess, Jim Lobsenz is a gifted vocalist who was part of an a cappella singing group while at Stanford. As they drove away from the airport, they rolled past countless highway signs directing traffic to destinations whose names are also imprinted in the South's civil rights history. Suddenly Jim had the urge to sing civil rights songs. And sing them loudly.

"I think Margie was just totally in shock," Jan says. "We're driving along, and he just starts singing out of the blue. And he just went through his entire repertoire. He sang all the way. So here we are driving into this incredible ordeal and we have Jim the entertainer."

His performance was just another reminder for Jan that her old friend had never been an ordinary lawyer. Their work together at the Edwards & Barbieri firm two decades earlier would have lasted longer had Jim not been fired. In addition to the volunteer work he was doing as the lead attorney on the Perry Watkins case, he had agreed to assist the defense in a high-profile death penalty case.

"I wrote a lengthy motion about why the Washington death penalty statute should be found unconstitutional. And I would have to admit that it was a lot of work and a lot of hours. And when you add that to the load of work and the hours on the *Watkins* case, the two cases, together, were truly a lot of time on pro bono work. And that didn't go over so well."

"On the one hand," he adds, "I think I was a little oblivious. On the other hand I don't think they were very forthright. Nobody wanted to come out and say 'You can't work on those cases that much, that's too much pro bono work,' because I guess, they were a little reluctant to say that. On the other hand, it was like, 'Don't you realize this is a for-profit law firm?'"

His dismissal from Edwards & Barbieri stung. It was the first and only time he had been fired from anything, and he learned from it. He was still representing Perry Watkins, and had taken on another high-profile death penalty appeal, also pro bono, when he joined Carney Badley in 1989.

"When I came to this law firm, before I came, I went around and talked to pretty much all the partners in the firm. And I said, 'Do you understand the kind of cases I do?'"

"I'm not going to change if I come here," he recalls telling the firm's partners, and then asking them: "Are you sure you want me to come here?"

The day-and-a-half hearing before the discharge board at Robins AFB was predictable and mostly unremarkable. There was, however, at least one moment Margie found darkly funny. Even though she was not contesting the fact that she was gay, the Air Force prosecutors obviously thought they should at least try to produce something to show she had actually told someone in uniform, or had said publicly, that she was a lesbian. So they produced video footage from her April press conference where ACLU's Aaron Caplan proclaimed "Major Witt is gay." The Air Force prosecutor contended that she was personally responsible for Caplan's statement. And it really was as simple as that. A more accurate shorthand for "Don't Ask, Don't Tell" would have been "If you are gay, you cannot stay."

For Margie, however, the longhand was excruciating. It was surreal being so far from home, sitting before three southern male colonels, whose main concerns at the end of the proceedings were how to fill out their worksheets and whether they actually had to "substantiate" their findings. (The answer from their legal adviser was that they did not.)

Then came the stark language of the board's findings and recommendation.

"The Board, after considering all the evidence in the case of Major Margaret Witt, has, in closed session, by secret written ballot, a majority of the voting members concurring, made the following findings and recommendation. The Board finds, by a preponderance of the evidence, that the Respondent, Major Margaret Witt, did engage in homosexual acts while a member of the United States Air Force Reserve; [and] number two, did make the statement that she is homosexual. . . . As a result of its findings the Board has determined the Respondent, Major Margaret Witt, should be separated from the United States Air Force Reserve under AFI 36-3209, based on the above findings of homosexual conduct."

With that, the proceeding adjourned at six minutes before noon.

Jan, who had come along for moral support, wasn't even permitted in the hearing room, so she spent the time downstairs, in an empty office. When the hearing was over, the three got back in their rental car and drove back to the airport in Atlanta. On the road north, Jim didn't sing. Instead he recited, from memory, Winnie-the-Pooh rhymes and other children's poetry he had shared with his young daughters at bedtime.

"Those rides could have been just awful," says Jan. "But they're delightful memories now."

The appeal of Judge Leighton's ruling to the United States Court of Appeals for the Ninth Circuit had actually been filed weeks before the discharge hearing at Robins AFB.

Even though Kathleen Taylor was enthusiastic about having the *Witt* case at the ACLU of Washington, Lobsenz would learn there was not nearly as much enthusiasm for the case in the ACLU's national offices. The reservations about the case had nothing to do with Margie's story, nor any lack of deep frustration with the military's policy. The concerns were about the likelihood that the case would fail and, in failing at the appellate level, only add to a trail of opinions further legitimizing and prolonging the policy. It was, after all, 2006. George W. Bush was still in the White House, and the Supreme Court, despite the *Lawrence* decision, still had a conservative majority.

In an internal memo he wrote in early April for the affiliate's legal director, Julya Hampton, Aaron Caplan elaborated upon "National's decision not to pursue challenges to the ban on gay and lesbian service members." Phone conversations he had had with Matt Coles, the leader of the ACLU's national Lesbian and Gay Rights Project, and Tobias Wolff, a law professor who had consulted on the *Cook* case (then pending before Judge O'Toole), had clarified the red flags.

Caplan informed Hampton that the two had shared "serious concerns about the risk of bad law that could come from pushing an overly expansive legal argument in a gays-in-the-military case." The risk of "bad law" wasn't just for how an adverse decision could affect other military cases, but for how it might also hurt the chances to advance gay rights generally. *Lawrence*, after all, had nothing to do with the military, and thus it didn't have to overcome the long-standing judicial deference to the military.

"In an ideal world," Caplan had written in his memo, "National's strategy would be to try to secure rulings about legal protections for gay people that expand upon *Lawrence*."

The concern, ACLU's Matt Coles said in a 2016 interview, was "that the military was a dangerous place to go" to secure such rulings. By that time (2006), Coles explained, it had become clear that cases against the government in which service members were plaintiffs were all the more difficult because "the courts are most likely to simply go along with whatever the military and Congress wanted."

To appreciate Coles's point—as to why it was "dangerous" to try to flesh out the implications of the *Lawrence* decision by advancing a DADT case—all one had to do was read Justice Sandra Day O'Connor's separate opinion in *Lawrence*. To be sure, Justice O'Connor sided with the majority in finding the Texas statute unconstitutional, because, in her view, it violated constitutional equal protection guarantees. Yet, in doing so, she noted, "Texas cannot assert any legitimate state interest here, such as national security or preserving the traditional institution of marriage" to justify the law. The clear implication was that, in Justice O'Connor's view, discrimination against homosexuals might still be justified on the basis of national defense—which, of course, was the sole underlying rationale for DADT.

In short, the national ACLU was justifiably worried that using *Lawrence* as a basis to challenge Don't Ask, Don't Tell was risky at best. The national security assertions built into the DADT statute would make it easier for judges to adopt rational basis review. They would therefore be more likely to dismiss the cases, and create adverse precedents that would hurt both military and civilian homosexuals experiencing discrimination. The wiser, more strategic approach would be to use *Lawrence* to expand the zone of gay rights through civilian cases, and then leverage those decisions to revisit Don't Ask, Don't Tell and the military.

By then, however, there was no chance that the ACLU of Washington was going to withdraw from the *Witt* case. Jim Lobsenz had grabbed the reins of Margie's case, and Kathleen Taylor was clear she wanted to help.

Attorney James Esseks, an ACLU litigation specialist who was tracking the *Witt* case, says, "Obviously, Jim's response was 'Well, I'm not here to fill out *Lawrence*, I'm here to defend a client.' And we totally get that."

Still, Caplan's memo summarizing ACLU national's concerns was prescient, given how the two district court judges would rule for the government in dismissing both *Cook* and *Witt*. As the *Witt* case proceeded to the Ninth Circuit on appeal, the *Cook* case went to the First Circuit Court of Appeals in Boston.

The next time Margie and Laurie would be in court, it would be in Coeur d'Alene, Idaho. It was May 17, 2007, and they were in the courtroom of Idaho district court judge John Luster. Judge Luster was presiding over the trial of Matt Kane, the young man who had attacked Dan McChesney. A jury had already decided that Kane was not guilty of felony assault charges but guilty only of misdemeanor battery.

The courtroom was literally divided, with Margie and Laurie seated on one side and a large crowd of Kane's family and supporters on the other. As part of the sentencing hearing, Judge Luster heard from a succession of Kane's friends, several of whom said the attack was out of character. His lawyer pleaded for leniency, saying that a long jail sentence could cost Kane his new job with a regional utility company. When it was his turn to speak, the defendant told the judge he had never been a fighter and "had no interest that night of getting into a fight."

When it was Laurie's turn, she walked to a chair at the top of the courtroom, from where she could look directly at the defendant, his family, and the rest of the people packing the room. She began by saying that she was there to speak as a mother and would address her statement to Matt Kane's mother, who was there in the courtroom.

"Mrs. Kane," she said, "I have lived a mother's nightmare, vastly different but tragic as your own. You know the initial timeline and details of this story. I want to tell you today about some particulars from my eyes."

She then spoke about her visit with Grethe Cammermeyer the previous summer, the day she, Margie, and Sam visited Grethe and Diane on Whidbey Island. She shared Grethe's solemn counsel that she bury the memory of her son before his devastating injury and regard him as a newborn with whom she could take heart at each and any improvement in his condition. She continued, describing the training she had received to suction his tracheotomy tube, the constant care he still needed, and how pieces of artificial bone, "the size of the palm of my hand," were being fashioned to encase his skull, and would be put in place by surgeons in Seattle the following month.

"Mrs. Kane, I can't say I've spent much time at all thinking about the actual point of the tragedy," she said. "When and how it occurred, because to dwell there doesn't change the reality of what my son has to face every day. To lose myself on the subject of your son would be another injustice."

The judge sentenced Matt Kane to sixty days in jail, with provisions for work release, and subtracted from the sentence the twenty-seven days he had already served. As the court adjourned, the relatively light sentence the judge had imposed induced an impromptu celebration among the crowd filing from the courtroom into the outer hall. One elderly man wasn't celebrating. It was Kane's grandfather, who stood and approached Laurie. She noticed he was tearing up.

"I'm so sorry for your loss," he told her.

Chapter 15

░░░░░░░░░░░░░░░

THE *WITT* STANDARD

If there is no crying in baseball, as Jim Lobsenz would say, then it could at least be conceded that some of the umpires were becoming sullen, if not mutinous.

This was certainly true of Thomas Zilly, the federal district court judge who had ordered the National Guard to reinstate Grethe Cammermeyer in 1994. In doing so, he had highlighted a disquieting rent in the fabric of American justice. It was a settled principle that "the federal government cannot discriminate against a class in order to give effect to the prejudice of others." And, yet, as a trial court judge examining the evidence, it was clear to him that Don't Ask, Don't Tell merely rewired and repackaged a policy "based solely on prejudice against a particular group."

Other federal judges had pushed back as well, especially in the Ninth Circuit, where, in addition to Grethe Cammermeyer and Perry Watkins, Army captain Carolyn "Dusty" Pruitt and Navy petty officer Keith Meinhold had each secured reinstatement through legal action.

In Watkins's case, a three-judge Ninth Circuit panel had seemingly completed the circle in 1988, ruling that the military's ban on homosexuals violated broad constitutional equal protection guarantees. Yet this thunderbolt of a ruling was withdrawn the following year when the en banc circuit judges replaced it with the equitable estoppel opinion, one narrowly tailored to Watkins's circumstances.

The *Pruitt*, *Cammermeyer*, and *Meinhold* cases were different. Sergeant Perry Watkins was an unapologetic, practicing homosexual whose life and career became a head-on challenge to widely held stereotypes and prejudices against gay people. Dusty Pruitt, Grethe Cammermeyer, and Keith Meinhold prevailed because judges ruled their dismissals were based upon their self-declared identity as homosexuals. They were neither charged nor found guilty of actually engaging in homosexual conduct. In Dusty Pruitt's case, a Ninth Circuit panel had taken the unusual step of putting aside a claim that her First Amendment rights were violated, while simultaneously framing a constitutional equal protection argument on her behalf, one that eventually led to her reinstatement. In *Meinhold*, the appeals court upheld a district court injunction against the Navy's efforts to discharge him after he told *ABC World News Tonight* in 1992 that he was gay. As in *Pruitt*, the Ninth Circuit judges were invoking equal protection rights and making a distinction (which the military had not) between a person's "status" as a homosexual and the acts of being a homosexual, which remained illegal under the Uniform Code of Military Justice.

All these cases arose prior to Don't Ask, Don't Tell. Proponents of the supposed compromise — beginning with President Clinton — offered it as a "major step forward" for both the military and gay service members. But DADT closed the equal protection loophole by forcing service members who disclosed their homosexuality to rebut the presumption they were also actively engaging in homosexual acts. The result was that there simply were no cases — either in the Ninth Circuit or elsewhere — that diminished the reach of DADT once the law took effect. In 1995, for example, Navy lieutenant Richard Watson took his challenge to DADT before Judge Zilly. The Seattle-based federal district court judge was still highly critical of the military's policy. But he nevertheless ruled in the military's favor, noting that Lieutenant Watson did not rebut the new statute's presumption "that service-members who state they are homosexuals engage in or have propensity to engage in homosexual conduct."

Judge Zilly wrote that his ruling "should not be interpreted as an endorsement of the military's 'Don't Ask, Don't Tell' policy or the way it has been applied in general."

"Regrettably, enforcement of the existing policy has resulted in the expulsion from the armed forces of many outstanding men and women who served their country with honor and dignity. This Court may not, however, question the wisdom of the policy or substitute its judgment for that of Congress."

Lieutenant Watson's case was taken up by the Ninth Circuit in 1997, with a similar appeal from Andrew Holmes, a lieutenant in the California National Guard. Both had disclosed they were homosexual, and neither attempted to rebut the presumption they were sexually active. "We must now face the question we avoided in *Meinhold*: whether the military's presumption from a service member's statement of homosexuality that he or she will engage in homosexual conduct bears a rational relationship to the military's interest in maintaining effective armed forces," the Ninth Circuit panel explained. Its answer: "Although the legislature's assumption that declared homosexuals will engage in homosexual conduct is imperfect, it is sufficiently rational to survive scrutiny."

In *Witt* and in *Cook*, the new argument was that by expressly overturning *Bowers* with *Lawrence v. Texas*, the Supreme Court had also removed in whole, or in part, the constitutional underpinnings of Don't Ask, Don't Tell.

By late 2006, however, nothing much had changed. In theory, things were better for gay people entering the military because they weren't supposed to be asked about their sexual orientation. On the other hand, it was now all the more clear that if you admitted to being gay (or the military otherwise concluded that you were), the "status" argument used to reinstate Pruitt, Cammermeyer, and Meinhold wouldn't shield you from discharge actions under DADT. In the aftermath of Judge Leighton's ruling for the Air Force in the *Witt* case and Judge O'Toole's ruling for the military services in *Cook v. Rumsfeld*, it was pretty clear that Don't Ask, Don't Tell wasn't yet unraveling in the courts. Where it was coming unglued in a somewhat more profound way was at the 446th Aeromedical Evacuation Squadron at McChord Air Force Base.

When Jim Lobsenz and Aaron Caplan submitted their opening brief to the Ninth Circuit Court of Appeals in October 2006, there were already nine unit members of the 446th—cited by name and rank—who had come forward to object. A half dozen were majors. Prominent in what they had to say was that the political cover story for Don't Ask, Don't Tell—that the presence of homosexuals was a detriment to unit morale—was simply not credible when it came to Major Witt. If anything, it was the Air Force's actions against her that were eating away at morale.

Stacey Julian, the twenty-year veteran tech sergeant who had traveled with Margie on their deployment to Oman in early 2003, made clear the move to discharge her had contributed to his recent decision to retire from the Air Force reserves.

"I no longer want to serve in an organization which mistreats people in the way the Air Force is mistreating her," he wrote in a declaration for the court.

The move to expel Margie also factored into Jim Schaffer's decision to retire from the 446th after twenty-six years in the military. With characteristic chutzpah, he invited her to attend his retirement ceremony at McChord. Because her discharge was not yet final, Margie still had her pass to get through the checkpoint onto the base. But when she reached the parking lot at the 446th's complex west of the flight line she was so overcome with emotion that she was trembling.

Fortunately, Stacey Julian was alert enough to spot her and help her out of her car. Upon entering the hall, she was greeted with an armful of roses and embraced by a succession of her former colleagues. A standing ovation followed when, during the ceremony, Jim called her forward to join him on the stage. There, he presented a gift from the squadron members, an enlarged photo of a C-17 Globemaster and C-141 Starlifter on the McChord tarmac; by evening's end, the photo would be completely bordered with handwritten messages and signatures from well-wishers.

Captain Ed Hrivnak's Air Force retirement gathering was in May 2007 at the Tacoma Firefighters Hall in south Tacoma. While most of the 150 or so people who came were friends and coworkers from his civilian job as a rescue specialist for Central Pierce Fire & Rescue, there were several faces in the hall from the 446th, including Janet Moore-Harbert, who by then had replaced Colonel Mary Walker as the squadron's commander.

Hrivnak was painfully aware of the post-traumatic stress he and his small team of flight nurses and med techs had carried home with them as a result of being fed into the maw of the Iraq War. Haunted by nightmares in which he and his crewmates were overwhelmed by scores of badly wounded soldiers wailing and calling out to them for help, he had struggled to keep his sanity and his marriage. Even at a retirement party, he was not going to put a gloss on what he had seen and been through. This included being honest with his anger about what had happened to his mentor and colleague Margie Witt. For his talk that evening, he had put together a PowerPoint presentation of the people he wanted to talk about. When Margie's photograph flickered on the screen at the Firefighters Hall, a gale of applause swept across the room.

"I said 'This *is wrong*,'" Hrivnak recalls. "I looked out into that room, and

I could see people who were retired or had quit since we got back from deployment, and I could see people who were still serving. Why in the hell isn't Margie out there serving? Give me one good reason."

Whether it was a good reason or not, the answer was "Don't Ask, Don't Tell." From 1994 to the end of 2007, the numbers of servicemen and women dismissed under DADT would surpass 11,500. During that time, the number of court-ordered reinstatements for service members discharged under DADT was zero.

In the meantime, the clocks were running on the parallel appeals of *Cook* and *Witt*, as both cases were taken up by the federal courts of appeals in their respective geographic circuits, the First Circuit for *Cook*, the Ninth for *Witt*.

When the First Circuit Court of Appeals ruling was announced, the jolt of disappointment for the *Cook* plaintiffs would be all the more intense because of how close they had come to prevailing. The June 9, 2008, decision was written by Judge Jeffrey R. Howard, the lone George W. Bush appointee on the court. Promisingly for the plaintiffs, the ruling first took up their constitutional due process challenge and did so by launching into a methodical dismantling of the government's primary defense. As in *Witt*, the government's attorneys insisted *Lawrence v. Texas* did not require anything more than "rational basis" review—the least rigorous standard of review in cases where plaintiffs alleged government discrimination. To be sure, the opinion noted, it was "difficult to pin down" whether *Lawrence* was prescribing rational basis review or "strict scrutiny" review that would almost certainly render Don't Ask, Don't Tell unconstitutional.

"But," Judge Howard wrote, "we are persuaded that *Lawrence* did indeed recognize a protected liberty interest for adults to engage in private, consensual sexual intimacy and applied a balancing of constitutional interests that defies the strict scrutiny or rational basis label."

For the *Cook* plaintiffs, the validation that the Supreme Court had recognized a "protected liberty interest" was golden. The notion they could win that argument but still lose their appeal was almost hard to imagine. But that is what happened.

Notwithstanding the "protected liberty interest" recognized by the Supreme Court in *Lawrence*, Judge Howard wrote, the Congress, with DADT, had proclaimed an overriding national security interest to justify discrimination against homosexuals in the military. Therefore, "judicial intrusion is simply not warranted."

Bam.

The concern reported in Aaron Caplan's memo two years earlier was that pushing a DADT case, even after *Lawrence*, could result in "bad law." But this was gruesome law, at least for the *Cook* plaintiffs. It was as though each had rounded third base and gotten crushed by a tank rolling up the base path from home plate.

The First Circuit's ruling would have gotten more national attention were it not for the Ninth Circuit's ruling in *Witt*, which had been announced nineteen days earlier, on May 21.

Margie and Laurie were working together that day on a pediatric physical therapy assignment at Lincoln Heights Elementary School, about a mile east of their home on Spokane's South Hill. It was toward the end of the school day when Margie's cell phone chimed to life as they were standing just outside the main school office. She quickly noticed it was displaying Jim Lobsenz's phone number.

"Margie?" he asked, and then she heard him check to make sure Aaron Caplan was also on the line. "You won!"

"What?" she asked.

"You won!" he repeated.

"And then I was just beaming," she recalls. "I won!" she explained to a passing faculty member who couldn't help but notice her delight. Jim had selected parts of the opinion to read aloud to her, and he read them, and explained them, and as Margie would usually do when Jim shared important news about the case, she began to choke up.

He paused.

"Are you crying again," he asked, playfully. "Didn't I tell you there was no crying in litigation?"

The news spread quickly among her friends and supporters. The calls and visits came, and invariably the question was "Do you get to go back?"

The answer to that question was no, or more accurately, not yet.

What she had actually won was the Plan B that Jim had presented to Judge Leighton two years earlier.

Plan A, of course, had been to win the argument that, after *Lawrence*, Don't Ask, Don't Tell was subject to strict scrutiny. If so, then the court could simply order the Air Force to return Major Witt to the 446th forthwith. There was, on the three-judge, Ninth Circuit panel, one voice for that remedy. It belonged to Judge William C. Canby—one of the three Ninth Circuit judges who had ruled in 1988 that Perry Watkins's discharge violated his constitutional right to equal protection. In a separate opinion filed in *Witt*, Judge Canby wrote that he would have gone further. His view, especially in light of *Lawrence*, was that "the so-called 'Don't Ask, Don't Tell' statute must be subjected to strict scrutiny." Judge Ronald Gould and Judge Susan Graber didn't agree that *Lawrence* required strict scrutiny, but they did agree with Judge Canby that the government's argument for minimal, rational basis review had to be rejected.

And that's where Plan B came to the fore.

"Because *Lawrence* is, perhaps intentionally so, silent as to the level of scrutiny that it applied, both parties draw upon language from *Lawrence* that supports their views," Judge Gould wrote for the court.

But after summarizing the respective arguments, he described how the Ninth Circuit panel resolved the question: "In these ambiguous circumstances, we analyze *Lawrence* by considering what the Court actually *did*, rather than by dissecting isolated pieces of text. In doing so, we conclude that the Supreme Court applied a heightened level of scrutiny in *Lawrence*."

Though there was no question from their analysis that *Lawrence* employed a heightened level of judicial scrutiny, "this leaves open the question whether the Court applied strict scrutiny, intermediate scrutiny, or another heightened level of scrutiny."

Substantive due process cases, like *Witt*, "typically apply strict scrutiny" when a fundamental right is involved, Judge Gould wrote. "Few laws survive such scrutiny, and DADT most likely would not."

But here, he continued, "we hesitate to apply strict scrutiny" because the *Lawrence* opinion hadn't provided sufficient guidance on how to construe the right in the presence of a compelling state interest.

At this juncture in the ruling, the *Witt* case could well have been crushed by the same national security argument that flattened the *Cook* plaintiffs. Instead, with surprising dispatch, the Ninth Circuit turned to an abstract recipe taken from another 2003 Supreme Court opinion—*Sell v. United States*—that Lobsenz and Caplan had injected into their appellate brief.

The sum of Judge Gould's thirty-four-page ruling is that it was a truly historic shift that said, in effect, it was no longer acceptable for the military (and Congress, for that matter) to trample at will upon the liberty and dignity of homosexuals in the ranks. The abrupt detour into the legalistic formulation in *Sell* was a dry exercise, given the judicial poetry of the moment. But it was necessary guidance for how the government and the courts should accord Major Witt—and others facing dismissal for being gay—their constitutional rights to due process.

Sell was a controversy about whether the Constitution allows the government to forcibly administer antipsychotic drugs to a mentally ill defendant in order to render the defendant competent to stand trial. The defendant (Charles Thomas Sell, a St. Louis dentist charged with fraud and money laundering) had a liberty interest to resist forcible medication, while the state had an interest in reducing the danger the defendant would pose to himself or others were he not medicated at trial. Through the "heightened scrutiny" analysis it applied in *Sell*, the Supreme Court recognized that a "significant" liberty interest had to be balanced against an important governmental interest. And the balancing mechanism imposed was a four-part test:

- First, a court must find that *important* governmental interests are at stake, and must consider the facts of the individual case in evaluating the government's interest, allowing that special circumstances may lessen the importance of that interest.
- Second, the court must conclude that involuntary medication will *significantly further* those concomitant state interests.
- Third, the court must conclude that involuntary medication is *necessary* to further those interests. The court must find that any alternative, less intrusive treatments are unlikely to achieve substantially the same results.
- Fourth, the court must conclude that administration of the drugs is medically appropriate.

The final factor, Judge Gould wrote, was specific to the medical context of *Sell*, "but the first three factors apply equally here."

Thus, he concluded: "We hold that when the government attempts to intrude upon the personal and private lives of homosexuals, in a manner that implicates the rights identified in *Lawrence*, the government must advance an important governmental interest, the intrusion must significantly further that interest, and the intrusion must be necessary to further that interest. In other words, for the third factor, a less intrusive means must be unlikely to achieve substantially the government's interest."

This part of the Ninth Circuit panel's ruling would become known as the *Witt* standard.

And then, from the perspective of Margaret Witt and her attorneys, it got even better. The analysis couldn't be done with a ministerial wave of the hand. It had to be "as-applied rather than facial."

"Under this review," Judge Gould wrote, "we must determine not whether DADT has some hypothetical, post-hoc rationalization in general, but whether a justification exists for the application of the policy as it applies to Major Witt. This approach is necessary to give meaning to the Supreme Court's conclusion that 'liberty gives substantial protection to adult persons in deciding how to conduct their private lives in matters pertaining to sex.'"

As she listened on her cell phone from Lincoln Heights Elementary School, Margie could tell her lawyers were elated.

Both lawyers well understood that heightened scrutiny (Plan B) wasn't nearly as dramatic as strict scrutiny. It was not a clarion ruling from the Ninth Circuit Court of Appeals that Don't Ask, Don't Tell was unconstitutional on its face.

But if it held, the practical effect would be, as Caplan put it, to "throw a lot of sand into the wheels of the discharge machine."

For the military, the *Witt* standard meant you couldn't discharge service members merely by learning, or forcing them to admit, they were gay. The military would actually have to show, in each case, that knowledge of a service member's homosexual orientation was adversely affecting unit cohesion and morale.

As a lawyer, said Lobsenz, "it puts me in a position where I can argue that you have to apply this case by case. You can't have a facial, just 'you're all gone.' You have to go one by one and decide. This soldier? A problem? Not a problem? This soldier? Not a problem? Problem? And the realization I had was, 'If I get them there it's going to collapse like a house of cards.' If the law can get to the point of saying 'You're right, it's mid-level scrutiny and you can do it on an as-applied basis.' If I can get them there, then every single time they want to throw out somebody who's gay or lesbian, they're going to have to have a hearing and prove a problem. Every. Single. Time."

In his chambers at Union Station in Tacoma, Judge Leighton noticed and read the e-mail telling him the Ninth Circuit panel and his "good friend," Judge Gould, had reversed him.

"Most of the time it's 'What are these guys doing? They don't know anything,'" he recalls. "This time I said, 'This makes some sense.'"

Judge Leighton really likes trials, so much so that he volunteers to be loaned to other federal districts where and when an additional trial judge is needed. He has presided over federal trials as far away as Florida. The reversal meant that the *Witt* case was going to be remanded to his Tacoma court to revisit the major's due process claims. He remembers discussing it with his longtime clerk James "Tiff" Seely.

"Tiff and I talked about it, and I said, 'You know, it's coming back, and we get a trial and we have the latitude to do the right thing. And I've got a saying that Judge [Robert J.] Bryan uttered at my swearing-in ceremony: 'Do the right thing in every case, every day, under the American justice system.' And that's what I was thinking about."

Chapter 16

OBI WAN OBAMA

Six weeks before the 2008 elections, John McCain surprised even members of his own party by attempting to call what amounted to a high-stakes, political time-out. With the first face-to-face debate between presidential rivals rapidly approaching, the Republican nominee hastily summoned reporters to a midtown Manhattan hotel. In the wake of the stunning bankruptcy of Lehman Brothers — Wall Street's fourth-largest investment bank — the nation's financial markets were teetering on collapse. Reading from a teleprompter, the senior senator from Arizona said he was suspending his campaign, returning to the capital, and asking that the highly anticipated debate set for Oxford, Mississippi, in three days, be postponed. He then declined to take reporters' questions and walked away.

McCain's misstep was easily cashed in by his Democratic opponent, Barack Obama. The forty-seven-year old, first-term U.S. senator from Illinois was able to say he understood the urgency of the financial debacle and appreciated the need to put aside partisan differences to solve it, but also calmly observed that the crisis made it all the more vital for the American people to hear from the two candidates. Besides, he added, "it's going to be the president's job to deal with more than one thing at once."

The debate in Oxford went on as scheduled, and in its wake, opinion polls showed Obama solidifying his lead on the way to winning the presidency.

To say that Obama had to "deal with more than one thing at once" when he took office on January 20, 2009, would barely describe what he faced. The unraveling of the U.S. subprime mortgage market had sent the world economy spiraling into a deep recession, with losses measured in the trillions of dollars and millions of jobs. An expensive war he had opposed was still raging in the Middle East, and the national security agencies now under his watch were implicated in unlawful surveillance and using torture to obtain intelligence. Then there was everything else, including his pledges to reform health care, squarely address the dangers of climate change, and bring an end to Don't Ask, Don't Tell.

In June 2008, Obama received the endorsement of the Human Rights Campaign, the nation's largest organization devoted to advancing equal rights for lesbian, gay, bisexual, and transgender (LGBT) people. In an open letter to the LGBT community, he had reiterated his support for several goals, including the repeal of Don't Ask, Don't Tell and of the Defense of Marriage Act. DOMA, as it was called, denied gay married couples the federal recognition and considerable benefits bestowed on straight couples; it had been signed into law by President Clinton in 1996. As encouraging as Obama's message was to those working on behalf of LGBT rights, the lack of a timeline for these goals did not go unnoticed. What drew more attention was that the president-elect invited a nationally prominent gay marriage opponent—Christian mega-church pastor Rick Warren—to give the invocation at his inauguration. The political embrace of Warren was especially upsetting to many LGBT advocates, raising questions about Obama's commitment to gay rights, or whether he would pay only lip service to avoid alienating evangelical Christians.

They were right to be concerned. When Obama's former top political strategist, David Axelrod, produced a political memoir in 2015, it drew national attention for Axelrod's admission that during the 2008 campaign he had successfully urged Obama to hide his personal view in support of gay marriage. (The online version of *Time* magazine's article on Axelrod's revelations included a copy of a 1996 candidate survey on which Obama—then running for the Illinois state senate—actually wrote out that he supported same-sex marriage.)

Compared to averting a second Great Depression and other challenges confronting the new president, ending Don't Ask, Don't Tell may have seemed straightforward and relatively inexpensive. But President Obama and his advisers would not have overlooked Bill Clinton's disastrous experience in trying to move quickly to end the ban on gays in the military. There were obvious similarities. Both Clinton and Obama were relatively young men at the time they took office, and neither had served in the military. Both had campaigned against a culturally potent military policy, and in Obama's case, his opposition to the Iraq War likely made the difference in his winning the Democratic nomination and the presidency itself.

Obama's oft-repeated vision was for a new, conciliatory approach to politics that would bridge partisan differences. Among the signals he sent as he took office was to include two Republicans in his cabinet. One was the secretary of transportation, Ray LaHood. The other was Robert Gates, whom Obama asked to continue serving in his role as secretary of defense. Inviting Gates to stay on was more than a signal. With two wars under way, the secretary's imprimatur and his credibility with the armed services and an increasingly intransigent opposition party were invaluable on several levels. If the new president was going to be able to deliver on his pledge to repeal DADT, there was no question he would try to work closely with Secretary Gates to make it happen.

Throughout this tumultuous period, Major Margaret Witt was just one among hundreds of gay service members enduring the frustration and humiliation of a DADT discharge. It deeply mattered that, by now, her parents accepted Laurie, and so many friends and colleagues had embraced and continued to support them. And, still, her continuing isolation from her Air Force colleagues was emotionally grueling, all the more so for how senseless and unfair it seemed. At times, she boiled with anger. The two-day Air Force discharge hearing at Robins AFB in Georgia was so obviously a military show trial that, when it was over, she literally started ripping off her uniform as she and Jim and Jan walked away from the building to their rental car. The shoes came off too, and when they arrived at the Atlanta airport she made a point of pitching them in a trash bin.

Fourteen months later, Margie was back in uniform for oral arguments before the three-judge panel of the Ninth Circuit Court of Appeals. To be sure, the abstruse arguments over rational basis review, strict scrutiny, and the substantive reach of liberty under the Constitution's due process clause seemed far removed from what she knew to be the basic truths about her experience. She couldn't help but wonder when the judges would turn their attention to the actual reality of the 446th Aeromedical Evacuation Squadron and to the loyalty, respect, and affection she had earned as a flight nurse and unit leader. Even so, watching and listening to a confident Jim Lobsenz present her case that morning in Seattle had given her hope and lifted her spirits. He was really good at this. And unlike the farcical discharge hearing at Robins Air Force Base, it was clear from the reactions of the judges that they were taking her challenge, her case, very seriously.

There was another reason for hope in the courtroom that morning. Her name was Sarah Dunne.

Although she had been hired by the ACLU of Washington months earlier to serve as its new legal director, Dunne was meeting Margie for the first time that day. A slim woman in her mid-thirties, with auburn hair and engaging eyes, Sarah was a self-described "military brat," whose father once served as an officer at McChord. Like Margie, she had grown up identifying herself through her passion for sports and disdain for bullies. She had also thrived academically, achieving a 4.0 grade-point average at Kent Ridge High School in a valley along Big Soos Creek between Tacoma and Seattle.

As a fifth grader she had mused in her journal, "Maybe if I study hard and get good grades someday I'll be able to go to Stanford University." Yet when she shared that goal with a guidance counselor at Kent Ridge in the fall of 1989, she was bluntly advised that "they don't take kids from this school." She applied to Stanford anyway, was accepted, and chose to pursue degrees in English and political science. She had become interested in law and justice in her early teens and thought about becoming a public defender. By the time she graduated high school, she had also formed an opinion that the world had too many lawyers. She did, however, take courses in civil rights and civil liberties at Stanford and found work as a paralegal to help pay her bills. She also began volunteering at the East Palo Alto Community Law Project, where she continued to work after she graduated from Stanford. By then she had mostly decided that maybe the world could use another lawyer after all.

Sarah Dunne was clearly intelligent and scrappy, but what Margie also quickly recognized and valued was how steeped and conversant Sarah was in the culture of the military. That attribute began to matter more in January of 2008, when Aaron Caplan accepted an invitation to join the faculty at the Loyola Law School in Los Angeles. Sarah would fill his seat as the ACLU staff attorney on the *Witt* case.

There was, in this twisting fabric of fate, something of a silver thread. A year out of Stanford, Sarah had been accepted at the University of Chicago

Law School. Like the university's internationally known school of economics, its law school has a reputation for being conservative. Sarah noticed how the rightward tilt influenced the professional and social pecking order among the faculty and how, in her view, it marginalized the public interest and civil rights law that most interested her. She remembers a lecture on property law by one of the school's prominent scholars who told the class that "if the word 'fairness' comes out of your mouth, you have nothing left to say."

In her third year, she turned to constitutional law and did a full quarter on equal protection and due process. Her instructor for that section was, by then, also a member of the Illinois state senate. He was a lanky, thirty-seven-year-old African American professor who—she quickly predicted to her classmates—would become the first African American president of the United States. It was Barack Obama.

Obama's radiant intellect was quickly evident, but what also inspired Sarah's admiration was how confidently he carried himself, even as he cut against the law school's ideological grain. "He was a rock star to me," she says, "and I also appreciated his kind of 'f-you' attitude. He never kissed up to certain professors."

There was another important detail Sarah could share with Margie. When Professor Obama turned to teaching constitutional due process, the case upon which he focused his attention was that of Sergeant Perry Watkins. In Sarah's view, Obama chose to highlight that particular case because of how outrageous the government's conduct had been in moving to expel Watkins after accepting and promoting him for so many years as an open homosexual.

Obama's focus on Perry Watkins and Sarah's deep admiration for her former law professor resonated with Margie. To her, Obama's interest in the Perry Watkins case revealed a basic decency and disposition for fairness that she connected to her own upbringing. When Washington State Democrats held their caucuses on February 9, 2008, Margie showed up at Spokane's Sacajawea Middle School to support Obama. He was, she began to say, her Obi Wan Kenobi.

What Margie couldn't have known then is that her case was headed Obama's way.

After the Ninth Circuit panel ruled in her favor in late spring 2008, there was no question about whether the Bush administration lawyers would appeal. Just as when Jim Lobsenz had secured what appeared to be a historic win from a Ninth Circuit panel in the *Watkins* case two decades earlier, government lawyers requested an en banc appeal—a review of the case by all twenty-nine of the Ninth Circuit's appellate judges—in *Witt*. In *Watkins* the en banc appeal resulted in the government losing the battle but not losing the war. The court order to reinstate Sergeant Watkins was affirmed, but the full court rescinded the panel's earlier finding that the antigay policy was unconstitutional.

That wouldn't happen this time. The Ninth Circuit Court of Appeals not only voted to decline the government's petition for an en banc appeal of *Witt*, but it announced its decision in early December, a month to the day after Obama had been elected. That meant it would be up to the Obama administration to decide what to do about Margaret Witt.

There were two choices.

The first was to simply honor the remand to Judge Leighton's district court for a trial. The second was to file a writ of certiorari, requesting the Supreme Court to hear an appeal of the Ninth Circuit's ruling. Filing such a "cert" petition with the Supreme Court would normally be premature, in that there hadn't been a verdict as yet from the trial court. But the Ninth Circuit's ruling in *Witt* was squarely at odds with decades of judicial deference to the military. The Ninth's ruling also delivered a new template for judicial review that had clear ramifications far beyond the *Witt* case. Hence, the government had a good argument that a pivotal question of law—whether the *Witt* standard was correctly derived from the Supreme Court's decision in *Lawrence*—still needed to be resolved by the Supreme Court. The government could also argue that if the Supreme Court granted certiorari, then ruled in the government's favor, it would make the time, hardship, and expense of a trial (and countless other DADT trials that were sure to follow) unnecessary.

In legal parlance such a challenge—to resolve an important legal question prior to trial—is known as an interlocutory appeal. It would have been all the more ripe in the *Witt* case because the First Circuit Court of Appeals, in *Cook v. Gates*, had looked at essentially the same question and come down on the opposite side, dismissing all claims of the *Cook* plaintiffs. Thus, there was a discernible split between two appellate circuits over how to interpret the *Lawrence* decision—a situation making it all the more likely the Supreme Court would accept an interlocutory appeal.

By all accounts, top officials in the new Obama administration—with their fire hoses trained on the flaming financial markets and other urgent priorities—were not ready to begin grappling with Don't Ask, Don't Tell in early 2009. But the *Witt* case would begin to force their hands. By early April, the Supreme Court had already granted two thirty-day extensions to allow the new administration time to decide whether it would seek an interlocutory appeal in *Witt*. The deadline for an answer was rapidly approaching.

Jim Lobsenz was spending a busy Easter weekend out of town when Steve Shapiro, the national legal director for the ACLU, reached him on his cell phone. He was needed for a meeting at the Justice Department on Monday, he heard Shapiro say.

Lobsenz protested. He and his wife were in southern Oregon, in the process of buying a new house. To get to DC on Monday he would have to fly back to Seattle and then cross-country to DC. Would some other day work?

Shapiro cut him short. "Jim, when the solicitor general of the United States says she wants to have a meeting with you, you don't get to pick your day, you just go."

With little time to spare, he was soon on his way to the airport in Medford, Oregon. Along the way, he knew he had to reach Margie, because there was a good chance the government would want to explore an out-of-court settlement. Sarah would be joining him at the meeting on Monday, and the two of them needed to know, from Margie, what she would be willing to put on the table. As with Perry Watkins twenty years earlier, the government could offer her a very generous payoff, including a full pension. What the government would likely request from their client, they figured, was for her to join in a motion to the Ninth Circuit, to request that the circuit's ruling in her case be withdrawn. If she accepted such an offer, and the Ninth Circuit agreed to rescind the ruling, then it would strip other DADT plaintiffs (especially those within the nine western states of the Ninth Circuit) of their right to invoke the *Witt* standard in challenging their discharges.

"We had to advise her of that possibility," says Sarah.

By this time, Margie's faith and trust in Jim Lobsenz's advice was airtight. What was different about this conversation, though, is that it had to be entirely her choice. She asked what he thought. He chose not to answer.

"I don't want to influence your decision," Jim recalls telling her. "And she said—God bless her—'I feel like I have a responsibility to the other gay and lesbian people in the armed forces that I can't just be looking out for myself. I just don't think I could do that.' So she decided, and once she said she didn't want to do that, then I felt free to say 'Good, I'm glad you decided on that.'"

A few days earlier, President Obama chaired a contentious meeting in the West Wing of the White House to try to work out what to do with the *Witt* challenge to Don't Ask, Don't Tell. Robert Gates would write about it in his 2014 memoir *Duty: Memoirs of a Secretary at War*. The Air Force was eager to push the issue to the Supreme Court, Gates noted. But the president "clearly hated the idea of upholding a law he considered abhorrent." The meeting ended, and the question lingered.

The next substantive conversation Gates reports he had with the president about Don't Ask, Don't Tell was on April 13. This was the same day that Jim Lobsenz and Sarah Dunne arrived at the Justice Department to discuss the case with the new solicitor general, Elena Kagan.

It's not clear which meeting happened first, or whether they happened simultaneously.

Joining Secretary Gates in the meeting with the president was Admiral Mike Mullen, the chairman of the Joint Chiefs of Staff.

"We understood his commitment to changing the law," Gates wrote, "but the question was how to fulfill that promise in a way that 'mitigates the negative consequences.'"

"The military had never had an open conversation internally about gays serving," Gates explained. "What dialogue there had been was, I suspected, mostly among groups of soldiers in the barracks or in small groups over a few beers. If the policy was to change, I cautioned him [the president] in the strongest possible terms, it should not be by presidential order; it could not be seen by the military as simply the fulfillment of a campaign promise by a liberal president. DADT was the law. Any change had to come through a change in that law by the elected representatives of the American people."

As to what should happen with the *Witt* case in particular, Gates wrote that he had agreed with Jeh Johnson, the Pentagon's top lawyer at the time, that they should not seek review by the Supreme Court. Gates said he trusted Johnson's analysis, which was that "the government's case as it stood was weak and that we might very well lose the appeal, resulting in my nightmare scenario of a Supreme Court–mandated change in the DADT law for the military."

If Elena Kagan agreed with Jeh Johnson and Robert Gates, it wasn't something she disclosed at the hastily assembled gathering with the *Witt* lawyers. She was the last to arrive for the meeting, Jim recalls, and drew chuckles with her apology as she explained she had been on the job two only weeks and was still learning her way around the building. Both were struck by her ease and cordiality. Sarah took note that Kagan purposefully declined to take the chair at the head of the table, leaving it empty and choosing to sit alongside her senior deputies, Neal Katyal and Edwin Kneedler.

The clearest purpose of the meeting was to push the *Witt* legal team to make the case for why the solicitor general should not pursue the interlocutory appeal to the Supreme Court.

It was not an easy question. Notwithstanding Jeh Johnson's advice to Gates that the government was vulnerable to a Supreme Court appeal, there were several reasons to think the government would have the upper hand. Justice Sandra Day O'Connor, who had joined the majority in *Lawrence*, had since retired and been replaced by a more conservative justice in Samuel Alito. Neither was there any guarantee that Justice Kennedy—now so clearly the swing vote—would agree that the zone of liberty created for gay civilians in *Lawrence* would apply to men and women in uniform. The argument that it shouldn't apply (that it should be precluded or subordinated to the military's national security interest) could be found in the First Circuit Court of Appeals ruling in *Cook v. Gates*, a ruling that had specifically rebutted the Ninth Circuit's reasoning in *Witt*.

It was no surprise that Kagan was personally sympathetic; but that just framed her dilemma.

Before accepting her appointment by Obama to be solicitor general, Kagan was dean of Harvard Law School. Part of what she had inherited as dean was a tense standoff involving Don't Ask, Don't Tell and military recruiters. Because the law school had a long-standing antidiscrimination policy, it had, for years, prohibited military recruiters from using the school's career services office to meet with students. That changed in 2002, when Harvard was threatened with a loss of hundreds of millions of federal dollars if it didn't allow military recruiters equal access. In trying to navigate the controversy as dean, Kagan not only criticized the government for trying to "use the power of the purse to force educational institutions to renounce their most foundational principles," but she personally denounced DADT as "both unwise and unjust."

Those statements did not go unnoticed by her conservative critics, including Republican members of the Senate Judiciary Committee. During her confirmation hearing to be solicitor general, she was pressed to reconcile her blunt personal views against DADT with the responsibility of the solicitor general to vigorously defend the nation's laws.

At their April 13 meeting at the Justice Department, Lobsenz says, Kagan told him "nobody dislikes Don't Ask, Don't Tell more than I do." But, he says, she also emphasized her vow to skeptical senators that she would put aside her personal feelings and represent the government's position as best she could. Given that reality, Lobsenz says he was asked to convince her why she shouldn't challenge the Ninth Circuit's ruling in *Witt* with a petition to the Supreme Court.

"And I didn't have much of an answer for her," he said. "It was sort of like, 'You got your job to do, I got my job to do, we're each going to do it well, goodbye and good luck.'"

The meeting ended cordially enough, but without a settlement and without an answer from Kagan as to whether she would seek Supreme Court review. That answer would come at the end of the following week, when Attorney General Eric Holder formally notified the U.S. Senate that the Justice Department would not seek Supreme Court review in *Witt v. Air Force.*

Reasons were offered in Holder's letter, but none of them was very persuasive, at least not to Senator Jeff Sessions, the ranking Republican on the Senate Judiciary Committee. The senator from Alabama—a former U.S. attorney whose nomination to the federal bench by President Ronald Reagan had been rejected by the Senate in 1986—was waiting for Elena Kagan when she returned to the Senate in June of 2010. This time the national spotlight was on both of them, because President Obama had nominated Kagan to replace retiring associate justice John Paul Stevens on the Supreme Court.

On the second day of her confirmation hearings, the two had tangled testily over Kagan's involvement in barring military recruiters from Harvard because of the university's objections to Don't Ask, Don't Tell. The next day, June 30, 2010, Sessions used the bulk of his time to go after her about the *Witt* decision.

"I'd like to follow up and go in a little different direction today," he began. "Ironically and almost amazingly, it fell to your lot as solicitor general to defend that very law, the law of the United States, the Don't Ask, Don't Tell law that you opposed so much there [at Harvard]. And let me focus on your responsibility and how you handled it."

Reading from a prepared script, the senator then spent several minutes reminding her of her promise, as the solicitor general nominee, to put aside her own views and represent "with vigor" the positions of the United States, including the constitutionality of Don't Ask, Don't Tell and the "doctrine of judicial deference to legislation involving military matters."

Senator Sessions described the Ninth Circuit's decision in *Witt* as "a severe damaging blow to the Department of Defense," especially given that the court had jurisdiction in states comprising 40 percent of the nation's land. "It was an oath you took," he said, to uphold the law. So why had she not pursued the interlocutory appeal of the case to the high court?

Broadcast highlights of Kagan's confirmation hearings tended to showcase her lightning wit and charisma. This was not a lighthearted exchange, though, and she seemed ill at ease as she responded, at length, to the senator's assertive questioning.

There were "very serious discussions" with the Pentagon about the *Witt* case and its threat to Don't Ask, Don't Tell, she said, "because I agree with you, Senator Sessions, that the Ninth Circuit decision undercuts that statute. It makes it harder for the government to carry out its policies under that statute."

The decision not to file certiorari in *Witt*, Kagan replied, evolved from two considerations. One was the general "presumption against interlocutory review" by the Supreme Court, which, she conceded, is "not a flat rule." But the primary consideration she offered appeared to catch Sessions off guard, in part because it borrowed so much from his explanation for why the Ninth Circuit ruling was so damaging to the military.

As Holder had noted in his April 24, 2009, letter, the government reserved its rights to come back to the Supreme Court in the event Margaret Witt prevailed at trial.

"And the reason that that approach was chosen," she continued, "was because we thought that it was—it would be better to go to the Supreme Court with a fuller record and with a fuller record about the particular party involved, maybe more importantly with a record that would show exactly what the Ninth Circuit was demanding that the government do.

"Because what the Ninth Circuit was demanding that the government do was, in the government's view, and—particularly in DOD's view—a kind of strange thing, where the government would have to show, in each particular case, that a particular separation caused the military harm, rather than that—rather than to view it in general across the statute. And one reason we thought that the remand would actually strengthen the case in the Supreme Court was because the remand would enable us to show what this inquiry would look like, what the Ninth Circuit's—the inquiry that the Ninth Circuit demanded would look like, and to suggest to the Supreme Court, using the best evidence there was, how it was that this inquiry really would disrupt military operations."

Senator Sessions stared back at her, looking over the rims of his reading glasses. He seemed taken aback, if not confused, by the reasoning of her answer.

"Well, I appreciate the position," he said, and then he fumbled for words. "I—I—I will look at it and review it." Sessions noted that "your position was in harmony with the position the ACLU took," added that he could "see no harm" in "attempting an interlocutory appeal" in *Witt*, and then he quickly changed the subject, moving on to ask her questions about the Constitution's commerce clause.

Two former White House officials, both of whom requested anonymity, corroborate Gates's account of how important the *Witt* case was in the president's decision making on Don't Ask, Don't Tell. Part of it was the timing of the decision that needed to be made, so quickly, about whether to seek review by the Supreme Court. And, as Gates suggested in his memoir, part of it had to do with the story behind the case, of "a highly respected nurse" who had been careful to abide by the "don't tell" handshake that was supposed to prevent gays and lesbians from being hounded out of the military.

But the most important postscript on the White House struggle over the *Witt* case comes from best-selling legal journalist Jeffrey Toobin, who also happens to be a former Harvard classmate of Elena Kagan's. In his 2012 book *The Oath: The Obama White House and the Supreme Court*, Toobin writes about a spirited argument between the president and his new solicitor general. Assuming Toobin's account is accurate, Kagan was taking a political bullet for the president during her Supreme Court confirmation hearing.

Even though Kagan thought DADT was a bad law and should be repealed, Toobin reports, she also thought it was constitutional and that the Ninth Circuit had just gotten it wrong with its 2008 ruling, reversing Judge Leighton and remanding *Witt* for trial. According to Toobin, Kagan *did* want to take the case to the Supreme Court, to file certiorari for the interlocutory appeal. He wrote:

"At the Justice Department and the White House, many people — most in fact — disagreed with Kagan. The president was already facing charges from his supporters in the gay community that he had betrayed his promises. Don't Ask, Don't Tell was manifestly unjust. If the Ninth Circuit made it a little harder to discharge gay service members, then so much the better. Pushing his appeal would be a needless insult to honorable members of the armed forces like Margaret Witt. With the administration split, there's only one thing to do. The president has to decide."

Thus, Toobin reported in *The Oath*, it was Obama who made the call not to take *Witt* to the Supreme Court, and that he did so over Kagan's spirited dissent. If so, Margie Witt's faith in Barack Obama was well-placed. While Attorney General Holder's letter offered plausible reasons for not taking the *Witt* case to the Supreme Court before trial, it's highly likely that, had the administration done so, the court would have granted certiorari.

Had the Obama Justice Department sought certiorari in *Witt*, says the ACLU's Matt Coles, "I think there's very little chance the court would have let a federal circuit's new interpretation of Don't Ask, Don't Tell — that was less favorable to the government — stand without looking at it. It's the court's job do that kind of case."

Coles's ACLU colleague, James Esseks, who attended the April 2009 meeting on the *Witt* case with Solicitor General Kagan, agrees. Had the Supreme Court granted the appeal, Esseks says, "that would have altered all the political dynamics that happened during that period, that sort of built up the pressure for repeal [of Don't Ask, Don't Tell]. Because everything would have been suspended while we all waited to see what in the world happened in the court."

Obama had to be deeply concerned, Esseks says, that taking the *Witt* case to the Supreme Court would "completely derail" the political campaign to repeal DADT.

"The other thing," Esseks added, "is I do think the trial that happened and Margie's story in particular were important parts of the discussion and the stories that people told on the Hill to create the political will and get people something that would push them over the edge to say, 'Okay, well it's time to do this.'"

Obama had the last word, Toobin reports in *The Oath*, but he also wrote that the argument revealed Obama's "strange affinity for people who disagreed with him"—that "Kagan's polite but resolute defense of a losing cause resonated with the president," and so much so that it was a key factor in his decision to appoint her to the Supreme Court a year later, in May 2010.

(When approached for an interview, Justice Kagan said that while she appreciated being contacted to comment on Jeffrey Toobin's account, she would decline to do so.)

On August 6, 2010, Elena Kagan would win Senate confirmation to become the 112th justice of the U.S. Supreme Court. The trial in *Major Margaret Witt v. Department of the Air Force* would get under way thirty-eight days later.

Chapter 17

▦▦▦▦▦▦▦▦▦▦

OUTING GOLIATH

Inside Tacoma's Union Station courthouse, even on cloudy days, knots and tendrils of spectral light emanate from ornate glass art pieces. The largest, *End of the Day Chandelier*, hangs directly beneath the ninety-foot-high copper dome and feeds on natural light pouring in from large banks of windows on the mezzanine level. Against the cream-colored walls and ceiling, the vertical chandelier suggests a giant, shimmering sea creature with air sacs and uncoiling tentacles. As with the other glass pieces, it is from the imagination of artist Dale Chihuly, a Tacoma native. The glasswork art spills into two, coffer-ceilinged federal courtrooms in the wings. In September 2010, during the week of the *Witt* trial, a green Chihuly, suggestive of a flower morphing into an old-style phonograph, was perched next to Judge Leighton's bench.

From the day Margie had been left trembling and all but speechless in her commander's conference room at McChord, it had now been six years and forty-nine days. Time was one way to measure what it had taken to put a branch of the military and Don't Ask, Don't Tell on trial. But it would take something like the eruptions and spirals of a Chihuly chandelier to reflect the range of emotions and perseverance involved. Given all she had endured, it would have been hard to ask for anything less than to have the trial here, in her hometown, in this vaulted landmark just above Commencement Bay.

She knew by day one who was in the lineup to testify in the coming week. She also knew the central question. Was Margie Witt a detriment to unit morale and cohesion in the United States Air Force?

It was not the sort of confrontation she would be cocky about, not with her eviscerating experience with what had ensnared her life, and Laurie's life, and the lives of so many thousands of gay men and women before her.

After finding the resilience to withstand the forced entry of her worst fears, she had used Grethe Cammermeyer's guidance to confront the Air Force and Don't Ask, Don't Tell. She now felt as though her entire career had prepared her for what was about to transpire in Judge Leighton's courtroom.

"Show me what you got," she was thinking as the four government lawyers were introduced to the court on September 13. "Because I'm not afraid of you anymore."

There were other reasons she felt like she had the home-court advantage. All she had to do was look behind her, to where her family and friends were sitting. There were Frank and Gloria, and there was Laurie, the love of her life, the woman her parents now embraced as their third daughter. In the three of them alone she had already won more than she could lose. Grethe Cammermeyer was there, as was Carla Savalli and Karyn Ingebritsen, now Karyn Gomez. As she had been from the start, Jan Gemberling was there too, with one of her sons. On most days a van arrived from Gig Harbor bringing members of the congregation from Agnus Dei Lutheran Church who were there to quietly support her and her family. To her right, where a jury would have been seated if this were a jury trial, a cluster of reporters looked on.

Among the newest of Margie's friends seated in the pew-style seats behind her was Lieutenant Colonel Victor Fehrenbach, an ace F-15E fighter pilot. In his nineteen-year Air Force career, Victor had flown nearly ninety combat missions in Kosovo, Afghanistan, and Iraq. As with Margie, he was also facing discharge under Don't Ask, Don't Tell, and also stood to lose his twenty-year pension if the Air Force prevailed. Yet, because the highly decorated pilot and trainer had been based in Idaho—within the Ninth Circuit's jurisdiction—Margie's 2008 court of appeals victory was also a victory for him, as it would all but certainly compel the Air Force to give him a trial as well.

Sitting alongside Margie was Jim Lobsenz. She well remembered the line from Randy Shilts's book, about how Perry Watkins saw Jim as the Atticus Finch character that Gregory Peck portrayed in *To Kill a Mockingbird*. So ironic, in some ways, that this brilliant but unassuming Quaker would devote so much of his life to advocating for two people whose basic demand was to let them serve in the military—an institution about which he cared naught. She so admired his preparation and advocacy on her behalf, his eloquence and the ease with which he presented himself in the courtroom, at times punctuating his statements or questions by thrusting a hand in a pocket, or adjusting the glasses on his nose.

Also sitting next to her was Sarah Dunne. The two of them had bonded so quickly, with their common competitive instincts as former athletes, and in the ways they understood military culture and rituals.

Their rapport was so intense at times, Margie joked, that "I couldn't talk to her fast enough."

It also helped that early in her career Sarah had served four years as a trial attorney for the Justice Department's civil rights division, focusing primarily on desegregation cases in the Deep South. Now she sat across the aisle from three Justice Department attorneys and an Air Force lawyer who were there to make the case for why Major Margaret Witt should not be allowed to return to her unit at McChord.

When Sarah and Jim and their associates — Perkins Coie law firm attorney Sher Kung and ACLU paralegal Nina Russell — packed up their cars for the trip down to Tacoma, they had loaded ten banker's boxes full of documents. And these were only a fraction of the more than thirty thousand pages of documents in exhibits, depositions, and other research they had compiled since 2004. Sarah would go first, delivering the opening statement for their case. In her final preparations the night before, in Seattle, she had reread her twelve-year-old notes from lectures on substantive due process at the University of Chicago law school, lectures delivered by Barack Obama.

If patriotism can be a last refuge for a scoundrel, then with Don't Ask, Don't Tell, national security had become one of the last places for bigotry against homosexuals to find a nest. The practical effect of the *Witt* standard, set out with the Ninth Circuit's remand order for trial, was to make that place even smaller, and that was part of what Dunne would focus on in her opening statement.

Nearly two decades earlier, Colorado congresswoman Patricia Schroeder had pointedly pressed a proposition that had long been a staple in Jim Lobsenz's courtroom arguments against the ban on gays in the military — that there really was no difference between the discrimination inflicted upon African American soldiers before 1948 and the discrimination perpetuated against gay service men and women. In May 1992, Representative Schroeder sent a letter to Joint Chiefs of Staff chairman Colin Powell after

General Powell told Congress that allowing homosexuals to serve in the military would make many heterosexuals uncomfortable and would thus be "prejudicial to good order and discipline."

"I am sure you are aware," Schroeder wrote to the nation's most prominent African American soldier, "that your reasoning would have kept you from the mess hall a few decades ago, all in the name of good order and discipline."

Powell took umbrage that Schroeder would compare bias based upon skin color with that due to a "human behavioral" characteristic. His highly publicized rebuke to the congresswoman helped galvanize political opposition to Bill Clinton's pledge to end the gay ban, and bolstered support for what became Don't Ask, Don't Tell. In February 2010, six months before the start of the *Witt* trial, the now-retired general announced he had changed his mind. He now supported President Obama in his push to repeal DADT because, in Powell's words, "attitudes and circumstances had changed."

In his ruling ordering the reinstatement of Grethe Cammermeyer in 1994, Judge Thomas Zilly reminded the government that the Supreme Court, in a pair of cases from the mid-1980s, had ruled there had to be at least a rational basis for a law, or policy, that discriminates against a group of people. These rulings (*Palmore v. Sidoti*, 1984, and *Cleburne v. Cleburne Living Center*, 1985) made clear that where bare prejudice was the evident motivation for a government action, the action was unconstitutional; nor could a law or policy give effect to private biases.

The authors of Don't Ask, Don't Tell had done their best to hide the prejudicial attitudes at the root of the law by wrapping them in national security and other patriotic bunting. What was left unspoken and unwritten is what Judge Zilly had called out in *Cammermeyer*, which is that it was the homophobic attitudes and actions of heterosexual service members that would undermine unit morale and cohesion. This was the uniformed thug hiding in DADT.

Sarah Dunne, whose father and four of her uncles had graduated from military academies, took it personally. If there was a way to do it, she would have seized the military by its epaulets and said, "C'mon guys, you're not bigots. This is ridiculous."

Instead, she would get the privilege of delivering the opening statement at the *Witt* trial, a trial that would level the playing field, that would force the government to convince a court that the dismissal of Major Margaret Witt was based on something other than poorly camouflaged prejudice.

"Good morning, your honor," she greeted Judge Leighton.

She let silence gather for a few beats, then started by simply reading phrases from her client's first Air Force performance review, more than twenty years earlier.

"Dynamic officer," she began.

"Consistently proves she can handle any task that comes her way."

"Ranks in the top 1 percent of her peers."

"A vital team leader."

"Dynamic nursing leader."

"Committed to continuing squadron cohesion and morale."

"Excellent role model."

"Knows and understands the worth and dignity of her subordinates."

Then she skipped forward to borrow words from Colonel Janet Moore-Harbert, the current commander of the 446th.

"Exceptional flight nurse. Always ready to support the mission."

The words were drawn from a performance review signed by the squadron commander *after* the *Witt* lawsuit had been filed, Dunne pointed out, and therefore after it had become known that the major was a lesbian.

"Your honor, we believe the evidence will show that Major Witt should be reinstated to her unit, the 446th AES. She does not cause a morale problem, and in fact her service and leadership builds and sustains unit cohesion within the 446th.

"We are here today because when the government intrudes on the personal and private lives of gay and lesbian individuals, in a manner that implicates rights identified in *Lawrence*—the right to engage in private, intimate sexual conduct—the government must advance an important government interest, the intrusion must significantly further that interest, and the intrusion must be necessary to further that interest. A less intrusive means must be unlikely to achieve substantially the government's interest.

"So while the Ninth Circuit believes the government has advanced an important governmental interest here in unit cohesion, morale, good order and discipline, the Ninth Circuit remanded for this court to hear evidence on whether discharging Major Witt furthers the Air Force interest in unit cohesion and morale, and whether less intrusive means, something other than discharge, would allow the Air Force to achieve unit cohesion, morale, good order and discipline. The Air Force bears the burden of proof that they had to discharge Major Witt; that there was no other alternative."

Anticipating the government's response, Dunne predicted its lawyers would rely upon the 1993 congressional findings, rather than address the circumstances of Major Witt's service and her experience with the 446th. By contrast, she said, the *Witt* legal team would present expert testimony to rebut the congressional findings, and then call current and former members of the 446th to testify about how they experienced Major Witt and her contributions to the squadron.

In conclusion, she said: "History has taught us that the U.S. military successfully integrated different races and integrated women in the last half century. No one can dispute the fact that these historical steps have improved the readiness and overall capabilities of our military. The U.S. military already has thousands of gay and lesbian members honorably defending our country. The time for Don't Ask, Don't Tell has ended. America is in a different place, and so is the military. We believe the evidence you will hear will show that Major Witt should be allowed to once again serve her country. Thank you, your honor."

The government's opening statement came from veteran Department of Justice trial attorney Peter J. Phipps.

"In this case, plaintiff Margaret Witt has sued the United States Air Force and officers of the United States," he began. "She has sued to have this court determine that the so-called Don't Ask, Don't Tell policy is unconstitutional as applied to her, specifically.

"Plaintiff's case fails. The United States Air Force's Don't Ask, Don't Tell policy is a valid regulation of the military by Congress, and it is constitutional."

The trial, he said, "will make clear the Air Force applied the policy correctly and the application of the policy is fully constitutional here."

Phipps didn't hesitate to criticize the Ninth Circuit's remand and its "new legal standard for evaluating a service member's substantive due process challenge" to DADT.

"Defendants disagree with the Ninth Circuit; its decision and its new test are incorrect."

Still, he submitted, he and the other government lawyers would show that the Air Force was well equipped to pass the new test. Not only would their evidence validate Congress's reasoning and its "predictive judgments," but they would reveal, at trial, "that each of the findings that Congress made at a general level apply at a specific level to the plaintiff here."

If there was any notion that the White House had instructed the Justice Department to play nice with Margie Witt, Phipps answered that question up front.

There were, he said, "several facts of plaintiff's conduct that plaintiff did not mention in her complaint and that were not before this court or before the court of appeals originally. For instance, plaintiff did not mention that she had engaged in adultery.

"We also learned that plaintiff had same-sex sexual relations with two other Air Force officers during her Air Force tenure. And plaintiff communicated or acknowledged her sexual orientation to enlisted service members. By making that revelation to enlisted personnel, plaintiff set an example of a disregard for Air Force policies, which is detrimental to unit cohesion and morale, good order and discipline."

Phipps also took issue with Dunne's contention that the burden of proof was on the government.

"That is not the case," he argued. At most, he submitted, the government had the burden of producing the factual evidence to support its case, but "the burden of persuasion still rests with plaintiff," a burden "she cannot meet."

As for the witnesses that the *Witt* attorneys would call, Phipps continued, they couldn't offer the sort of evidence that would allow her to prevail.

"Beyond the individualized problem with the testimony of those witnesses, which can be addressed through cross-examination, there's a far bigger problem. The constitutionality of the United States statute and regulation is not dependent on the viewpoints and experiences of a few members of plaintiff's former squadron who were her friends or who were impressed with her service. Nor is the constitutionality of the United States statute dependent on the experiences of other service members who never served with the plaintiff, and who were discharged under the Don't Ask, Don't Tell policy. Likewise, the constitutionality of the United States statute is not contingent on the viewpoints of a psychology professor, or the viewpoints of a political scientist, or the viewpoints of a historian."

In his opening statement, Phipps named two witnesses whom the government would call to the stand. Neither of them knew Margie Witt.

But first the court would hear from plaintiff's witnesses. At the front of that line was someone who knew Margie Witt, the 446th, the Air Force, and the nature of the mission as well as anyone. And he was eager to tell his story.

Chapter 18

TRUE STORIES

If in the trial of *Witt v. Air Force*, the government's lawyers wanted to spend the bulk of their time trying to varnish and reinterpret Don't Ask, Don't Tell in light of the Ninth Circuit's ruling, then Judge Leighton wasn't inclined to stop them.

When he had met with the lawyers in pretrial conference the morning of September 2, he moved swiftly through a list of procedural, jurisdictional, and scheduling issues before turning to what they could expect of him, and he of them.

"I don't tether," he said, as he went over his rules of comportment. "Judge Coughenour [now a senior federal district court judge] threatened to shoot me once as a trial lawyer if I ever moved from behind the podium again."

He wouldn't force them to seek his permission before approaching a witness. "But I will require that you keep a respectful distance to the witness and not do anything to intimidate a witness, other than asking difficult questions."

On the broader issues of what lines of argument and testimony he would allow, he said, "both sides are going to get a chance to tell their true story."

"I will rule on objections," he added. "But I don't know whether you've talked to anybody who's had the misfortune of going to trial with me, but I am pretty liberal on the evidentiary rules. I don't say 'sustained' without stuttering."

"I didn't want it [the case] to come back to me again," Judge Leighton would later explain, in a post-trial interview. "I believe in lawyering; cross-examination—when in doubt, if it's marginally relevant and not unfairly prejudicial, it's coming in, deal with it. I tell them that. And that's what their job is. And so I wanted as full a record as I could have."

In his opening statement on September 13, Phipps, the lead government attorney, asserted that with DADT, "Congress did not determine that the open service of gay and lesbian service members would actually harm unit cohesion and morale *in any specific instance*, but Congress' concern was the risk that open service presented." (Emphasis added.)

Phipps then insisted that the congressional findings "are entitled to extremely high deference" by the courts, and now, at trial, he and his cocounsel "will reveal that each of the findings that Congress made at a general level apply at a specific level to the plaintiff here."

How that would actually occur in ways that might satisfy the Ninth Circuit's heightened scrutiny test (a.k.a. the *Witt* standard) was, to put it mildly, something of an open question.

Don't Ask, Don't Tell had survived legal challenges for over a decade because the courts had accepted the congressional findings that the presence of known homosexuals in the ranks was ipso facto an unacceptable risk to unit cohesion and morale. And Phipps was correct that, in doing so, the courts had accorded Congress and the military "extremely high deference" under rational basis review. But the only reason a federal trial was now under way in Tacoma was that a U.S. Court of Appeals had ruled—after the Supreme Court's ruling in *Lawrence*—that rational basis review was no longer sufficiently protective of Margaret Witt's rights to due process. That ruling begged for some evidence that Major Witt was, or would be, an actual threat to the morale and cohesion of the 446th. Of the two witnesses the government expected to call, however, neither had ever met Major Witt nor had any direct involvement in or knowledge of the day-to-day functioning of her unit.

As it turned out, the work of revealing why Major Witt had been rightly banished from the Air Force would be done largely by subtraction, by using cross-examination to try to undercut her character, and try to chisel away at the credibility of the witnesses who came to testify on her behalf. As Phipps had done in his opening statement, the government was also going to make adultery an issue at trial, even though the Air Force had never charged Margaret Witt with adultery nor raised the issue in her discharge proceedings.

Judge Leighton's "it's coming in" approach meant that the Witt lawyers would be given a wide berth as well. They would have the opportunity not just to try to show that DADT was unconstitutional "as applied" to their client, but that the law itself now belonged in the dustbin of history.

As the *Witt* trial would unfold in the coming days, Lobsenz, Dunne, and Kung elicited ample testimony about how valuable and respected Margie had become as a member of the 446th. At the same time, though, the Witt legal team was also marshaling a much deeper argument—that Don't Ask, Don't Tell, by officially encouraging dishonesty, was a cancer upon the nation's military ethos.

Sarah Dunne's answer as to who their first witness should be was formed in December 2009 when she and ACLU volunteer attorney Sher Kung traveled to Spokane to meet Jim Schaffer at the fire station where Schaffer works as a fire captain and paramedic.

"Oh sweet Jesus!" she found herself thinking, as the two ACLU lawyers were listening to him share his history with the 446th, including his tour into the bloody chaos of Somalia in 1993. Beyond that, there was just the essence—in Jim's barrel chest, deep voice, demeanor, and expressive eyes—of a man who, day after day, was used to putting himself on the line in order to tend to people in dire straits.

Schaffer would take the stand just moments after Peter Phipps ended his opening statement with his assertion that the only relevant evidence to be produced during the trial would come from the government. Within the first minute, Schaffer would disclose that the main reason for his retirement from the Air Force reserves in 2007 was the "rather dishonorable act" by the Air Force in discharging Major Witt. From there Dunne walked him through his quarter-century career in the military and his work as a specialist in trauma care.

As one of the top noncommissioned officers in the 446th, Schaffer was on the executive board that selected the officer who would be the unit's chief of standards and evaluation. In explaining why the board had selected Major Witt for that assignment, he said the demands of the position required the board to "choose the best of the best" of the squadron's officers. Later, he added, "I would put Major Witt in about the top two percent" of flight nurses he had worked with during his Air Force career.

He testified about serving with her, and training with her, and becoming friends during their travels together. He talked about being deployed to

Oman with her. And then, under questioning from Dunne, he described how a remark she made talking about the Harley-Davidson motorcycle she used to own led him to asking her if she were a lesbian.

"Well, yeah, duh," he said, characterizing her response.

"Did you think less of her as an officer or flight nurse because of her sexual orientation?" Dunne asked.

"No," he answered. "At that point I would say I probably thought more of her because she was honest with me."

Asked about the unit's reaction to the news that she had been suspended from the 446th for being a lesbian, he replied: "About the same as mine; shock, anger."

He talked about his retirement ceremony, about calling Margie up to the stage and presenting her with the photograph of the medevac aircraft on the tarmac at McChord, signed by dozens of her former colleagues in the 446th.

In his cross-examination by Justice Department attorney Steve Buckingham, Schaffer was asked three times whether he had actually polled each member of the 446th about whether each felt as he did about the suspension of Margaret Witt. He said no, and reiterated that all with whom he spoke voiced support for the major.

Buckingham cross-examined him about the number of signatures on the photo she was presented at his retirement party.

"Would you estimate there were over a hundred members there?" he asked.

"I would think, yes," Schaffer replied.

"Can you tell from looking at [the photo] whether there are over a hundred signatures on it?"

"There are not over a hundred signatures on there," Schaffer replied. "But there are even less on mine, to be honest with you."

When Buckingham was finished, Judge Leighton chose to ask several of his own questions, about the role of unit culture, and specifically about the culture of the 446th.

Schaffer answered by telling the judge that when he joined the 446th "it was a very broken unit" on account of frequent worldwide deployments that created cliques within the squadron. A counselor had to be brought in to help rebuild unit morale, and, within a couple of years, the squadron became a "cohesive unit" built upon recognizing competence and building trust.

"What about the characteristic of openness and tolerance?" Judge Leighton asked.

"It was an extremely tolerant unit," Schaffer answered. "We had members of different races, people of frankly different lifestyles, and the unit was pretty open about it."

Racism and other forms of bigotry weren't tolerated in the 446th, Schaffer said, and people with "a chip on their shoulder" were "kind of ostracized." Under questioning from Dunne, Schaffer said it was understood even by the unit's commanders that there were "a dozen or so" gay men and women serving in the 446th. The prevailing attitude was, "It's your life, I don't need to know the details of your life. I don't know what happens in the bedroom, I just want to know are you there doing a good job, are you worthy of the position you are placed in, are you worthy of my respect? That's the important thing."

For the next three days, testimonials from current and former members of the 446th dominated the media coverage from the trial. In order, they were:

- Lieutenant Colonel Vincent Oda, a veteran flight nurse and member of the 446th's executive management committee, who at the time of the trial was chief of training.
- Major Heather Julian (retired), a veteran flight nurse married to Sergeant Stacey Julian.
- Sergeant Stacey Julian, the burly, now-retired medical technician with whom Margie had deployed to Oman in early 2003.
- Lieutenant Colonel Thomas Hansen, a former Army officer and nurse who transferred to the Air Force reserves in 1994. He became a flight nurse and, at the time of the trial, was commander of readiness for the 446th. Hansen began a deployment to Afghanistan on September 2, so his appearance was in the form of a deposition conducted by Jim Lobsenz on August 30.
- Captain Jill Robinson (retired), who served both as an enlisted flight medic and flight nurse.
- Major Heidi Smidt (retired), a flight nurse who served with Margie in 1995 and 1996.
- Major Judith Krill (retired), a former intensive care nurse and Army reservist who switched to the Air Force reserves and even-

tually became the 446th's deployment manager. She also served as mayor of DuPont, Washington, from 2000 to 2003.

- Major Faith Mueller (retired), an assistant chief with the Tacoma Fire Department who served as a flight nurse and flight nurse examiner for the 446th for sixteen years before retiring in 2007.

Although there was a "Margie Witt, this is your life" dimension to the testimonials about her personal and professional qualities, there was as much time devoted to the culture of the 446th, and attitudes toward gays and lesbians in the unit. The portrait that emerged was of a dedicated and extremely capable unit in which Margie was a central cog. No one seemed to care one way or the other whether or not she was gay; and the reaction to the law and system that had yanked her from the unit was shock and exasperation.

Among her secondary duties in the unit, Captain Robinson served as executive assistant to Commander Moore-Harbert. Before being chosen for that assignment, Robinson had sent a letter to the review board in Georgia that would process Margie's dismissal.

In questioning her, Lobsenz read passages from the letter, including:

"I fundamentally believe Major Witt's absence during the last Middle East conflict was a detriment not only to the Air Force but to the soldiers who were unable to fall within her incredible skill set of care." And, "her absence as a fundamental leader was overwhelming to those she has guided and mentored over the years. In essence we were forced to leave behind the most constructive and supportive leader many of us will ever come to know."

Lobsenz asked how the unit reacted.

"It was kind of like extracting a parent out of a family," she replied.

Major Smidt said the news of Margie's suspension was "devastating."

Major Krill said she was "horrified" when she heard.

"Why?" Dunne asked her.

"It was unfair," Krill explained. "It wasn't anybody's business what her sexuality was. It doesn't enter into it in a professional setting. She had been an exemplary officer and flight nurse. She was the epitome of what you want people to be. And all of a sudden, now you can't be part of this anymore, and it was very sad."

The cumulative testimony from the past and present unit members was rich in complexity, emotion, and irony.

At one point, during the reading of Lieutenant Colonel Hansen's deposition, an exhibit Hansen was asked about seemed to offer the perfect rebuttal both to the prejudice built into Don't Ask, Don't Tell and the contention of the government lawyers that testimonials praising Major Witt ought to be dismissed because they were anecdotal and biased by her friendships. The moment came when Lobsenz was reviewing, with Hansen, "officer performance reviews," or OPRs, as they were known. As one of the senior officers in the unit, Hansen regularly served on the 446th's executive management committee. In that capacity he had been assigned by Lieutenant Colonel Moore-Harbert, the 446th's commander, to write Margaret Witt's OPR for the period of April 2004 to April 2005, the year encompassing her removal from the unit. It was a glowing review, including the comment: "Dynamic senior nursing leader recognized by peers for strong character, leadership skills and knowledge base."

The review also included the comments that Major Witt was committed "to continuing squadron cohesion and morale" and that she was "first in line to promote barbecue luncheon, softball game."

The last live witness on Wednesday, September 15, was retired major Faith Mueller, a Tacoma fire captain in her civilian life. Sarah Dunne's last question to her was whether she would hire Margaret Witt if she applied for a position at the Tacoma Fire Department.

"I'd hire her tomorrow," Mueller replied.

Justice Department attorney Bryan Diederich then stepped forward to cross-examine her.

Diederich said he noticed that when Mueller was arriving to testify, she had exchanged a greeting with another retired major, Judy Krill, who had testified earlier in the day.

"Do you know her," he asked.

"Yes," Mueller replied.

"A friend of yours?"

"Yes."

"Are you friends with Ms. Witt?

"Yes."

"I take it you have other friends at the 446th; is that right?"

"I have some great friends at the 446th," Mueller replied, unfazed.

This line of questioning continued until Diederich tripped over Jim Schaffer, suggesting that Schaffer and Mueller were friends because they both worked at the Tacoma Fire Department.

"If you are referring to James Schaffer," she replied, "he works for the Spokane Fire Department. I work for the Tacoma Fire Department."

When Diederich finished, Judge Leighton made a point of sending a not-so-subtle message to the government's lawyers.

"Ms. Mueller," he said, "I am going to ask you a question that may seem a little strange. If someone were to suggest that the folks that are coming and testifying on behalf of Major Witt, including yourself, were sort of carefully selected friends that don't accurately reflect the views of the 446th, would you have a response?"

"Well, I would dispute that," she answered.

Interspersed with testimony from past and present members of the 446th was testimony from three other service members, Jenny Kopfstein, Darren Manzella, and Anthony Loverde. All three had been removed from the military because they had disclosed their homosexuality. None had served with Margaret Witt or the 446th. Their common experience—each in a different branch of the service—was in having to confront the moral hypocrisy embedded in the law that led to their discharge.

JENNY KOPFSTEIN

Former Navy lieutenant Jenny Kopfstein was second in line to testify on day one, after Jim Schaffer. A Naval Academy graduate, she had become the chief ordnance officer aboard the USS *Shiloh* in 2000. The *Shiloh* is a state-of-the-art guided missile cruiser with a crew of over four hundred, then based in San Diego.

"Ms. Kopfstein," Sher Kung asked, after leading her through a few introductory questions, "when you were first stationed on the USS *Shiloh*, did you tell any of your fellow shipmates that you were a lesbian?"

"I did not tell," she answered. "I tried very hard not to."

What made it difficult is she was a new officer on board a ship that was seldom in port. Her shipmates were eager to get to know her. They would ask about her life, "and so I did an awful lot of avoiding people's questions. I would try to change the subject, or I would say that I had to be somewhere and I couldn't talk, various strategies for not getting into a personal conversation with my shipmates."

It was lonely and it was very stressful, she said, "because you have to think ahead, and you have to anticipate these sorts of situations in order to avoid them. It was very tough for me."

She had served on an honor staff at Annapolis, she told the court, and was deeply committed to her personal integrity and to the Navy's core values of honor, courage, and commitment. For that reason, she found herself feeling "extremely conflicted about the difference of what Don't Ask, Don't Tell was telling me to do and what the core values of the Navy say."

"To me," she added, "I felt like I was being forced to lie. But then I was also being told never to lie, that an officer should always tell the truth and make sure the whole truth be known, which is part of the honor concept."

On July 17, 2000, she decided she would write a letter to her commanding officer, to do the honorable thing, to tell him she was a lesbian.

Suspecting she might be claiming to be gay to get out of the Navy, her commander didn't act on the letter immediately, though he eventually sent a request for an investigation to the secretary of the Navy. In the meantime, Kopfstein stopped lying to her shipmates. Word travels fast on a ship, she said, and before long she was stopped in a passageway by a senior chief petty officer, who asked to speak with her privately. When they were alone, he pulled from his wallet a photo of a teenage boy. It was his son, he told her; "He's gay, and I am really proud of him."

The overall reaction to people knowing, she said, was positive, and allowed for trust-building that could not have existed had she continued to hide the truth from them.

In early 2001, the *Shiloh* got a new commander, and there was a traditional, informal celebration, a "hail and farewell" party at the new commander's residence in San Diego. The new commander invited Kopfstein and her partner to attend, and, Kopfstein said, the commander's wife embraced each of them on their way in the door. "And the party was fun," she added. "All the other officers and their spouses were there, including the new captain, and everybody talked to us and we had a great time."

In May of that year she was promoted from ensign to lieutenant. Her new commander—for whom she also served as legal adviser—chose her to represent the ship in a prestigious ship-handling competition. She won. The admiral in her chain of command—who was well aware of the letter disclosing her sexual orientation—congratulated her by giving her the traditional commendation of the admiral's coin. Then, in her officer fitness report in early 2002, was this observation: "Due to her admission on sexual orientation, a board of inquiry was convened. The board determined her in violation of Navy policy and recommended separation from naval service. Her sexual orientation has not disrupted good order and discipline aboard USS SHILOH." And, "Lieutenant JG Kopfstein has been an asset to the ship and the Navy, but unfortunately her sexual orientation precludes further naval service."

The government lawyers repeatedly objected during Jenny Kopfstein's testimony, to challenge its relevance.

"Overruled," Judge Leighton snapped on each occasion.

Her tenure aboard the USS *Shiloh* ended in December 2001. At her discharge hearing in 2002, both her commanders from her time on the *Shiloh* testified on her behalf. And it didn't matter. She was discharged on October 31, 2002.

DARREN MANZELLA

The last witness on day one was Army sergeant Darren Manzella, a medical technician who served two tours in Iraq between 2004 and 2007. Sher Kung greeted him and led the questioning.

In his first week on patrol in Baghdad, one of Manzella's best friends was killed by sniper fire. Coupled with the intense violence he was confronting day after day, the tragedy pushed him to look at himself differently. He realized he had to come to terms with the truth about his sexual orientation, admit to himself that he was gay, and commit to a new level of honesty with those closest to him. Back at his home base in Texas, he summoned the courage to tell his Army roommate, with whom he had served in Iraq. He dreaded his roommate's reaction, "and I was actually expecting to lose a friend over this." Instead, he told the court, "he reacted the complete opposite. He was very accepting. He said, 'I love you, you are like my brother.'"

Manzella then came out to others with whom he had served in Iraq, and their acceptance of him, he said, was a great relief. In 2006, however, his feelings of stress and paranoia returned as he heard rumors that he was being investigated. When his supervisor, a lieutenant, asked him if there was something wrong, Manzella decided to tell the truth, and that led to him being investigated for violating Don't Ask, Don't Tell. He cooperated, answered honestly, admitted he was gay, and then, a month later, was told that the investigation had been closed, "and they found no proof of homosexuality."

The news that he had been cleared was very confusing, he said, but the bottom line is that he was still in the Army and now all the more relieved that he was not living a lie, nor expected to live a lie.

In October 2006 he again deployed to Iraq. While there he was promoted to be the medical liaison officer for the First Cavalry Division and was transferred to Kuwait; there he was stationed at a Navy hospital, where he worked with all the armed services and other allied forces as well.

Manzella was still on the witness stand when day two of the trial began, on Tuesday morning, September 14. Although he didn't flaunt his homosexuality, he continued, neither did he hide it. He openly displayed photos of his boyfriend in his living quarters, he explained, and spoke honestly about his sexual orientation when asked. Several times in his testimony he attributed his acceptance and the lack of harassment to the high level of professionalism in the military. In Kuwait he was contacted by CBS News to take part in a story about how, given the demands on an all-volunteer force fighting two wars, a growing number of commanders were allowing known gay service members to serve. It became a *60 Minutes* segment, with Manzella appearing in uniform on camera from Kuwait, being interviewed by correspondent Leslie Stahl.

"Did you tell any of your supervisors in Kuwait that you were doing this interview?" Kung asked him.

"I did," Manzella replied. "I told my supervisor."

"How did your supervisor respond?"

"He was very supportive," he replied. "Again, I didn't know what to expect. But I wanted to make sure he knew before this aired. He shook my hand and patted me on the back. That was about it."

The segment aired on December 16, 2007. The following March he was told by his company commander that he was being recommended for discharge under Don't Ask, Don't Tell. The discharge occurred in June 2008.

"I was very proud of my service," Manzella said near the end of his testimony. "I thought I was a very good soldier, and my promotions and awards, I think they verify that for me. But being true to yourself and being proud of your accomplishments regardless if you are gay or straight, man or woman, I think that's what honesty and integrity mean to me."

ANTHONY LOVERDE

Anthony Loverde's videotaped deposition was played in court at the end of day three, following retired major Faith Mueller's testimony. Loverde had enlisted in the Air Force in early 2001 when he was twenty-one, with the goal of learning a trade and securing tuition for a college degree in exchange for a six-year commitment. As with Manzella, and Margie Witt for that matter, he was quietly struggling with his sexual identity when he was accepted and began his training.

Given his upbringing in a small town and in a church that taught that homosexuality was a "temptation I had to overcome," it was difficult for him to accept that he was gay. Meeting other gay service members early in his Air Force career, and noticing that many of them seemed content with their sexuality, brought him "to a point where I realized my life would be happier if I accepted myself for who I was."

The sheer number of interactions and new relationships that came with joining the Air Force inevitably increased his stress. An Internet search led him to the Servicemembers Legal Defense Network (SLDN), an organization created in 1993 specifically to assist gay members of the military. SLDN published an online "survivors guide," Loverde said, and it was from that guide that he learned in detail about the Don't Ask, Don't Tell policy.

What he took from it, he told the court under questioning from Sher Kung, is that his main vulnerability to DADT was in telling the truth about being gay. Yet, withholding the truth, in practice, was not so easy, and it regularly included having to mislead his heterosexual friends about his interests and relationships.

"So it was a fear of opening that door," he said; "so I would usually say I had to study. Or if they asked what did I do this weekend, I'd say, 'Well, I just studied.' I really played myself to be a boring person and didn't really comment on much of my actual activities, because I didn't want to open that door to being found out."

"So would you say you had to lie?" Kung asked.

"Yes, I did," he replied.

He spoke to having to memorize, as part of his military training, the Air Force core values of "integrity first, excellence in all we do, and service before self."

"So given that you had to lie to guard your sexual orientation," Kung asked, "did you feel that you could maintain the Air Force core value of integrity while serving?"

"No," Loverde replied, "I couldn't. I constantly had to sacrifice my core values and integrity, and it was something that was a black cloud over me, my entire service. It was something I never felt I could fully embrace, because this law directed me otherwise. It told me to lie."

Loverde's advanced training was in calibrating electronics, a trade he described as "ensuring the precision part of precision warfare." He worked for three years at a special laboratory at Ramstein Air Base in Germany, and advanced quickly to the rank of staff sergeant, gathering more responsibilities along the way. He was assigned to another advanced laboratory at Edwards Air Force Base in California in 2005 and then to a similar lab in Qatar to support military operations in Iraq and Afghanistan. In Qatar he was given broad leadership responsibilities as the "non-commissioned officer in charge" of the lab.

When he returned to Edwards AFB in 2006, Loverde said he realized he wanted to stay in the Air Force, but that he also wanted a less traditional job, one that would allow him to be less conspicuous and reduce the pressure on him to lie to shield his sexual identity. He decided to become a loadmaster for C-130 cargo planes. After receiving new training, he was again sent to Ramstein, but this time as a loadmaster. From Ramstein he was repeatedly deployed to Iraq, where he flew on sixty-one low-altitude combat support missions in C-130s.

During crew rest periods in Kuwait, he began to develop even closer bonds with his fellow C-130 crewmates, both men and women.

"And in time," he testified, "we'd go out and we'd eat together. We'd go to the movie theaters together. We would play Rock Band together."

Eventually, though, "it got too hard for me to not disclose myself, that I just stopped. I started to avoid them. I really liked them. I respected them.

This was a great group of people, but I felt that I couldn't put them in a situation where if I disclosed anything, then I'm going to burden them with the secret. So I stopped hanging out with them."

There was, however, one superior, a master sergeant supervising the loadmasters in his chain of command, whom he couldn't abide. The sergeant made repeated comments that were derogatory toward homosexuals, using the word "fag" often and making crude jokes that conveyed fear of and contempt for homosexuals. Loverde's discomfort with the homophobic remarks, coupled with his fear that filing an official complaint against the flight chief might backfire and implicate him as a homosexual, led finally to his decision that he had had enough of hiding his sexual identity in order to stay in the Air Force.

When he returned to Ramstein from Kuwait, Loverde testified, he decided to come out, to disclose to his supervisors that he was gay, and that he was struggling with Don't Ask, Don't Tell.

"I felt I could no longer abide by its policy," he told the court.

His commander was sympathetic, but also forwarded the e-mail Loverde had written, disclosing his homosexuality, to his legal advisers. In the meantime, Loverde was assigned to a desk job, and in May 2008 he learned he was going to be discharged. By that time, he said, he had begun telling his Air Force comrades that he was gay and that he was being discharged as a result. The reaction, Loverde testified, was an outpouring of support from his comrades, many of whom sent e-mails and letters to the discharge board, commending him and opposing his expulsion from the ranks.

Ultimately, though, he decided not to engage in what he thought was a futile effort to stay in the Air Force, and he accepted an honorable discharge.

Loverde was discharged from the Air Force in July 2008. In May of that year, aware of his fate, he had applied for a job with a defense support contractor, KBR, and was offered the job in June. KBR gave him three weeks to visit with his family, and then sent him to Iraq, knowing he was gay, knowing he had been discharged from the Air Force under Don't Ask, Don't Tell.

Before long, Loverde had come full circle, working for KBR doing electronic calibrations in support of U.S. combat missions in Iraq and Afghanistan.

"It is exactly the same thing," he said in his deposition. "The only difference was I was not wearing the uniform, and I was working with the Army mostly, rather than the Air Force."

Not only was he doing the same work, he said, in response to Kung's questions, but he was working and eating and recreating in the same facilities as the U.S. military personnel at the base where he was living and working as a KBR employee. And doing so as an openly gay man. He returned to the states in the spring of 2009 and, with a new contract, was sent to work at Andrews Air Force base in Washington, DC, where he again was able to live and work as an openly gay man, even exercising his free speech rights by driving on and off the base in a car "that was decorated" with messages supporting the repeal of Don't Ask, Don't Tell.

Near the end of his videotaped deposition, Kung asked him why he was unavailable to attend the *Witt* trial in person. His answer was that he was scheduled to report for a new calibration assignment in Iraq and Afghanistan.

Kung's last questions to him were about what effect he thought he had in his last months in the Air Force, after he had revealed his sexual orientation.

"It brought my unit closer," Loverde said. "We worked well together when I was open. And as a contractor, it's a huge relief. I don't have to worry about being fired. I can just be honest, and people can know who I am. They can trust me. I can trust them. We've got each other's back."

"If Don't Ask, Don't Tell were not the law today," Kung asked, "and you could serve as an openly gay man in the U.S. military, would you consider reenlisting?"

"I would," Loverde replied. "I miss the Air Force. I love the Air Force. I would serve again tomorrow, if I could."

"Thank you," Kung replied. "That's all I have."

Ed Hrivnak would be the last of Margie Witt's peers to come to the witness stand, at the end of the day on Thursday, September 16. He had had no hesitation when Sher Kung called to ask if he would be interested in being a character witness.

"Oh yeah, without a doubt," he recalled in a 2016 interview. "In fact I remember telling her, right from the get-go. I said, 'Can I wear my uniform to the trial?' And she said, 'Why would you ask that?' And I said, 'Because I have served honorably twenty years. My uniform represents that and they need to see it, they need to see a professional officer willing to stand up and defend another officer who is professional. They need to see that.'

"I don't know if there's a picture of me, but I had my best dress uniform on, with all my service ribbons and medals, even got a crisp military haircut. I walked into that trial room to give a representation of what a professional officer is supposed to be, and that was my point. 'You guys trained me, you made me who I am today. I'm a professional officer. I have served with honor and distinction in two wars, and I'm coming in to tell you that you're wrong. You made a mistake by letting this officer go.'"

It was a lot about Margie. But it was also about something Hrivnak knew as well as anyone could, about how Margie Witt was forced out of the Air Force at a time when qualified flight nurses and other medical personnel were badly needed. The emotional fatigue of having to care for so many wounded soldiers over such a long period of time was depleting their ranks. And it wasn't just that he had experienced it himself. Unknown to him, one of the most attentive readers to his dispatches from the war zone was General Melissa Rank, the Air Force's assistant surgeon general. He was ready to retire, but she talked him out of it. She was deeply concerned, he was told, about flight crews and ground crews "melting down" under the stress, with some crews even becoming too overwhelmed to function.

"General Rank asked me to specifically interview returning medics, nurses, doctors, to find out how they felt about prolonged exposure to taking care of trauma patients," he testified under questioning from Jim Lobsenz. "And it's a diagnosis, a condition now referred to as 'compassion fatigue.' So I was trying to ascertain were our medics and nurses suffering from compassion fatigue after being exposed to excessive trauma for months and years on end, an extreme form of burnout for trauma medicine."

Because of the overlap between his deployments and Margie's removal from her duties at the 446th, he missed saying goodbye to his former colleague and mentor.

"So what was your reaction when you were informed she was discharged for being a lesbian?" Lobsenz asked him. "Were you surprised that she was a lesbian?"

"I wasn't surprised she was a lesbian," he replied. "I was surprised that the Air Force, in a time of war, when we are short on qualified flight nurses, would take the time to discharge a professional officer. That's what really shocked me."

As his testimony continued, Hrivnak spoke bluntly about the damage to the 446th's morale caused by Margie's removal, and the fear it caused among both gay and straight members of the squadron about who might be next.

In a statement he submitted to support Margie in 2006, Hrivnak had written, among other things, that "it would be a disservice to taxpayers, but more importantly, the wounded, to discharge Major Witt."

Near the end of his testimony, Lobsenz asked him about that sentence. This is how he responded.

"Not once did I ever have a wounded casualty ask me, when I was treating them, 'Hey, before you give me that morphine, or before you put that splint on me, are you gay?' The wounded don't care. They want the best professional health care provider taking care of them. They want the best possible care they can get for the sacrifices they made. Margie is the type of nurse who gives that kind of care."

Chapter 19

▬▬▬▬▬▬▬

THE LAST DAYS
OF SUMMER

Just as she had each morning the week before, Sher Kung quietly greeted Margie with a smile in the main lobby of the Marriott Courtyard Tacoma. It was Monday, September 20. In addition to examining witnesses and her other duties in the courtroom, the soft-spoken, twenty-seven-year-old lawyer was Margie's designated escort to and from the courthouse at Union Station.

One reason Sher was shadowing Margie was to try to shield her from the sort of ugly encounter Grethe Cammermeyer had to endure in June 1992, the day she announced she would bring her lawsuit against the government. As the TV crews were packing up their cameras, a woman approached Grethe, her fists waving in the air, shouting that her husband had spent his career in the military "trying to protect our country from people like you." When Grethe held her ground and replied that she had nearly given her own life for the country, the woman yelled back in her face, "I wish you had."

As Sher and Margie reached the glass doors to Pacific Avenue, there was an awkward moment as they looked out to see the government's lawyers and their entourage of assistants just beginning their paces toward Union Station. They loitered for a minute to allow a comfortable separation. Outside, beneath a lumpy, gray sky, there was just enough light rain coming down to warrant an umbrella as the two chatted and walked eastward, side by side, along the wet sidewalk. Strolling just a few steps behind them, beneath another white-and-green umbrella with Laurie, was Margie's old friend Karyn Gomez.

Karyn had spent Sunday night with Margie and Laurie in their hotel room and was growing concerned about the emotional toll the trial was taking on the two of them.

"I didn't think about it as my friend Margie Witt who's making history," Karyn says. "I was really worried about my friend Margie Witt who'd been through some very dark days. And all I could think about was how she was hurting, about how she was exhausted. And I was worried about her and Laurie because Laurie was exhausted too."

The exhaustion was no surprise, given the stakes. Margie was the plaintiff, but from the outset it was clear the government lawyers would aggressively put her and her witnesses on the defensive at every opportunity. Today was going to be Margie's day on the witness stand, and the government's lead attorney, Peter Phipps, would get his chance to cross-examine her.

Laurie was bracing herself. By her own description, she had been living "under a rock" in the years leading up to the trial. Her low profile was largely at the behest of Margie's legal team because they wanted to keep the media and legal focus on the injustice of Don't Ask, Don't Tell and avoid distractions involving the allegations of adultery. But now that the trial was at hand, she would come out of the shadows. For the length of the proceedings, Laurie would be seated right next to Margie at a table built into the railing just behind the attorneys. This was purposeful, to show Judge Leighton they were a committed couple. The legal team was well prepared to address the adultery issue. But, like Margie, Laurie had to prepare herself emotionally. She fully expected that when the subject came up at the trial she would be made to feel like the woman wearing the scarlet letter. She resolved to hold her head up and show no sign of shame or remorse.

Only those closest to them had seen the extent to which their love for each other is rooted in a shared sense of humor. It was Laurie's inspiration, as she went through the daily ritual of prepping Margie for the walk to the courthouse, to lead her partner in reenacting a scene from *Cool Runnings*, the Disney movie about the Jamaican bobsled team that competed at the 1988 winter Olympics. In the scene, one of the movie's main characters, Junior Bevil, is taken to a mirror by another team member and asked to describe what he sees in his reflection.

"I see Junior," Junior replies.

"You see Junior," his teammate replies in a thick Jamaican accent. "Well, let me tell you what I see. I see pride! I see power! I see a bad-ass mother who don't take no crap off of nobody!"

The powder room skit served its purpose, especially on this last day of summer. When Margie walked into the courtroom that morning, she was wearing a St. John knit with red silk sleeves beneath her dampened coat. But she might as well have been wearing her old PLU basketball jersey. "Put me in, Coach," was all she was thinking.

She was sworn in shortly after 9:30. Jim Lobsenz then led her through her biography and Air Force career, in which she added the detail that both Commander Janette Moore-Harbert and the commander's assistant were in tears the day Moore-Harbert informed her she had to leave the premises at McChord. The news of her eventual discharge, she recounted, was indirectly delivered by her dentist in Spokane the day she found out, from him, that she had been dropped from the Air Force's dental coverage.

It was shortly after eleven o'clock when Lobsenz got to the point of asking her about how she came out to her parents, the night before her press conference, announcing her lawsuit against the Air Force.

"I figured they should hear it from me instead of seeing it on the news," she explained.

"How did they react when you told them?" he asked.

"They didn't miss a beat. They had been behind me the whole time. It's the best thing that's come out of this."

A couple of minutes later, he asked: "Do you know a woman named Laurie McChesney?"

Yes, she replied, and yes, they had been together for seven years now, and yes, she was in the courtroom today.

"Did you wait until Laurie had separated and was no longer living under the same roof with Pat McChesney before you began your intimate relationship?" Jim asked.

"No," she replied.

"Since that time, have you thought about that?"

"Yes."

"What have you thought about?

"Although I don't regret our relationship, I do very much regret the way I handled it in the beginning and apologize for that, and I have apologized to all of the parties involved."

There was more, after that, to cover, including her account of coming out to Jim Schaffer, about how she regarded Jim as a brother and realized she couldn't lie to him. Lobsenz ended by asking her why she wanted to be returned to the 446th.

"I miss the people tremendously," she said, the emotion squeezing on the edges of her voice. "I miss the mission. I miss being able to be the one that the soldier looks at and I can do something for him. I am not complete, and it kills me to not be there."

Lobsenz then excused himself with a simple "thank you," and Judge Leighton beckoned to Peter Phipps. As Margie worked to rein in her emotions, she looked out and made eye contact with her parents, who were seated in the front bench just behind Laurie.

"I am happy to give the witness a couple minutes if she needs it," Phipps offered.

"Do you need any time?" the judge asked.

"No, sir," Margie replied, determined not to show weakness to Phipps. "I'm fine."

Phipps's cross-examination moved first to Jim Schaffer and others from the 446th who had testified before her—again reaching to the familiar theme that just because she had made some really good friends in the Air Force, this didn't necessarily refute the congressional presumption that she was, nonetheless, an unacceptable risk to unit cohesion and morale.

After that, it was only a matter of a few minutes for him to corral her toward the adultery issue.

As he did, one of the exhibits he sent to the projection screen at the front of the courtroom was a declaration from Pat McChesney, reporting the intimate relationship between Laurie and Margaret Witt. Not that either Margie or Laurie could ever forget where this all had started, and the humiliation inflicted upon them by two people whose sole purpose was revenge. Laurie looked briefly at the screen, enough of a glimpse to see her ex-husband's name, and then she shifted her eyes away from it, while reminding herself to hold her head high.

At the outset, Phipps suggested that it was really the fault of the Ninth Circuit Court of Appeals that he was having to put Margie through a detailed examination of her sex life.

"We argued for a different legal standard or this wouldn't be relevant," he said. "But we are back here under this legal standard."

Of course, by the legal standard that Phipps and the government continued to advocate, Margie's connection with the Air Force would have ended, for good, the day she got the news from her dentist.

On the witness stand, Margie stiffened as Phipps then asked several questions about her sex life since she had joined the military, leading up to her relationship with Laurie.

"And you agree," Phipps asked, "that adultery is not consistent with high standards of integrity, correct?"

"Yes."

"And you agree that adultery is not consistent with the concept of officership, correct?"

"Yes," she again replied.

It was now shortly before noon, and Phipps decided to move on. After the noon recess, he wrapped up his cross-examination by getting her to acknowledge her public opposition to Don't Ask, Don't Tell and admit to the fact that she had spoken critically of the policy to journalists, including a reporter from the *New York Times*. He offered no explanation for why exercising her First Amendment rights to seek repeal of DADT should matter to the court.

The government's turn to put on its case came the following day. It was Tuesday, September 21.

There were only two witnesses. One of them, Chief Master Sergeant Janice Kallinen, was called to clarify long-standing confusion over the timing and content of Margie's discharge. That issue was pertinent, because Judge Leighton had also been charged by the Ninth Circuit panel with resolving the procedural due process claim that had been part of Margie's original complaint. (This was the same claim Jim Lobsenz was so eager to pitch to Judge Leighton at the outset of the oral arguments back in June 2006—when the case was first heard—offering the judge a quick route to reinstating Major Witt without "making a broad, sweeping constitutional ruling." Judge Leighton didn't bite.)

The government's featured witness—the one who would speak in defense of the merits of DADT and the correctness of Margie's discharge—was Lieutenant General Charles Stenner, a thirty-eight-year former pilot, of average height, thinning brown hair, and six bars of ribbons on his blue uniform. He was testifying in his capacity as the head of the Air Force Reserve Command based at Robins Air Force Base in Georgia, where Margie's discharge hearing had been held in the fall of 2006.

On direct examination, Phipps guided General Stenner through a re-cital of command structures and Air Force personnel policy. There were no surprises.

Stenner's testimony would have been all the government needed to win a Don't Ask, Don't Tell challenge prior to May 21, 2008, the day the Ninth Circuit Court of Appeals issued its stunning decision in the *Witt* case. But as Sarah Dunne well knew and expected, the general's answers to Phipps avoided the very reason the Ninth Circuit had sent the case back to Judge Leighton. On cross-examination, it took Dunne less than a minute to zero in on just how little the government's lead witness could contribute to an-swering the main question before the court—how exactly had Margaret Witt jeopardized the morale and readiness of the 446th?

> *Dunne*: "Now, you've never met Major Witt before; is that correct?"
> *General Stenner*: "That's correct."
> *Dunne*: "I know that you would want to put a human face on your testimony, and I did want to let you know that Major Witt is in the courtroom. And she's sitting over there."
> *General Stenner*: "Okay."
> *Dunne*: "Now, at the time of your deposition in May, you knew noth-ing about Major Witt's Air Force career, and today, you still know nothing about her service career. Is that correct?"
> *General Stenner*: "That's correct."
> *Dunne*: "You've never read any documents from her personnel file?"
> *General Stenner*: "I have not."
> *Dunne*: "You've never read any of her officer performance reports; is that correct?"
> *General Stenner*: "No, I have not."

Dunne: "And I believe you've never interviewed any service member who has served with Major Witt about Major Witt?"

General Stenner: "No, I have not."

Dunne: "You've never done any research on Major Witt; is that correct?"

General Stenner: "That's correct."

Dunne had mostly made her point. But she decided to dig a little deeper.

Dunne: "Now, other than this case, you haven't had any personal experience with investigations, suspensions, or discharges of any service member on the grounds that they were suspected of being a homosexual, correct?"

General Stenner: "I have had a lot of experience with discharges, but not for that very specific reason."

Dunne: "Now, you've never served with a service member that you knew for a fact to be a homosexual, correct?"

General Stenner: "Correct."

Dunne: "And you've never served with a service member that you suspected to be a homosexual, correct?"

General Stenner: "Correct."

Dunne: "You don't have any friends that are homosexual; is that right?"

General Stenner: "I don't."

Dunne: "And you don't have any family members that are gay or lesbian either, do you?"

General Stenner: "I do not."

Dunne then tied the knot on this part of her cross-examination.

Dunne: "Major Witt is the first person you are meeting who is gay or a lesbian?"

General Stenner: "I guess that's true."

From her seat next to Laurie, just behind the attorneys' table, Margaret Witt aimed a perky smile at the government's lead witness. She then turned her head toward Laurie and (picking up on a line made famous by Ellen

DeGeneres in the comedienne's on-air coming out moment in 1997) asked: "Do I get a toaster oven for that?"

There was something else Sarah Dunne had in her quiver of questions for General Stenner. Only weeks before the trial, in the final stage of preparation, it occurred to her that it would be a good idea to run a criminal background check on some of the government's possible witnesses. One of them was Colonel Janette Moore-Harbert, the current commander of the 446th who was listed, at the time, as a "may testify" witness for the government. According to court documents, Moore-Harbert, if called, would testify to the effect that Major Witt's "potential return would have on unit cohesion, morale, good order and discipline" on the squadron.

Dunne asked Eric Nygren, the ACLU of Washington's intake manager, to run the background check. In little more than an hour, Nygren was back with the news that not only had Colonel Moore-Harbert been cited criminally, but it was a recent offense.

From the online search, Nygren couldn't tell what the offense was, only that it involved a criminal charge. The ACLU dispatched a messenger to pull the case file. The file showed that the commander had not only been cited for drunk driving, but for hit and run. The material on file also disclosed that she had retained one of the best attorneys in the state at fighting charges of driving under the influence. That retainer had proven extremely valuable to her. As a result of a plea bargain, her prosecution had been deferred in exchange for her agreeing to treatment. If she played by the rules of the plea bargain, after two years the charges would effectively be dismissed.

Dunne's purpose, of course, was to expose the military's hypocrisy. She had disclosed the finding to her client, but she had asked Margie to keep it a secret, even from Laurie.

Dunne worked her way toward this explosive revelation as she was cross-examining General Stenner on the subject he was listed as being expert in — the importance of uniformity and consistency to unit morale and cohesion.

Responding to her questions, Stenner said he "didn't believe" the U.S. military made individual exceptions to personnel policies. She then promptly presented him with an exhibit showing that the Army had done precisely that in the case of a Sikh captain who had been formally excused from the Army's grooming standards for hair and beards. She then asked him if he had information to show that the morale or conduct of U.S. soldiers had been adversely affected by their serving—side by side—with other coalition forces in Iraq and Afghanistan, like the British and Canadian forces, whose ranks were integrated with gay soldiers.

"I have no knowledge of that," the general replied.

After a few more questions, she moved abruptly to the case of Colonel Moore-Harbert.

Dunne: "Colonel Moore-Harbert, do you know her?"

General Stenner: "I do not."

Dunne: "For the record—she took command in October 2005; would you accept that representation from me?"

General Stenner: "Yes."

Dunne: "So, she took command in October of 2005, so she's now been leading the unit for almost five years; is that right?"

General Stenner: "Yes."

Dunne: "And you would agree with me that she does a pretty good job commanding the unit, is that fair to say?"

General Stenner: "That's fair."

Dunne: "Now, sir, I am going to ask you some questions about what it means to be an officer and commander in the United States Air Force. And to be clear, I am only asking these questions because the Air Force has raised officership as an issue in this trial. And I don't ask these questions to embarrass or humiliate anyone. It's simply to allow the court to resolve this issue. Now, you, to echo some of the questions of the government, you believe that officers are expected to lead, is that correct?"

General Stenner: "That's correct."

Dunne: "And you think it's important for officers to have high integrity, isn't it?"

General Stenner: "It is."

Dunne: "Now, you would agree with me, in fact, that command of a squadron, colonels and generals in command positions—not staff positions, command positions—are held to a higher standard of conduct than junior officers. Is that right?"

General Stenner: "They do uphold those standards and are held to a higher standard."

Dunne: "You believe colonels and generals in command positions establish respect by leading by example, isn't that right?"

General Stenner: "That's correct."

Dunne: "Now, isn't it fair to say that driving drunk is not leading by example?"

General Stenner: "That's correct."

Dunne: "And in fact if an Air Force officer drives drunk, off base, they are endangering not only their life, but the lives of other civilians, isn't that right?"

General Stenner: "That's correct."

Dunne: "Now, you would also agree with me that an Air Force officer getting arrested for fleeing the scene of an accident after hitting an occupied car, that isn't an example of integrity or honesty, is it?"

General Stenner: "No, it's not."

Dunne: "Now, Your Honor, at this time I would like to show—again, I am going to bring forward some exhibits that are certified copies of Moore-Harbert's criminal records. I have the certified original copies unredacted that I want to give to the government in case they have any question about their authenticity, but I would like to show the witness redacted copies, because we do have personal information on these criminal records."

By this point, Laurie's heart was pounding, and she was physically shaking. Both she and Margie could hear the gasps coming from the benches behind them. From their vantage point they could also see how alarmed the government's lawyers were as they hurriedly began whispering to one another and flipping open laptop computers. In the meantime, Dunne moved to get as much as she could on the record before one of the government attorney's entered an objection, which Peter Phipps finally did as Dunne moved to enter copies of Colonel Moore-Harbert's DUI and criminal hit-and-run citations before the court.

"Your honor, we are going to lodge a couple of objections here," Phipps finally interjected. Even if the records were properly obtained via a subpoena, and authentic, Phipps protested, the questions Dunne was raising were "entirely irrelevant" to the matters before the court.

No subpoena necessary, Dunne shot back; the documents were in a public file at the courthouse. And as for relevance, she said, the government was putting Margaret Witt's integrity at issue by raising questions of adultery at the same time General Stenner and the Air Force were allowing Moore-Harbert to serve despite a recent criminal offense.

The judge listened and then spoke decisively.

"In terms of relevance, they are not closely similar," he said. "We are not going to—it is totally unnecessary to bring somebody else down, in order to lift someone else up in this context." He took a small detour to talk about the "officership issue on a theoretical plane" and "the fact that we are all flawed individuals," and then drew back. "I know that sounded like jargon, but we are not going to go there, is what I'm saying."

As he spoke to not bringing someone down to lift someone up, Laurie noticed that Margie's head was nodding in agreement with Judge Leighton. She intuited, correctly, what was on Margie's mind, that the point about the double standard had been made. They had gotten it out. She could also hear and sense the dramatic effect it had in the courtroom, among both the lawyers and the spectators.

Judge Leighton's statement hadn't frozen Sarah Dunne, but it caused her to quickly evaluate her options. Whatever Judge Leighton decided, his ruling was likely to be appealed. It wasn't possible to foresee how the Ninth Circuit or U.S. Supreme Court would treat the issue of the Air Force expelling a gay flight nurse, while ignoring a criminal offense by her commander. But having it in the trial record couldn't hurt.

"I am just pausing to think about the record for a second," she explained to the judge as she considered her options.

It was Dunne's prerogative, at that moment, to challenge the judge and insist upon an offer of proof—an explanation for the record as to why the issue was properly before the court or would lead to proper, admissible evidence. If she did it, she would be doing it to protect Margie's rights on appeal.

Still, Judge Leighton's message—we don't have to tear someone down to lift someone up—was echoing in her mind.

"He's basically looking me in the eye," Dunne recalls, "and telling me, counsel, don't go there.'"

Dunne concluded she had what she needed.

"Your honor," she said, "I have no further questions."

"Thank you, Ms. Dunne," Judge Leighton replied.

By late morning, only one witness remained. Dunne had tried to line up retired general John Shalikashvili, the popular, Polish-born, former chairman of the Joint Chiefs of Staff (1993–1997) to rebut General Stenner. General Shalikashvili—an outspoken critic of Don't Ask, Don't Tell—had retired to the small, picturesque town of Steilacoom, just south of Tacoma, the same town in which Frank Witt had landed his first teaching job. But as the *Witt* case was in its discovery phase, General Shalikashvili had suffered a severe stroke that left him too weak to testify.

Dunne then sought help from C. Dixon Osburn, the well-connected executive director of Servicemembers Legal Defense Network, the resource organization devoted to ending discrimination against gays in the military. Osburn quickly led her to retired major general Dennis Laich, a highly decorated graduate of the U.S. Army War College.

"Wait till you see *our* general," a beaming Dunne had confided to Margie.

Dunne was delighted she had been able to line up a classic "boots on the ground" heterosexual general to rebut General Stenner. And General Laich didn't disappoint. By pure coincidence, Laich had been prominently cited and quoted in that morning's *Wall Street Journal*. The shout-out to the retired general had come in an eye-opening piece by Bret Stephens of the paper's notoriously conservative editorial board. The column was entitled: *Why the GOP Should Repeal DADT*. Stephens's column not only underscored General Laich's ethical objection to DADT as a policy, but included such facts as the high cost ($600 million since 1993) to taxpayers of investigating and expelling gay service members even as the Army and the Marine Corps were now offering "moral waivers" to recruits with previous felony convictions.

Moments after Judge Leighton confirmed the government had rested its case, General Laich was announced. "Our general" was six and a half feet tall, buff, bald, and, as he all but bounded over the low rail separating the lawyers from the public, radiated a commanding physical presence.

On the witness stand, Laich recounted his command experience and how he had reached the conclusion that Don't Ask, Don't Tell undermined the military. It was the *Witt* legal team's coda on the moral bankruptcy of DADT, a theme present from the first morning of the trial in the testimony of Jim Schaffer and Jenny Kopfstein.

"What is your opinion of the Don't Ask, Don't Tell policy?" Dunne asked General Laich.

"I think it's wrong. I think it's counterproductive to the objectives we are trying to achieve. And my two principal objections — I am not gay, I am not — I don't have an emotional story to tell about this, but I do think that there are two principal arguments that I have consistently written about and spoken about over the last number of years. The first one is, in my professional and personal judgment, Don't Ask, Don't Tell is a lie of omission. When a values-based organization, like the U.S. military, has a policy that says we will encourage lies of omission, it is a slippery slope, that you to begin to ask where does it begin, where does it end. And when trust and loyalty are fundamental to an effective military operation, this is something that to me is unacceptable."

Laich's questioning from Sarah Dunne and cross-examination by Peter Phipps filled the rest of the morning and spilled into the afternoon.

After the towering retired general was dismissed, the lawyers and the judge politely wrangled over several exhibits that remained to be submitted for the record, with Judge Leighton saying, at one point, that he was going to employ the "Dick Butkus theory" (a reference to a famous Chicago Bears linebacker) of evidentiary rulings. "We sort of let everything in and we just ferret out until we find the guy with the ball."

Then it was time for closing arguments.

They were really closing conversations, as Judge Leighton freely interjected questions and offered strong opinions on how at least some of the arguments from the lawyers were being received. One of the absurd ironies that Lobsenz highlighted is that, with the exception of Margie affirming Jim Schaffer's suspicion, it was the government that disclosed Margie Witt's sexual orientation to her unit, then turned around to say that because it was known she was a lesbian, she posed an unacceptable risk to her unit's performance. And even with the Air Force asking and then telling, he argued, "there's still not an iota of evidence that it would disrupt unit morale and cohesion. No one cares."

A poignant and clarifying interjection from Judge Leighton came mid-way through Lobsenz's closing. After crisply punctuating his argument about how the government failed to offer "an iota of evidence" that Marga-ret Witt's continued service with the 446th would disrupt unit morale or co-hesion, Lobsenz quickly pivoted to preemptively rebut what he anticipated would be the government's last-ditch effort to raise the red flag of adultery.

He had barely gotten the word "adultery" out of his mouth when the judge interrupted.

"Mr. Lobsenz," Judge Leighton said, "I view the adultery allegation from the government, and your allegation on procedural due process, to be frolics in detour."

"Okay," Lobsenz replied, "then I will not spend any of the court's time on it."

To which Judge Leighton added: "That [adultery] was not the basis for the action by the military. And this is a substantive due process claim, focused on the application of Don't Ask, Don't Tell. That's the way it's going to be decided."

In short, Judge Leighton was sending an unmistakable message to both legal teams that his decision was going to tightly adhere to the primary constitutional issue involved in the case. It was not going to be about the government's late-hour attempt to play the adultery card, and, as the judge had so bluntly told Sarah Dunne, neither was it going to be about the criminal record of the 446th's commander.

After Judge Leighton's admonition, Lobsenz quickly refocused. In the final minutes, as he reached the close of his argument, Lobsenz reminded the judge not just of the testimony about Margaret Witt's acceptance by the unit, but about the fiercely negative reaction from unit members when they learned she had been discharged. The last point he hammered home was the dishonesty required by Don't Ask, Don't Tell. His last words were these:

"I would like it if I could ask you to invalidate Don't Ask, Don't Tell on its face, strike it down in all its applications everywhere, but I cannot do that, because those are not the rules set by the Ninth Circuit in this case. I can ask you to invalidate it as applied to Major Margaret Witt. So I would now ask you to let her go back and serve. And if she can go back and serve, the nice thing about the truth of that will be that she can go back and serve, and no one in her unit will have to lie."

The problem Phipps faced as he launched into his closing argument is that the government presented nothing in the way of evidence to address the Ninth Circuit's demand that the Air Force show how "the application of DADT *specifically* to Major Witt significantly furthers the government's interest" in maintaining unit cohesion and morale.

All the government had really produced was General Stenner, who had placidly admitted to knowing nothing at all about Margaret Witt and her experience with her unit. And because Phipps had nothing else, he started drawing interruptions from Judge Leighton as soon as he tried to re-anchor the government's case in the legislative record of Don't Ask, Don't Tell, by suggesting his court could still use "the facts Congress considered" to uphold Margaret Witt's expulsion.

"Aren't you asking me really to overrule the Ninth Circuit?" Judge Leighton pointedly asked Phipps.

Phipps kept trying, at one point arguing that because the 446th was subject to sudden worldwide deployments, this was enough of a case-specific factor that the judge could use it as a basis for upholding the constitutionality of Witt's dismissal from the Air Force.

But it was clear he wasn't gaining much traction. The same was true when Phipps tried—despite the judge's earlier admonition—to raise the adultery issue. In the end, Phipps tried to nullify the strength of the evidence—the moving testimony from Margie's former colleagues in the 446th—by saying that it would be wrong to turn the application of Don't Ask, Don't Tell into a "unit referendum" on the popularity of an individual service member.

"The unit referendum approach makes the United States Constitution contingent on my friends in the unit that testify for me," Phipps argued.

"But it is *some* evidence," Judge Leighton responded, not needing to add that the government hadn't presented *any* evidence to suggest that Margaret Witt was, or would be, a detriment to the 446th.

Judge Leighton then continued with what, in retrospect, was his own closing argument about the role of the court: "As I say, I understand and appreciate the admonition that the military is a particular field that is fraught with difficulty when the courts enter. I am one of those federal judges that thinks we don't run school districts very well. We don't run prisons very well. We don't do a lot of things very well. But what we do is we adhere to the rule of law, and we do that to a degree better than anybody else in the world, and we have a Constitution. And I made my call with regard to whether this act was constitutional in the face of *Lawrence versus Texas* and what Justice Kennedy said and what he did not say. And my colleagues, my friends, said: 'Ron, you got it wrong.' And in a democratic society, the only thing we have—we have a military to defend us, but the only thing we have to keep us together is respect for an adherence to the rule of law. And that's—this trial, I think, has been a testament to that principle. And you have come here with Mr. Buckingham and Mr. Diederich and made your arguments very, very well. I am proud to be a lawyer. And Mr. Lobsenz and Ms. Dunne and Ms. Kung have done the same. And we've done it in an environment of respect, which I know pervades our military culture.

"This case is not going to be decided based on a referendum," he added, picking up on Phipps's last line of argument, "but it will be decided on all the evidence before me. And I will make that decision. End of sermon."

With that, the trial was over. Judge Leighton announced he would render his verdict in writing, and in court, Friday afternoon. He thanked the lawyers again.

His last words were addressed directly to Margie.

"Major Witt, I am going to tell you a story about judges. There are some who look at the law and say, if that's the law, it shouldn't be. And they set about to change it. We live in a world where they are considered to be heroic, and indeed, some of them are my friends, and they are indeed heroic. I am not one of those judges. For me, my own personal views about Don't Ask, Don't Tell are not germane. I treat this as a law school exam, and all I want to do is get it right. And you have, regardless of the outcome, fought the good fight, and you have brought a timely, important and vital issue to the Court. And Don't Ask, Don't Tell was a product of a compromise, it seems to me, between the hopes and aspirations of people whose sexual orientation is different than the traditional. And the traditional folks who— taken at their best it seems to me—were of the view that, you know, can't we just slow down in the change, the rapidity of change? I know that if, or whenever, gays are allowed to openly serve in the military, that they will be treated with respect, and that they will treat their fellow officers with respect, because that's what the military does. And you have my admiration, as you had my admiration the first time we met."

Chapter 20

AN EXEMPLARY OFFICER

Judge Leighton's closing remarks, his "story about judges" and sober commentary about the kind of judge he is, were enough to keep Margie's expectations in check.

The last time she had placed her hopes in his hands she had been roundly disappointed. Given how painful her and Laurie's lives were in 2006, it was difficult to isolate his dismissal of her lawsuit from the humiliations and emotional shocks the two of them were enduring at the time. Yet, even then, she had been able to separate her disappointment from her measure of the judge himself. In his courtroom, he had treated her with dignity and respect. Her sense, then, was that the judge was a decent man trying to do the right thing. His ruling did not change her opinion of him.

She had no idea how much that ruling had pained him.

The truth is that on Don't Ask, Don't Tell, Ron Leighton disagreed with the Republican president who had appointed him to the federal bench just four years earlier. He thought it was a lousy, discriminatory statute. It was a personal view tightly connected to his upbringing. As an educator to Hispanic migrant workers in California in the 1950s, Judge Leighton's father made a point of enrolling Ron and his brother and sister in the same schools that he taught in and administered. Those schools, Judge Leighton remembers, were in the worst parts of town, so it was a purposeful act on his parents' part to embrace humanity and live in acceptance of people of all races, creeds, and cultures. "That's just part of who we are."

It is also part of who Ron Leighton is that he and his first wife, Sally, adopted two boys. The younger of their two beloved sons, they would eventually learn, was gay.

Still, as he tried to explain directly to Margie in his closing remarks on

September 21, he has never envisaged himself as a "heroic" activist judge. His regret about first dismissing her case, four years earlier, was personal, not professional.

"I am as traditional as anyone. The judge can serve the highest, best use by retaining and enforcing consistency, even if it is occasionally bland, or even ugly," he explains. "You know, that's what I did, with apologies."

Looking back, years after the 2010 trial, he expressed gratitude for "my friend" Judge Ronald Gould, who had written the Ninth Circuit panel's decision in Witt, sending the case back to Tacoma for trial.

"He opened it up," he said of Judge Gould. "I mean, he gave me the opportunity to make it right."

After Judge Leighton excused himself at the end of closing arguments on September 21, he retreated to a ski cabin near Packwood Lake in the Cascades, just south of Mount Rainier. There he would settle in to write his opinion, in longhand.

In the emptying courtroom, the immediate situation confronting Margie was the passion of her anchor witness, General Laich. Within moments of Judge Leighton exiting to his chambers, the buff and towering retired general called out to her and then led her over to the opposite side of the courtroom, where he could speak to her one on one, away from the crowd that had gathered around her. He was already sure that she would prevail and win reinstatement.

"This is your O-eight to O-four talk," he said, borrowing from the military shorthand for a conversation between a general and a major. "Can you meet the weight standards?"

"I believe so, sir," Margie replied.

"Can you pass the fitness test?"

"Sir, I'm not sure what it is today," she answered. "Because it has changed over the past six years. But I'll be ready."

"You'd better be," the general declared with full-metal eye contact. "Every eye will be upon you. You represent every one of us. Don't let us down."

After the initial jolt, the admonition from General Laich was just a brusque and comical reminder of the length and restlessness of the journey she and Laurie had undertaken. There was always something else rushing toward them, always something else that had to get done next.

It would be three days before court would reconvene, on Friday morning, for announcement of the verdict. But the *Witt* case and her story were already having their effects on a national scale.

In the week before the *Witt* trial got under way in Tacoma, federal district court judge Virginia Phillips had issued a broad ruling from her Riverside, California, courtroom attacking the constitutionality of Don't Ask, Don't Tell.

Judge Phillips had been presiding for several years over *Log Cabin Republicans v. United States of America and Robert M. Gates, Secretary of Defense*, a challenge brought by a national organization of gay Republicans. In early July 2010, she issued a critical pretrial order, formally notifying the parties that she would adjudicate the case employing the heightened scrutiny prescribed by the Ninth Circuit Court of Appeals in *Witt*. The case then went to trial in mid-July and included testimony from experts and several gay former service members, including Anthony Loverde and Jenny Kopfstein, both of whom later testified in *Witt*. Nathaniel Frank, an author and expert on the history of the military's antigay culture and policies, also testified in both trials.

Because Judge Phillips also presides in the Ninth Circuit, the Ninth Circuit Court of Appeals ruling in *Witt* not only applied to the case, but packed important leverage within the circuit. In her September 9, 2010, ruling in *Log Cabin*, Judge Phillips found the government and Defense Department had failed to "satisfy their burden under the *Witt* standard." The enforcement of DADT, she concluded, violated both the First and Fifth Amendments to the Constitution. She also announced her intention to issue an injunction barring the military from enforcing its DADT discharge policies.

On September 23, the day before Judge Leighton was set to announce his verdict in *Witt*, sixty-nine members of Congress wrote a short letter to President Obama requesting that he not appeal Judge Phillips's ruling in *Log Cabin*.

"Some of the most accomplished and lauded members of our military are gay," the letter reported in its third paragraph. "Air Force Reserve Major Margaret Witt is one of those talented defenders of peace who has suffered at the hand of DADT policy. After 17 years of service to the United States Air Force, receiving regular recognition for her devotion and excellence, Major Witt was discharged after it was discovered that she was a lesbian. Her worth to the military and the American people was outweighed by her sexual orientation. Her story is not uncommon, and neither is the unnecessary grief and hardship that is added to the shoulders of the gay and lesbian members of our military."

No doubt General Laich was right. If Margie prevailed and was reinstated, it would be a historic victory. It would bring her even further into the national spotlight.

But something else had happened along the way. Sure, winning the case would matter, and if Margie were to rejoin the 446th as a result, that would matter too. Yet, what mattered much more to both Margie and Laurie was that they had survived the journey and had arrived in Tacoma having already won more than they could possibly lose.

The two were not alone in what they were experiencing. Carla Savalli had carried a burden for over five years, feeling deep remorse that she was so late in accepting her best friend's account of how Tiffany Jenson had participated in outing Margie to the Air Force. She and Margie had finally begun to repair their friendship in the months leading up to the trial. Carla would make two trips to Tacoma during the course of the trial and was determined to be there for Margie and Laurie on the day of the verdict.

For Nancy Mellor, it had been nearly thirty years since she had been banished from the Witt family after Gloria learned she was gay and forbade Margie to see her. She and Margie had stayed in touch and had spoken at length shortly before Margie had come out to her parents in 2006. Nancy now worked in Sumner, Washington, only a few miles east of Union Station, and though her work schedule prevented her from sitting through the entire trial, she made a point of coming for part of every day. Inside the courthouse, Frank and Gloria had recognized her, and the three came together.

"It was very emotional for me," Nancy recalls. "I didn't show it there, because the court was about Margie. They hugged me, and they said they were sorry." As Nancy recalled the embrace, her voice trembled, and she fought back tears. "It was a long time coming."

On September 22 and 23—in the two days between closing arguments and the delivery of the verdict—Laurie would wake up not in the Marriott but on the other side of the Tacoma Narrows, in Frank and Gloria's home in Gig Harbor. It had been ten years since Laurie had lost her father, and by now her mother was deep in a well of dementia. From the day she knew that she and Margie were meant to be together, she had dearly wanted to be accepted into Margie's family. And now she was. On that Wednesday and Thursday she rose at dawn to walk all the way around the harbor in misty, autumn light. It was the same route Frank Witt still walked every day, and as Laurie made the loop around Gig Harbor she imagined she was striding in Frank's footsteps.

To the extent she imagined what Friday would bring she thought she was well prepared either way, that her reaction to a verdict against Margie would not be much different from her response to a verdict in Margie's favor.

Thursday night they returned to the hotel on Pacific Avenue. Jan Gemberling had rented an apartment in Tacoma so she could stay for the duration of the trial and also have a place to keep up on her legal work. That evening, when Jan met Margie and Laurie in the hotel bar, her son Bob was with her. He had recently had oral surgery and was in considerable distress. It was clear what needed to happen to help relieve his suffering. Margie ordered a shot of vodka for him, and there, in the bar, she stanched the pain by removing his stitches with the scissors and tweezers he had purchased on his way to the hotel. She is, after all, a flight nurse.

Judge Leighton was up earlier than usual Friday morning because he was also in distress. His marriage of thirty years was unraveling. Before he arrived to render his verdict in *Witt*, he and Sally were in a mediation session.

"One thing this job does, is that when you sentence people to jail repeatedly it sort of takes a piece of your soul," he reflects. "Every day. And it's been very hard. I love and respect my ex-wife, but I just wasn't happy."

He was as aware of his unhappiness as he was of the pain Sally was feeling, and he was enduring both with considerable remorse.

"It's tough," he says. "It's like a death."

The verdict he had written up at Packwood was in hand. But now, with less than ten minutes before he was scheduled to appear, he realized he had something else to say to Margaret Witt. He quickly wrote a postscript.

Then it was time. Margie remained standing as Judge Leighton settled behind his bench and began reading his ruling. Jim Lobsenz and Sarah stood on either side of her, each lightly clasping an arm.

The first several minutes were devoted to summarizing and highlighting the history of the case, including an extensive account of the congressional findings underlying Don't Ask, Don't Tell. To those findings, he made a point of adding the government's main argument—offered with the testimony of General Stenner—that "uniformity" was crucial and that treating Margie Witt differently from other gay members of the military would result in a different personnel policy and thus cause harm to unit morale and cohesion.

"The argument proves too much, however," he said.

It was at that point that both Jim Lobsenz and Sarah Dunne knew they had won, and, from behind, Laurie noticed as each reached for and squeezed Margie's hands on each side. The argument that uniformity must prevail, Judge Leighton explained, was contrary to the Ninth Circuit panel's ruling, and he was compelled "to reject any notion that the overriding need for uniformity trumps individualized treatment of Major Witt."

He then turned to the case that Margie's legal team had mounted, from the testimonials of her peers in the 446th, to the testimony of the expert witnesses. And then he was in full stride, voicing the words that would ring like church bells and be so prominently featured in national and international news stories that afternoon and the following morning.

"The evidence produced at trial overwhelmingly supports the conclusions that the suspension and discharge of Margaret Witt did not significantly further the important government interest in advancing unit morale and cohesion. To the contrary, the actions taken against Major Witt had the opposite effect. The 446th AES is a highly professional, rapid response, air evacuation team. It is comprised of flight nurses and medical technicians who are well-trained, well-led and highly motivated. They provide a vital service to our fighting men and women around the world. Serving within that unit are known or suspected lesbian service men and women. There is no evidence before this court to suggest that their service within the unit causes problems of the type predicted in the congressional findings of fact referenced above. These people train together, fly together, care for patients together, deploy together. There is nothing in the record before this court suggesting that sexual orientation—acknowledged or suspected—has negatively impacted the performance, dedication or enthusiasm of the 446th AES. There is no evidence that wounded troops care about the sexual orientation of the flight nurse or medical technician tending to their wounds.

"The evidence before the court is that Major Margaret Witt was an exemplary officer. She was an effective leader, a caring mentor, a skilled clinician, and an integral member of an effective team. Her loss within the squadron resulted in a diminution of the unit's ability to carry out its mission."

A minute later, he added, in reference to the *Witt* standard test: "For the reasons expressed, the court concludes that DADT, when applied to Major Margaret Witt, does not further the government's interest in promoting military readiness, unit morale and cohesion. If DADT does not significantly further an important government interest under prong two of the three-part test, it cannot be necessary to further that interest as applied to prong three. Application of DADT therefore violates Major Witt's substantive due process rights under the Fifth Amendment to the United States Constitution. She should be reinstated at the earliest possible moment."

Judge Leighton says he didn't notice the body language from Jim and Sarah when they realized he was going to rule their way. He was focusing on the words, he explained, all the while mindful that his estranged wife was in the balcony, listening and watching as he delivered a verdict, the historic importance of which he well understood.

When he finished reading, he paused and asked if there were any questions. Then his eyes went to the postscript he had written just minutes before coming into the courtroom.

"Major Witt, you and I are unlikely to see each other again, at least under this context, and I would like to make a couple points before you leave.

"One, I hope you will request reinstatement with the Air Force Reserves in the 446th. Your service will provide the best evidence that open service of gays and lesbians will have no adverse effect on cohesion, morale, or readiness in this or perhaps any Air Force or military unit.

"Second, you have been and continue to be, a central figure in a long-term, highly charged civil rights movement. The role places extraordinary stresses on you, I know. Today you have won a victory in that struggle, the depth and duration of which will be determined by other judicial officers and hopefully soon, the political branches of government.

"You said something in the trial that resonated with me: You said that the best thing to come out of all this turmoil is the reaction of your parents when you told them of your sexual orientation, their unfailing love and support for you. Notwithstanding the victory you have attained here today, for yourself and others, I would submit to you that the best thing to come out of all this tumult is still that love and support you have received from your family. You are truly blessed as a family, and I am sure they will see you through whatever obstacles and difficulties you may encounter along the road ahead."

Judge Leighton's voice strained with emotion as he reached toward the end of his parting message. He appeared to be in tears, or at least on the verge of tears, but he made it through.

"Court will be at recess," he announced before he briskly departed to his right. It was five minutes after two o'clock.

Chapter 21

HEARD

Out of respect for Judge Leighton, the tightly packed spectators restrained themselves until the door closed behind him. The courtroom then erupted in cheers, more than loud enough for the judge to hear the outburst in his chambers.

For Margie, it had been a surreal experience to stand there between Sarah and Jim knowing this was perhaps the most important public moment of her life. She was trying to concentrate on what Judge Leighton was saying. It had never been easy to comprehend the legal abstractions underlying the case, and she listened closely as he walked through it all again. And then, after some twenty minutes, Judge Leighton's voice emerged from the analytical thicket. He explained his conclusions in clear language, in unequivocal terms that everybody could understand. Finally, Margie thought, the truth—the truth about her life and work, and the truth about her experience with her companions in the 446th—was being unshackled before everyone.

In the last minutes, as he added his personal postscript and talked about the "unfailing love and support" of her family, she found herself feeling compassion for him as he paused to collect himself and struggled with his emotions.

Near the back of the courtroom, the part of Carla Savalli that had grown into a well-seasoned, professional journalist was simply amazed to be hearing such a personal and emotional outpouring from a judge.

"And then it just dawned on me," she says. "'Oh wow.' And I burst into tears. Margie was a lot more composed."

What ensued was the best sort of bedlam. Margie and Jim turned to each other and shared a long embrace, and then there was a succession of tearful celebratory hugs. After several minutes, in which she tried to give hugs and talk to everyone who had come to support her, Margie finally turned to Sarah for direction about what to do next. "You know," she recalls with puckish sarcasm, "because I don't move without my legal team."

The news cameras were waiting outside the courtroom. It was time to talk to the press.

"Go!" Sarah said, giving her a playful shove toward the door at the rear of the courtroom.

"So we eventually headed that way," Margie recalls, "and we're just this giddy mob."

Among the timeless news photos from that afternoon is one of Margie and Laurie emerging from the courtroom dressed in broad smiles, Laurie with her left arm around Margie's left shoulder, and Margie with her arms wrapped around Laurie's waist. An obviously delighted Sher Kung looks on behind them.

Just outside the security gate, as Margie's giddy mob spilled from behind the glass partition into the Union Station rotunda, the television cameras were rolling. Margie emerged followed by Frank, and then Laurie leading Gloria by the hand, then Victor Fehrenbach, followed by Margie's two young nieces, seemingly walking on air, and then a very happy looking Sarah Dunne. As the hand-held microphones converged upon her, Margie smiled broadly, deftly removed her glasses with the sweep of a hand, and started answering questions.

"I was just stunned," Carla remembers as she watched the reporters gather around Margie in the foyer beneath the dome. "It's like you're in shock. I was looking at her, looking at her parents. Thinking how far everyone had come."

One of the first stories, from KOMO-TV, included a quote from a woman who had been there before.

"This is such an exciting day," Grethe Cammermeyer said. "For the first time, the military had to show a cause why somebody gay could not serve in the military. And they could not do it. This is just huge. I could cry."

There was champagne back at the hotel down the street where the celebration continued. In the midst of it all, Margie noticed that Frank had separated himself and taken a seat in a chair next to a window. She came over to her father, sat on the floor, and reached for his arm as she noticed the tears flowing down his cheeks. He was overwhelmed.

"Just talking about it tears me up," he says. "I wanted to get away from the hullabaloo. We had a lot of people there, and they were all celebrating, a whole lot of staff, our minister, all the friends that came with Margie. I just wanted to get alone."

"It was the end of something," Gloria added. "And it was kind of a letdown because we knew we'd never again have to go through that. It was a once-in-a-lifetime experience. But we knew. The verdict didn't surprise us at all."

The party rolled on in Tacoma, but Margie and Laurie and Sarah and Victor Fehrenbach had to go. Victor had been on the phone with MSNBC, where he had been making periodic appearances on the *Rachel Maddow Show*. Now he and Margie were scheduled to be linked in, live, to be interviewed by Maddow a little after 6 p.m. Pacific time. After a last round of hugs and toasts, they piled into Victor's rental car and sped north, up Interstate 5, to the NBC studios at KING-5 TV in Seattle.

"A bit of big breaking news late on a Friday," Maddow announced as she introduced her two guests. "A federal judge appointed by George W. Bush in 2002 has issued a federal court ruling late today, essentially dismantling the Don't Ask, Don't Tell policy."

Emblazoned beneath Maddow and courtroom sketch images of Margie on the witness stand was a caption, in all caps: "Devastating Court Ruling Quashes Military Gay Ban."

Maddow continued,

"This is the second very strong federal court ruling against the military's gay ban in less than a month. The plaintiff in this case has not done a national TV interview before; she will be joining us in just a moment for an exclusive discussion, along with someone whose face will be familiar to those who've been following our coverage of this issue."

The familiar face was Victor's, and the other federal ruling was, of course, Judge Phillips's ruling in the *Log Cabin* case, which significantly relied on the *Witt* standard.

After recapping other recent court rulings expanding gay rights in California and Florida, Maddow turned to a recap of the *Witt* case. Photos of Judge Leighton, and then of Margie and Laurie, appeared on the screen, then of Margie and Victor. Then came the video footage of Margie greeting the press, earlier that afternoon in the Union Station rotunda. Maddow, a

Rhodes scholar who thrives on meaty stories, actually did a short, on-air tutorial about how the case had come back to Judge Leighton.

"If you want to know anything about how this part of civil rights in America goes," she said, "if you want to know how Don't Ask, Don't Tell is going to get struck down by the courts and that's how it's probably going to die," then you needed to know how Judge Leighton had been instructed by the Ninth Circuit to review the *Witt* case.

"Under what is known as the *Witt* standard," Maddow explained, "Judge Leighton ruled today that the Air Force must reinstate her, in his words, 'as soon as practicable.'" Maddow then read for nearly two minutes, quoting directly from Judge Leighton's ruling. Then, as the live faces of Margie and Victor appeared side by side from Seattle, she asked Margie if the ruling meant she could rejoin her unit soon.

"I sure hope so," Margie answered. She had changed from the light green jacket she had worn to court earlier and was now wearing a dark blazer. Plus a huge smile. "I'm ready whenever they are."

Victor explained how the judgment had "solidified" the Ninth Circuit's ruling creating the *Witt* standard, "so it gives me a lot of hope that we can be successful in my fight" to rejoin the Air Force. He reminded Maddow how he had been notified by the Air Force of its intent to discharge him just two days before the appeals court ruling in *Witt* was rendered.

"And that gives me hope, but it just doesn't give me hope. There are thousands of others out there confronted with a Don't Ask, Don't Tell case right now, and I hope Margie's victory today gives them hope as well."

Turning back to Margie, Maddow said:

"Margie, after the ruling, the judge in this case, Judge Leighton, I know that he brought himself to tears and much of the courtroom to tears, when he read a statement describing the stresses on you as a person, to be what he called 'a central figure in a long term, highly charged civil rights movement.' He described how much it resonated with him personally when you said how important your family was in supporting you. I imagine that was surprising. What did it mean to you that the judge addressed you in those very personal terms?"

"It was very surprising," Margie replied. "It was very heartfelt. He spoke to me directly. I think he really understands the impact that it has on everyone around you, particularly family, and how thankful I was to have my parents behind me. I think he really gets that, and he knew it was a big struggle, and a big event."

Maddow's last question, to Victor, was the most politically charged, and referenced Air Force major Mike Almy, a friend of Fehrenbach's since high school who had been discharged under DADT in 2006. It was Almy who approached Margie the year before—just after she had given a speech at a Servicemembers Legal Defense Fund rally on the Capitol grounds in Washington, DC—to tell her about Victor and his legal challenge to DADT.

"I know that you told us here on this show that the president told you man to man, eye to eye, that he was going to end this policy. He told you he was 'going to get it done,' I remember hearing you saying it, here on this show. I wonder, as things have changed so much since you and I first talked, over a year ago, I wonder if you are starting to think that maybe it's going to be people like you, and Margie Witt, and Mike Almy who are going to change this policy despite the president, uh, not because of him?"

"I've been disappointed over and over again by the lack of leadership and courage we've seen from so many of our political leaders," Victor replied. "Thanks to Major Witt and people like her, I've had hope, I've been able to fight." Victor added he would "love to visit" with Senator John McCain—an outspoken opponent of ending DADT—"and take him to work with me on Monday and see how today's military operates and see how this is a nonissue to the military."

Maddow ended the interview by congratulating Margie on "this big freaking deal of a ruling" and wishing she were in Seattle "to take you both out for a beer." Before cutting to a commercial break, she also directed a barb at the Obama administration and Congress, saying "the administration and the Senate are unwilling or unable to do what the federal courts appear to have no problem doing."

This was just the sort of high-profile criticism that stung at the White House. For the reasons Secretary Gates would later share in his memoir, the president and the senior military leadership thought it crucial that the nation's elected leaders, not the courts, be the instrument for ending Don't Ask, Don't Tell. As 2009 came to an end, White House staffers working on the issue were assured by the president's top advisers that 2010 would be the year. This was publicly confirmed in early February 2010 when Vice

President Joe Biden told NBC's Andrea Mitchell that "by this year's end, we will have eliminated the policy," meaning Don't Ask, Don't Tell.

Rachel Maddow had made the salient point, though. The courts were now beginning to outrun Congress and the White House by striking at the constitutionality of a law that—as the evidence before Judge Leighton and Judge Phillips well demonstrated—was actually eroding military capability, morale, and credibility. With the verdict in the *Witt* case, and Judge Phillips's rulings in *Log Cabin*, the courts weren't idly waiting for the political branches to take action.

Unlike many of her contemporaries—a half dozen of whom put on their uniforms and chained themselves to the White House fence in an April 2010 protest—Margie hadn't lost faith in President Obama. Yet, neither was it lost on her, especially during the grueling run-up to her trial, that Barack Obama was commander-in-chief. The lawyers on the other side, rummaging through her private life, were working for him. It was puzzling and frustrating.

Sarah Dunne, who had worked for the Justice Department and developed an appreciation for the politics behind high-profile cases, offered an explanation.

"Here's the way the puzzle's going to work," she remembers telling Margie in the summer of 2010. "They need the circus. They need the trial in order to push Congress. They need you to be the face."

On the other hand, according to one White House official who worked on LGBT issues and followed the *Witt* case, there was certainly no joy in the Obama White House for the ordeal that Margie Witt was having to endure. Their hope, she said, was to have the president sign the repeal of Don't Ask, Don't Tell before her case went to trial. When Margie half-jokingly apologized to another White House staffer "for making his job so hard," he had quickly replied that she was actually making it easier.

A pillar of the White House strategy in 2010 was to be a new Department of Defense study, providing a fresh and thorough evaluation of the effects on the U.S. military of a repeal of Don't Ask, Don't Tell. The intended audience for the study—chaired by Army general Carter F. Ham and Pentagon general counsel Jeh Johnson—was Congress. The 267-page report was released the last day of November at a press conference led by Secretary Gates and Admiral Mike Mullen, the chairman of the Joint

Chiefs of Staff. By then, Admiral Mullen had already become a hero to many for his congressional testimony, not just calling for an end to Don't Ask, Don't Tell, but hammering away with the same argument that Sarah Dunne felt so strongly about as a former military brat: that Don't Ask, Don't Tell was deeply contrary to the military's core values.

The Department of Defense report concluded there would only be limited and isolated disruptions in the military if the law were repealed. But the more direct political message was delivered by Secretary Gates at the press conference. It was, he said, "a matter of urgency" for the Senate to vote on the repeal so the military could initiate an orderly transition. Otherwise, he warned, congressional inaction ran the risk that repeal would be "imposed immediately by judicial fiat."

Still, even into the second week of December the prospects for getting a vote in the Senate to end Don't Ask, Don't Tell looked bleak at best. With Senator McCain and other Republican senators threatening to filibuster any defense authorization bill that included DADT repeal language, Senate Majority Leader Harry Reid called for a vote on whether the Senate should bring such a bill to the floor. That vote took place on December 9. Although it passed 57–40, it was actually a stinging setback, because it was short of the sixty votes needed to overcome the promised filibuster.

With only a few days remaining on the 2010 legislative calendar, Senator Joe Lieberman, an independent from Connecticut, and Senator Susan Collins, a Republican from Maine, cosponsored a stand-alone bill to repeal DADT. The bill secured eight Republican votes (including that of Collins) and passed 65–31.

"This was one of the great moments that I had the privilege of being involved in," says Senator Lieberman. "And in some sense it was one of the most emotionally satisfying moments. Part of this—and I know it's true for Susan Collins, too—is that we're such fighters and competitors and we just believed so much. You know, the story here is we just refused to give up."

Jim Lobsenz was on a family vacation in Paris as the Senate voted. He was just coming out of the shower when one of his daughters shouted from the other side of the bathroom door that Don't Ask, Don't Tell had been repealed. He thought she was joking. When he accepted she wasn't pulling his leg, he sent Margie an e-mail: "I just heard. C'est magnifique!"

Among those who supported the repeal there was no shortage of strong opinions as to what finally brought it about. Andrew Sullivan, a widely read conservative gay writer and activist, offered his assessment the following day in a piece entitled "Obama's Long Game, 65–31."

"This process took time," Sullivan wrote on his *Daily Dish* blog at the *Atlantic*. "Without the Pentagon study, it wouldn't have passed. Without Obama keeping Lieberman inside the tent, it wouldn't have passed. Without the critical relationship between Bob Gates and Obama, it wouldn't have passed. It worked our last nerve; we faced at one point a true nightmare of nothing . . . for years. And then we pulled behind this president, making it his victory and the country's victory, as well as ours."

In the aftermath of a bitterly partisan, year-end legislative scrum, Senator Lieberman was widely praised for his leadership in securing the votes needed for the repeal. Looking back on that period, he says he well understood the importance of the *Witt* case and the effect that Margie's story and her gutsiness in refusing to go quietly was having on his congressional colleagues.

"There were a lot of things that enabled us to repeal Don't Ask, Don't Tell," Lieberman says. "But one was Major Witt's case, because of the effect it had on public opinion, because of the inequity of how she was treated."

On Margie's end, she awoke on December 21 amazed at how quickly things had turned around in the Senate. At the same time, she was coping with the growing realization that while she had fulfilled her mission of vanquishing Don't Ask, Don't Tell, she hadn't yet won the battle to be reinstated. Although Judge Leighton ordered that she be allowed to rejoin the 446th "as soon as is practicable, subject to meeting applicable regulations," that process was replete with obstacles. It had also become clear the Air Force was trying to draw the process out as long as it could.

To try to resolve the logjam, Margie was on a predawn flight to Seattle that morning to meet with her ACLU legal team. She had turned her cell phone off for the flight, but when she landed at Sea-Tac airport, she noticed a new e-mail message had arrived. It was from the White House—an invitation for her to attend the DADT repeal signing ceremony the next morning in Washington, DC.

Her pulse started racing when she noticed that a reply was requested by 8 a.m., and it was now two minutes after 8. She quickly responded to the e-mail, then immediately called Sarah Dunne, knowing Sarah had worked in DC and would likely know the best way to get there in a hurry. Within a matter of seconds, Sarah directed her to a gate in another concourse, where a flight was in the last stages of boarding for the nation's capital. She hustled and got there just as the agents were closing the door on the aircraft. Desperate to make it onto the plane, she held out her iPhone to show the gate agents the e-mail from the White House. That was good enough. There was one empty seat left on the plane, and she was in it. She had no idea where she was going to stay in DC, but Laurie would take care of that and book her a hotel room while she was en route.

To accommodate a large audience, the signing ceremony was held in a six-hundred-seat auditorium at the Department of the Interior, three blocks from the White House. Margie got there early and quickly connected with Grethe Cammermeyer. As the two were catching up with each other, one of the organizers approached Grethe and invited her to lead the Pledge of Allegiance. What not even Margie knew at the time is that Grethe—as a private act of protest against the government's discriminatory policy—had stopped reciting the pledge. This would be the first time in seventeen years that she would give voice to it.

For Margie, it was all part of a dreamlike experience. It just seemed that one moment she was on her way to Seattle, and in the next instant "there I was standing amongst the giants of the historical battle over gays in the military. It was unbelievable, the energy in that room."

From his position on the stage where President Obama addressed the room, Senator Lieberman was also struck and deeply moved. It wasn't just the "pulsating excitement and pride in the hall," he said, but a realization that something transcendent was occurring, that the vote to repeal DADT "was also a reflection of a broadening acceptance by America of the justice of the LGBT equality and treatment cause."

After the president finished an emotional speech, Margie was delighted to find Grethe being interviewed, in Norwegian, by a Norwegian reporter well familiar with Grethe's family roots in Oslo. When Grethe was finished with the interview, she turned to Margie and told her, in English, "I started it, and you finished it."

As she was leaving the ceremony, Margie noticed Senator Lieberman and worked her way through the crowd to thank him personally for his leadership role in ending DADT. His gracious response—about how vital her case and her story were in persuading members of Congress to vote for the repeal—was deeply moving and made her feel as though she really had made a difference in the historic effort that culminated in this once-in-a-lifetime ceremony.

The next stop was CNN, which had requested an interview with her and Victor Fehrenbach about the repeal. As she departed, she handed Grethe her hotel room key so Grethe could relax and continue doing interviews from there. After the interview with CNN, Margie and Victor and Mike Almy came back to Margie's room to do a telephone interview with the *Air Force Times*.

The dreamlike day rolled on. After saying her goodbyes to Fehrenbach and Almy, it was time for her and Grethe to catch their flight back to Seattle. As they got to their gate at Reagan International Airport they found Senator Patty Murray, who had spoken passionately about Margie's story on the floor of the Senate, and Congressman Jay Inslee, who two years later would be elected governor of Washington. It was all smiles and laughter as they greeted one another and posed for pictures before boarding for the long flight home to the other Washington. And that was how this day ended, with Margie and Grethe sitting next to each other, flying home from the nation's capital, enjoying the last precious hours of a day that so thoroughly validated some of the deepest and darkest struggles of their lives.

It was ironic, perhaps, that Ron Leighton, a federal judge, had given voice to the deeper victory of that year. The law really matters to a society that values human dignity and equal opportunity—and he had said so, as well as anyone could, in the opinion he wrote in his cabin up by Mount Rainier. And, still, in a voice trembling with a deeper truth, he had finished by saying that love matters even more than law.

When she and Margie stepped inside Tacoma's Union Station courthouse the first morning of the trial, Laurie had felt overwhelmed. It was a beautiful and formidable space. If circumstances were different, she would have allowed herself to bask in the full spectrum of the light, to absorb the richness of the sound shaped by the unusual acoustics beneath the dome, and let her fingers feel the smooth coolness of the Italian marble skirting the passageways.

On that first day, she had tried to imagine how the two of them, and the spirit and energy of the people who had come to support them, might fill the vast space around and above them. But it was just too overwhelming to fathom. They all seemed so small by comparison. By the second week of the trial, she had begun to feel differently. Beneath the game faces she and Margie had put on every morning for their walk into the courtroom, they were deeply and constantly moved by the outpouring of support they were receiving, not just from friends and family, but from people they hadn't known before, including the court reporter who, during the midday break during Margie's testimony, rose from her seat and told Margie, with great earnestness, what an honor it was to meet her.

To the extent Laurie thought about what the verdict would deliver, she thought she was prepared either way, that her reaction to a judgment for the Air Force would not be much different from her reaction to a verdict in Margie's favor. But after Judge Leighton had spoken, and said what he said, and the way he had said it, the enormity of it all began to sink in. To this day she can't go past Union Station without getting tears in her eyes.

"I was raised Catholic," she explains. "I did a lot of churchgoing, and when I drive by that building now it feels like that is my church."

Margie was having much the same experience, albeit at a different level of intensity. In Seattle, just before she was to go on the air with Rachel Maddow, the woman prepping her for the camera shared her memory of applying makeup to Grethe Cammermeyer before Grethe was interviewed in the same KING-5 studio nearly twenty years earlier. It was that kind of day, and the victory celebration continued long into the night. As a KING-5 Lincoln Town Car whisked her back to the hotel in Tacoma, Margie received a coded text message from a deployed gay member of the 446th, serving in Germany. He had just seen a news photo of Margie wearing her green coat as she was leaving the courthouse in Tacoma that morning. "Green looks good. It's your lucky color!!!"

On Saturday, Ed and Jennifer Hrivnak hosted a party for them at their home in Spanaway, Washington, where cups continued to runneth over.

On Sunday morning it was time to go. They both had to be at work on Monday back in Spokane, and Margie was already well aware of the physical conditioning and the 160 volunteer nursing hours she would have to add to her calendar in order to be certified for reinstatement at the 446th.

Gloria, as was her habit, had sent them off with a couple of paper sacks filled with multigrain chips, fruit, carrots, roast beef sandwiches, and a couple of boiled eggs for their long trip back. And, as usual, the food had been eaten by the time they emerged from the mountains and drove into the Kittitas Valley. After a solid stretch of gray and rainy skies during the trial in Tacoma, the sunshine lifted their spirits as they reached Ellensburg in the middle of the state and continued over the high, treeless ridge at Ryegrass and down toward the Columbia River.

"I felt we were just floating," Laurie remembers. "Traffic was moving along, the sky was blue, everybody had the same worries, the same destinations. But we're different. And we're in our little capsule, and nobody knew it but us."

Just east of the Columbia, the interstate climbs from the river gorge and passes within a half mile of Frenchman Coulee, one of the epic scars of the ice age floods that gouged deep canyons and braided channels in the basalt bedrock between the Columbia River and Spokane. In some places, enormous granite boulders delivered by ancient riots of water from Montana rest in pasture, or in wheat or potato fields where tractors navigate around them. Although this isn't the vaulted blue-and-green expanse that makes for Evergreen State postcards, the sparse and gently rolling terrain invites an open sky and majestic sunsets framed by distant, folded ridges and the mountains on the western horizon. On a clear day, you can see as far as Mount Rainier.

Their next-to-last stop was at a rest area smack in the middle of this boundless piece of nowhere, with hundred-mile views in every direction. On the southern flanks of the little oasis is a parklike expanse of grass, where families can picnic, dogs can be walked, and children can climb in the now mature elm trees the Washington Department of Transportation planted decades ago.

The sunset that evening was breathtaking. As it began to fade in the sky over the Cascades, Major Margaret Witt and Laurie Johnson got back in their car and headed farther east toward home, just the two of them.

Epilogue

████████████

OUT OF THE BLUE

The hardest part was letting go.

From the day she found the path to becoming a flight nurse, the Air Force had been a near perfect fit. It offered the physicality and adventure she sought. It was the opportunity to serve her country and serve the men and women in uniform who needed a skilled nurse when they were badly ill, injured, or wounded. It made possible the lasting bonds of honor and respect that come with proving yourself to your peers under intensely stressful and sometimes life-threatening circumstances.

There was a reason she became the one to lead karaoke. There was a reason she could sleep with her head on Stacey Julian's shoulder on the long flight to Oman, or engage Jim Schaffer as a brother in whom she could confide. And there was a reason Jill Robinson told the court that removing Margaret Witt from their unit at McChord was like extracting a parent out of a family. Her comrades in the 446th had become her second family, and they knew and experienced her in ways that her first family could not.

And that was why she wanted to go back. The comically direct pep talk from General Laich after court had recessed on September 21, 2010, had no doubt gotten her attention. But the motivation to rejoin her unit was more than enough to propel her to get back in shape and fulfill the nursing-hour requirements the Air Force now stipulated.

The physical fitness part of it would have been easier had she not by then entered her late forties with a pair of knees that had endured six surgeries, two of which were recent and major. But she did it. Three months after Judge Leighton's order, she had worked herself into shape, met her weight-loss goal, and fulfilled her nursing hours requirement.

She had done her part, but the Air Force seemed to be moving not at all, which is why she was on her way to meet with Sarah Dunne early on

December 21 when she got the e-mail from the White House, inviting her to the Don't Ask, Don't Tell repeal signing ceremony.

It turns out that it had been a lot easier to get into the Air Force than it was to get *back* into the Air Force after they had wrongly discharged you. To come in as a second lieutenant had required only a physical. Now, she was told she needed a more arduous physical fitness test. Next she was informed that since she was going to be returning to her position as a flight nurse, she was going to need an even more demanding flight physical. The darkness of this Catch-22 comedy was complete when the most openly gay woman in the U.S. Air Force saw that the flight physical paperwork included a list of disqualifying factors. At the bottom of the list was homosexuality. The regulation hadn't been updated yet.

Nor was it at all clear where the test would be administered, and by whom. Among other things, she learned of a bureaucratic tug of war between the Air National Guard and the active-duty Air Force, as each insisted the other should administer the flight physical.

Although Don't Ask, Don't Tell was legislatively repealed in December 2010, the law required the president, the secretary of defense, and the chairman of the Joint Chiefs of Staff to certify that the military had put in place the necessary policies and procedures. After certification, which occurred on July 22, 2011, there would still be sixty days before DADT, at long last, would expire.

Notwithstanding Judge Leighton's order, it was clear the Air Force intended to delay Margie's reinstatement at least until after the sixty-day period expired on September 21, 2011.

The delay was frustrating, but other realities intervened as well. When Margie attended Stacey Julian's Air Force retirement party in August 2011, she couldn't help but take notice of how many new, young faces were there. It had been seven years since she was told to leave the 446th. The squadron was changing, and many of those to whom she had been closest were now retired. Moreover, the equipment and procedures had changed. In returning to the 446th as a flight nurse, she would have to work extra hard to come up to speed on new technology and practices.

But the darkest cloud was her deepening sense that she wouldn't be welcome.

There was no escaping the serious rift between her and the 446th's commander. The disclosure by Margie's legal team of Colonel Janette Moore-Harbert's DUI hit-and-run records at trial was intended to hit a nerve, and surely it did. Margie and several of her supporters also strongly believed Moore-Harbert had dishonored herself in a February 2010 deposition when she said she didn't know there were other gay men and women serving in the 446th. In the same deposition, the colonel said she couldn't remember the standing ovation Margie received at Jim Schaffer's retirement party, couldn't remember what Margie said from the stage, and couldn't remember signing the large photo given to her as a gift, even though her signature was clearly on the photo. The colonel also said in her deposition that she was concerned Major Witt might make other service members "uncomfortable" if they encountered her in a deployment situation and learned she was a lesbian. When pressed on that claim by Jim Lobsenz, Moore-Harbert admitted she had no actual evidence of anyone's discomfort.

Grethe Cammermeyer had seen this coming, because she had lived through it herself, in 1994, after the Ninth Circuit Court of Appeals upheld Judge Zilly's order that she be reinstated to the National Guard.

"You don't want to go back," Margie remembers Grethe telling her during their long visit together, on Whidbey Island in the summer of 2006.

Grethe brought it up again, on the long flight home after the DADT repeal ceremony in December 2010.

"Now what do you want to do?" she had asked.

It just wasn't something Margie wanted to hear. Although she had accepted Grethe's admonition in 2006—that her new mission was to take on Don't Ask, Don't Tell—she had not given up her hopes for rejoining her comrades in the 446th. Part of this came from Frank. Her father had raised her not to be a quitter, and with her unit being stretched by continuous deployments to support troops wounded in Iraq and Afghanistan, she ached to be there with them.

Says Laurie: "It was such a final decision that we really didn't want to wrap our arms around it, and we had that whole year to think about it, which felt like an eternity. And I knew we were being taken advantage of during that year. I was so frustrated. But, yeah, that whole year. We put off the finality of it."

Says Margie: "So Laurie and I, when we talked about it, it was another heartbreaking decision. It was really final this time, and I was the one making the decision to leave my family, or the memory of what my family was."

On May 10, 2011, the ACLU of Washington announced Margie had reached a final settlement agreement with the Air Force. She would forgo reinstatement. In exchange, the Air Force agreed to drop its appeal of Judge Leighton's ruling, to remove her discharge from her military service record, and provide her with full retirement benefits.

Margie would later tell an audience in Spokane that she and Laurie were now committed to moving ahead, trying to focus on the good energy in their lives and not dwell on the parts that brought remorse and pain. She began to welcome speaking invitations for graduations and from civic groups, and to allow herself to appreciate the ways in which her story had resonated with people, especially young people. A month after the settlement with the Air Force, she was invited to be the grand marshal in the Spokane Pride Parade, an honor extended to Grethe two years earlier. As the parade was gathering, a young man approached her. He was, he told her, a flight attendant with Alaska Airlines and a reserve Air Force sergeant.

"I'd like you to meet Jacob," the flight attendant said. "He's from Deary, Idaho, and he's the only out student in his school."

Deary is a small town of five hundred people about two hours' drive from Spokane. The boy, who looked to be about twelve years old, had come to Spokane for the parade, and with him was his stepfather, a big guy in a baseball cap. Jacob wanted to meet Margie, and when he did he asked if they could be Facebook friends. By the end of the day, they were.

"Jake," said Margie, "call me anytime."

There were two more trips to Washington, DC. In late September, Lieutenant Colonel Victor Fehrenbach invited Margie to join him at his very public retirement celebration near the Capitol. The repeal of Don't Ask, Don't Tell had led to an abrupt end to his lawsuit, as the Air Force granted him full retirement benefits, effective September 20, the day the repeal of DADT took final effect.

As 2011 came to an end, another invitation arrived from the White House, this time in writing, to attend a holiday reception in mid-December. Laurie had been ill the day before, and by the time the two got from their hotel near Dupont Circle to the White House, her feet were hurting from the new shoes she had bought just for the occasion. Yet when she walked into the East Wing of the White House, sore feet and all, the enormity of their journey sunk in. The soaring, angelic voices she could hear were coming from the Baltimore City High School choir. Looking out through a window, she could see to where the dark-green and white "Marine One" helicopter, bearing the president, had just landed on the White House lawn.

"So the moment I walk in and I look out the window, I see the president stepping off the helicopter. And I hear this music and I start to cry. There are people around me, and I can't stop. It was so beautiful, and so surreal, I finally broke down."

A couple of days after the White House reception, they were home in Spokane, still basking in the joy of the trip, but also reflecting on how difficult it was to let their guards down, after so many years of feeling besieged. Laurie's divorce proceedings had dragged on for years, including a state appeals court ruling, in early 2007, upholding a contempt of court citation against her ex-husband for failing to make timely child support and other payments. For years it seemed there would be a daily delivery of legal documents to their door, such that both were living with the conditioned response of flinching every time they heard the rumble of a FedEx or UPS truck.

After the Dixie Chicks released their song "Not Ready to Make Nice" in 2006, it had quickly become one of their anthems. But so had the John Prine song "In Spite of Ourselves," with their favorite line—"We'll end up a'sittin' on a rainbow / Against all odds / Honey, we're the big door prize."

Having been raised Catholic and ostracized by other Catholics as whispers of her relationship with Margie had spread like a virus, Laurie was drawn to deep reflection about God and how she imagined God was watching not just the two of them, but those who had condemned them. She didn't feel pious, and she didn't feel angry. But she did feel as though she had "walked into the fire" in ways that those who scorned her would never understand, that she had found the courage to be true to her heart.

For Margie, the pace of her life had at least distracted her from the psychological trauma inflicted by the ambush meeting with Major Torem. She didn't blame Adam Torem, as he was just doing his job, and, under the circumstances, she felt he had done his best to treat her as a fellow officer. Still, the experience had been a knife in her back. This was her country coming after her, the Air Force she had served, treating her as a common criminal.

The depth of that wound would become clear on a late winter's day in 2012. By then, she had been working as the rehabilitation coordinator at the Veterans Administration hospital in Spokane for three years, a job she had sought in part because she wanted to be connected to service members during her exile from the Air Force. During the last week in February she and a small group of coworkers from the VA made a routine site visit to the hospital at Fairchild Air Force Base, just a few miles away on Spokane's west plains. The idea was simply to meet senior staff members, tour the Fairchild hospital, and identify ways they might cooperate in providing health care and rehabilitation services to both Air Force and VA patients.

During the tour, without warning, she began to feel anxious and then to tremble. She excused herself from the tour and tried to compose herself.

It was a deeply perplexing mix of things she had loved about being in the Air Force and things she dreaded, like the miserable experiences with her supervisor in the similar-size hospital at Castle AFB, when she was a young, vulnerable lieutenant.

A short while later she rejoined the group as they were finishing the tour and about to sit down for a meeting. The meeting was in the hospital commander's conference room. Margie walked in and found a seat, but not comfortably. Her friend Barb—the nursing director at the Spokane VA who had been so helpful when Margie needed to log the nursing hours required for reinstatement in the 446th—then recognized what was happening.

"This has got to be a really hard day," she remembers Barb saying, trying to comfort her.

"Barb, I have to go," Margie replied.

With that she left, again, got in her car, and drove around until she parked at the base car wash, sobbing, trying to understand what was happening to her.

"It was the combination of missing it, and then the terror of it," she explained a couple of days later, her eyes still puffy. She was still feeling vulnerable and deeply unsettled. The worst part was that it seemed to be something she had no control over.

The experience could have become an excuse to withdraw and shield herself. It didn't.

Even while pursuing her challenge to Don't Ask, Don't Tell, she and Laurie had been talking with Jim Lobsenz about the prospects of bringing a lawsuit to secure the right to be married. Yet, in a good way, events overtook them, especially in Washington State. A couple of weeks before her unexpectedly dreadful visit to Fairchild, she and Laurie were in Olympia at the invitation of Governor Chris Gregoire. Grethe Cammermeyer and her partner, Diane, were also there for a deeply emotional ceremony at which the governor signed legislation allowing for same-sex marriage in Washington.

Under Washington's constitution, however, opponents of legislation can prevent it from taking effect by prevailing in a statewide referendum. Even as Governor Gregoire signed the marriage equality bill into law, signatures were already being gathered to put the issue on the November 2012 ballot.

It was in this context that Spokane City Council member Jon Snyder crafted a resolution that would put the council on record in support of marriage equality. A public hearing on such a measure would draw a crowd almost anywhere. But Spokane resides uneasily on a cultural fault line between the coastal liberalism of Seattle and Idaho's gunsmoke conservatism. It was sure to be a long, intense evening, radiating with moral opprobrium and flecks of rage. On April 16, the council chamber was overflowing with more than three hundred people, nearly a hundred of whom would testify. Margie and Laurie were there, standing, waiting their turns to speak.

Even before the session began it was gaveled to a halt to quell an outburst. Once order was restored, the first to come forward was Claudia Johnson, a large woman in a beige overcoat, her short brown hair in a tidy perm.

"In seven places the Bible refers to homosexuality as a sin" she began, before turning to her primary complaint—that homosexuality is an instrument of communism.

"In order to destroy our government, it is necessary to destroy our society. In order to destroy our society it is necessary to destroy our family structure. In order to destroy our family structure it is necessary to promote homosexuality, and that is exactly what the communists are doing."

A disproportionate number of those who signed up to speak were passionate opponents of the resolution, and many, like Claudia, invoked the Bible. A few argued—one in the most graphic terms—that homosexuals were a danger to public health.

After two hours, Margie's name was called, and she approached the podium wearing the same moss-green jacket she had worn to court the day

Judge Leighton rendered his verdict in Tacoma. At the start of the meeting, a mayoral proclamation was read to mark the "Days of Remembrance"—a weeklong commitment to honoring those who died, survived, and who rescued survivors of the Nazi holocaust. She chose to make reference to it.

"I am Margaret Witt, retired Air Force major," she said. "Before I go on I just want to reflect that we started this meeting with a proclamation for those who were persecuted and murdered by the Nazis, and that included homosexuals. Recently, I won an eight-year battle against Don't Ask, Don't Tell. I have been and I continue to be, believe it or not, overwhelmed with kindness and support from the Spokane community. For six of the eight years I was in a very public court battle to basically prove that I was the same officer who'd served honorably for eighteen years prior to them discovering who I love. All I wanted to do was serve my country. Today I want to do what would be considered the honorable thing to do in everyday society. I want to marry my partner of nine years, Laurie. I want to support, love, and protect my family. Marriage is about love and commitment to each other. It's so strange and hurtful to me that our love and commitment is seen as somehow different and undeserving of social recognition. And yet, picture this, tomorrow I could go down to the courthouse with a male friend, perhaps even an acquaintance, and apply for a marriage license. I would automatically receive praise and a hearty congratulations from those present because they would assume that we were in love. We wouldn't be asked over and over again to prove it. He would automatically be given rights to my property, my military and my federal pension. And he would not have loved me, nor been in a committed relationship with me for even one moment. Laurie and I are committed to each other and our family. She deserves to be that person.

"Thank you," she concluded.

Because the council president, Ben Stuckart, had warned he would evict people for hooting, booing, or applauding, there was only loose silence.

Laurie was next to speak.

"Good evening," she began. "My name is Laurie Johnson. I'm here tonight to talk about marriage, a powerful affirmation of love and commitment. It is a source of social support, of stability in the community that we live in, and I know that everyone here agrees with this. Margaret Witt has been my partner for nearly nine years. God willing, we will have many more years together on this earth. We share a bond. We are a family. The marriage issue is as basic as the golden rule, as basic as treating others as one would want to be treated. This includes allowing marriage for couples who are truly committed to each other. I've been, one time, married. I have three grown, loving and supportive children from that marriage who are among my greatest sources of pride and strength. I know what it feels like to live in a heterosexual marriage. I know the steps I needed to take to make that marriage survive as long as I could. I also know what it feels like to have a late in life recognition that heterosexual is not who I am. For those of you tonight who are not gay or lesbian, I can assure you that what I feel for Margie is no different than what you feel in your heart for the one you love. It is everything. In fact it has taken an extraordinary quality of effort for us. We've had to prove our relationship in a very public setting, full of public inquisitions and private intrusions, for the simple act of wanting to pursue the love of a lifetime. And we're still standing. I want to end the exclusion of committed couples from marriage. I want to participate in this existing institution, to have access to legal protections that other committed people enjoy. I want to marry Margie. Thank you."

By chance, Laurie was followed by George McGrath, a gruff, white-haired, former city council candidate who has been an archconservative fixture at Spokane council meetings for nearly two decades. He declared it "atrocious" that some members of the Spokane community had testified in support of marriage equality, which he compared to "people marrying animals."

"Table it forever," he growled, "because this is not what Spokane is all about."

By that time, Margie and Laurie were gathering themselves in the cool, night air outside City Hall, shaken less by what they had heard than by having to share the same crowded space with those who harbored such fear and contempt. They were home in bed, after midnight, watching the end of the hearing on the city's cable TV channel. Council president Stuckart spoke last. Before calling for a vote on the resolution, he complimented several who had spoken during the long evening.

"I listened to Margaret Witt," he said, "and if I could repeat what she said, I would be the most eloquent man in the world. That was beautiful."

The resolution failed on a 4–3 vote.

On Election Day, however, state voters approved Referendum 74 — confirming the new law — with nearly 54 percent approval, making Washington one of the first three states to approve marriage equality by popular vote. Four days later, before an audience of nearly five hundred people, Margie was giving a short speech after being presented with an award at the ACLU of Washington's annual Bill of Rights dinner.

"I have a final, short personal thing to say," she announced. "Laurie, I have a question to ask you. Will you marry me?"

The room erupted in cheers.

The R-74 election results were certified on December 5, and the next morning the two were all smiles, snapping selfies at the front of the line to receive their marriage license from Spokane County auditor Vicky Dalton. Among the first to embrace them as they gleefully departed with their license was an ebullient Carla Savalli.

Across the state, on Whidbey Island, Grethe Cammermeyer and her partner of twenty-five years, Diane Divelbess, were first in line to get their marriage license from Island County. They were married three days later in a private ceremony at their home overlooking Saratoga Passage.

Margie and Laurie's wedding was on December 15, at a winery banquet room in downtown Spokane. Laurie wore a black short-sleeve dress, and Margie a dark-blue uniform with her service ribbons. They were surrounded by close friends and family who dined on center cut steaks and goat cheese–stuffed chicken breasts before watching the couple exchange vows administered by Jim Lobsenz. Jim Schaffer and Stacey Julian were there with their wives. Sarah Dunne was there with her husband, Bob, a naval officer she had met during the *Witt* trial. Frank and Gloria were there, as were Abby and Sam, Virginia and her daughters, and Carla and her husband Steve. Karyn Gomez, Margie's dear friend from eighth grade, was there as well. Jan Gemberling, all smiles, moved nimbly through the revelers, taking snapshots with a pocket-size camera. Six months later, when the weather had warmed, Debbie and Steve Duvoisin hosted a second reception, to allow those who hadn't been able to attend the wedding in December to share in the celebration. The gathering was poolside, in the garden at the Duvoisins' home on the back ridge of Spokane's South Hill. The party lingered long into the night with gales of laughter, the clinking of champagne glasses, and open views of the high, gauzy clouds above, drifting lazily in starlight.

Years before they could have any idea whether their trials would end well, Margie and Laurie made a rule about always having champagne in the refrigerator and a practice of saving the corks in a large stainless steel bowl. Both were gestures of a will to celebrate the victories in a journey they knew could break their hearts at any turn, of a resolve to build loving lives together, no matter what the storms washed in. The mound of corks is now above the rim of the bowl.

On the last Friday in August 2014, Sher Kung was making her morning commute on bicycle, riding in downtown Seattle. The driver of the truck that collided with the bike said he never saw her as he made a turn at the corner of Second and University. The corner was a notoriously dangerous one for bicyclists and was scheduled for bike safety improvements, including a new signal system, in two weeks. The gentle, thirty-one-year-old lawyer who had done so much to advance Margie's case, and who was her faithful guardian during the trial, died at the scene. She and her partner were engaged to be married, and the two women were mothers to a seven-month-old girl.

The tragedy stunned Seattle and flickered into national news. Within hours, two whitewashed "ghost bikes" framed a memorial at the corner, a few steps away from the entrance to Benaroya Hall, where the city's symphony orchestra performs. As word of the tragedy spread, dozens of bouquets, mementos, and notes were placed on and near the white bikes and then along the stone wall fronting the "Garden of Remembrance," a memorial to military veterans adjacent to the stairs leading into Benaroya Hall. Nearly all the broadcast and written tributes to Sher's lifework underscored her contributions to winning the *Witt* case.

Among the flowers piled along the corner at Second and University was an ACLU poster with a handwritten message spanning two large Post-it notes.

"Sher: Thank you for bringing your light and love to our community of Seattle LGBT attorneys and advocates for LGBT rights. You will be forever remembered for your contributions and positive spirit that you brought to us."

ACKNOWLEDGMENTS

This is a story about a journey I wouldn't have chosen.

A decade ago I was serving my country as a flight nurse when my country served notice of its intention to expel me from the Air Force because I'm a lesbian. As this book explains, it was an assault instigated by an act of vengeance, aimed not just at me but at the love of my life. It was an effort to ruin us. We chose not to let it.

Somehow we found the strength to resist, and through this resistance, grace emerged. With the support of our families, some dear and devoted friends—and the inspired legal work of Jim Lobsenz and Sarah Dunne, Aaron Caplan, Nina Jenkins, and Sher Kung—a prolonged trial by fire became something larger than us all. If, in the beginning, the struggle defined us, then, in the end, our struggle would redefine how our government must treat gay men and women in national service.

Foremost, I wish to thank Laurie for her unwavering devotion and loving resilience. I'm so grateful for the boundless support from my family, and especially my parents, Frank and Gloria, for living out what they had instilled in me as a child—the importance of equality and fairness, and the resolve to fight to make things right. While the talents of my lawyers and the support staff at the American Civil Liberties Union of Washington speak for themselves, I remain humbled by their devotion and skill. To my brothers and sisters in uniform who stood by me and testified with such courage and distinction, I am forever honored to have served alongside you.

To Grethe Cammermeyer, my hero, mentor, and dear friend, no words can convey the depth of my gratitude. To my wingman for the cause, Lieutenant Colonel Victor Fehrenbach, and to Anna Curren and Jan Gemberling, who did so much behind the scenes to help us through, your support was invaluable. I would need a second edition to list the precious friends of my lifetime who've always been there for me and who helped me become who I am. Likewise, there isn't nearly enough room to list all those who helped bring this story to print. But we are especially grateful to UPNE editor Stephen P. Hull and copy editor Glenn Novak for their encouragement and fine tuning. One of the better days of our lives was our first long-distance phone call with literary agent Rayhané Sanders, who had read the book proposal and, from day one, deeply believed in this story, in all its human, legal, and social dimensions. We would not be here without her.

And, finally, thanks to my coauthor Tim Connor, whose love for us and commitment to the story made this book possible.

NOTES AND SOURCES

1. HOMECOMING

1 *That was the day Ramzi Yousef* Federal Bureau of Investigation, "FBI 100, First Strike: Global Terror in America," February 26, 2008, https://archives.fbi.gov/archives/news/stories/2008/february/tradebom_022608.

4 *By September 2001, more than seven thousand service members* Servicemembers Legal Defense Network, *A Guide to "Don't Ask, Don't Tell,"* 2009, http://sldn.3cdn.net/52cda64370ee816e52_zvm6bekat.pdf.

9 *In the mid-1960s, Beale became the first* U.S. Air Force online library, *Beale's History: Past to Present*, February 23, 2016.

10 *Six crew members died in the crash* Aviation Safety Network report, March 15, 1981, RC-135 crash at Shemya, https://aviation-safety.net/database/record.php?id=19810315-1.

10 *Somali militants shot down* National Public Radio, *All Things Considered*, "What a Downed Black Hawk in Somalia Taught America," October 5, 2013.

3. CROSSING INTO THE BLUE, PART I

30 *Fewer than two dozen of the C-9As* Air Mobility Command Museum, C9 A/C Nightingale, http://amcmuseum.org/at-the-museum/aircraft/c-9ac-nightingale/.

4. CROSSING INTO THE BLUE, PART II

39 *Likewise, the premise that homosexual service members are inherently a threat* Randy Shilts, *Conduct Unbecoming: Gays and Lesbians in the U.S. Military, Vietnam to the Persian Gulf* (New York: St. Martin's, 1993), 281, 647–49. See also Nathaniel Frank, *Unfriendly Fire: How the Gay Ban Undermines the Military and Weakens America* (New York: Thomas Dunne, 2009),

suppression of the 1957 Crittenden Report prepared for the secretary of the navy, 118; suppression of the 1988–1989 Personnel Security Research and Education Center (PERSEREC) reports, 199; and suppression of the 1993 Rand Corp. study whose findings challenged the premise that homosexuals harmed military readiness, 114.

39   *Still, there had been approximately one hundred thousand*   Rhonda Evans, *U.S. Military Policies concerning Homosexuals: Development, Implementation and Outcomes*, report prepared for the Center for the Study of Sexual Minorities in the Military, University of California, Santa Barbara, November 1, 2001, 73.

41–42   *when it came to gathering evidence against gay officers and enlisted personnel, OSI regularly employed highly coercive techniques, even though the Uniform Code*   Uniform Code of Military Justice, subchapter 6, section 830, article 31.

5. FLIGHTS OF THE NIGHTINGALES

49   *The battles lasted only one hundred hours*   George M. Watson Jr., "A Salute to Wiesbaden," *USAF Medical Service Digest*, Fall 1992.

50   *Because a main purpose of the mission*   NASA mission archives for STS-58, http://www.nasa.gov/mission_pages/shuttle/shuttlemissions/archives/sts -58.html.

51   *The plane broke apart*   Mary Ellen Condon-Rall, *Disaster on Green Ramp: The Army's Response*, Center of Military History, U.S. Army, 1996.

54   *Watkins had been raised in Tacoma*   Randy Shilts, *Conduct Unbecoming: Gays and Lesbians in the U.S. Military, Vietnam to the Persian Gulf* (New York: St. Martin's, 1993), 385.

55   *A federal appeals court in 1989*   Sgt. Perry Watkins v. United States Army, et al., 875 F .2d 699 (9th Circuit. 1989), U.S. Court of Appeals for the Ninth Circuit.

56   *The shattering result of her admission*   Cammermeyer v. Aspin, 850 Supp. 910 (W.D. Wash. 1994).

7. HALLOWEEN

69   *Top administration officials*   Barton Gellman, *Angler: The Cheney Vice Presidency* (London: Penguin Books, 2009), 215–53; Mark Mazzetti and Scott Shane, "Senate Panel Accuses Bush of Iraq Exaggerations," *New York Times*, June 5, 2008.

69   *Twenty-three U.S. senators*   govtrack, H.J. Res. 114 (107th): Authorization

for Use of Military Force against Iraq Resolution of 2002, https://www
.govtrack.us/congress/votes/107-2002/s237.

69 *Then came U.S. secretary of state Colin Powell's* United Nations press release,
"Briefing Security Council, U.S. Secretary of State Powell Presents
Evidence of Iraq's Failure to Disarm," February 5, 2003.

70 *The U.S. military had taken so few casualties* Gerry J. Gilmore, "Sickness,
Injury Took Toll of Gulf Troops," American Forces Press Service,
February 23, 2001.

71 *His first-person accounts* "Soldiers' Stories: Dispatches from Iraq," *New
Yorker*, June 12, 2006.

9. MEETING MAJOR TOREM

90 *Six weeks earlier, a two-page letter had been sent by e-mail to General John Jumper,
the Air Force chief of staff* Report of Major Adam Torem, Memorandum
for 446 AWCC, Commander Directed Report of Investigation of Alleged
Homosexual Conduct of Major Margaret Witt, 446 AES, October 20,
2004. Attachment 2.

11. SILVER WINGS

102 *In a 7–4 opinion issued on May 3* Sgt. Perry Watkins v. United States Army,
et al., 875 F .2d 699 (9th Circuit. 1989), U.S. Court of Appeals for the
Ninth Circuit.

103 *In the Pentagon and in Congress* Rhonda Evans, *U.S. Military Policies concerning Homosexuals: Development, Implementation and Outcomes*, report prepared
for the Center for the Study of Sexual Minorities in the Military, University of California, Santa Barbara, November 11, 2001, 8.

103 *"As a general rule," the policy stated* Ibid., 14.

12. "MAJOR WITT IS GAY"

109–110 *Torem e-mailed a copy of his interview* Report of Major Adam Torem,
Memorandum for 446 AWCC, Commander Directed Report of
Investigation of Alleged Homosexual Conduct of Major Margaret Witt,
446 AES, October 20, 2004.

112 *Notably, it was not a case challenging* United States v. Technical Sgt. Eric P.
Marcum, United States Court of Appeals for the Armed Forces, No. 02-
0944, Crim. App. No. 34216, August 23, 2004.

13. A SOJOURN TO LANGLEY

121　*In that dissent, Justice Stevens asserted*　Michael J. Bowers, Attorney General of Georgia v. Michael Hardwick, et al., 478 U.S. 186 (1986).

129　*For Pruitt, it had taken four years*　Pruitt v. Cheney, et al. U.S. Court of Appeals for the Ninth Circuit, 943 F.2d 989, August 19, 1991.

14. THE WILDERNESS

130　*"I did not realize," she wrote in her memoir*　Margarethe Cammermeyer with Chris Fisher, *Serving in Silence* (New York: Viking Adult, 1994), 231.

130　*She became a cause célèbre*　Nathaniel Frank, *Unfriendly Fire: How the Gay Ban Undermines the Military and Weakens America* (New York: Thomas Dunne, 2009), 24. See also Cammermeyer, *Serving in Silence*, 295.

132　*His twelve-thousand-word decision*　Cammermeyer v. Aspin, 850 F. Supp. 910, (W.D. Wash. 1994), No. C92-942Z, Order, United States District Court. W.D. Wash., Northern Division, June 1, 1994.

132–133　*Instead, the appeals court ruled*　Cammermeyer v. Perry, et al., Nos. 94-35600, 94-35674, United States Court of Appeals, Ninth Circuit, October 7, 1996.

133　*The ruling from Judge Leighton*　Witt v. Department of the Air Force, et al., Case No. C06-5195 RBL, United States District Court, Western District of Washington at Tacoma, Order, July 26, 2006.

136　*"Though the matter is not free from doubt"*　Cook et al. v. Rumsfeld, U.S. District Court, District of Massachusetts, Civil Action No. 04-12546-GAO, Memorandum and Order, April 24, 2006.

139　*The Air Force prosecutor contended*　Record of Discharge Board Proceedings, Air Force Reserve Command, Maj. Margaret H. Witt, September 28, 29, 2006, Transcript, vol. 3.

141　*Caplan informed Hampton that the two*　ACLU of Washington internal memo, Aaron Caplan to Julya Hampton, "Choice of Legal Theories in *Witt v. Air Force*," April 2006.

141　*Yet, in doing so, she noted, "Texas cannot assert*　John Geddes Lawrence and Tyron Garner v. Texas, Supreme Court of the United States, No. 02-102, June 26, 2003. Justice O'Connor's concurrence.

15. THE *WITT* STANDARD

145 *In* Meinhold, *the appeals court upheld* Meinhold v. U.S. Department of
Defense, 34 F3d 1469, United States Court of Appeals, Ninth Circuit,
Nos. 93-55242, 93-56354, August 31, 1994.

145 *Judge Zilly wrote that his ruling* 918 F. Supp. 1043 (1996) Lieutenant
Richard P. Watson v. William J. Perry, Secretary of Defense, No. C95-
1141Z, Order, March 7, 1996.

146 *"We must now face the question we avoided"* Holmes v. California National
Guard, Watson v. Cohen, Nos. 96-15855, 96-15726 and 96-35314, United
States Court of Appeals, Ninth Circuit, Sept. 5, 1997.

148–149 *Notwithstanding the "protected liberty interest"* Cook et al. v. Gates,
United States Court of Appeals for the First Circuit, Nos. 06-2313, 08-
2381, June 9, 2008.

151–152 *Thus, he concluded: "We hold that"* Witt v. Department of the Air Force,
United States Court of Appeals for the Ninth Circuit, No. 06-35644, D.C.
No. CV-06-05195-RBL, May 21, 2008.

16. OBI WAN OBAMA

154 *Reading from a teleprompter, the senior senator* Elisabeth Bumiller and Jeff
Zeleny, "Obama Rejects McCain's Call to Delay Debate," *New York Times*,
September 25, 2008.

155 *In an open letter to the LGBT community* Barack Obama's Open Letter to the
Gay Community, February 28, 2008, http://slog.thestranger.com/2008/02/
barack_obamas_open_letter_to_the_gay_com.

155 *When Obama's former top political strategist* Zeke J. Miller, "Axelrod: Obama
Misled Nation When He Opposed Gay Marriage in 2008," *Time*, February
10, 2015, http://time.com/3702584/gay-marriage-axelrod-obama/.

159 *The Ninth Circuit Court of Appeals* Order, No. 06-05195-RBL, D.C. No.
CV-06=05195-RBL, Witt v. Department of Air Force, Dec. 4, 2008.

161 *A few days earlier, President Obama* Robert M. Gates, *Duty: Memoirs of a
Secretary at War* (New York: Knopf, 2014), 332.

163 *In trying to navigate the controversy* Supreme Court Review, profile of Justice
Elena Kagan, http://supremecourtreview.com/default/justice/index/id/46.

163 *Those statements did not go unnoticed* Hearing before the Committee on the
Judiciary, United States Senate, February 10, 2009, S. Hrg. 111-361 (U.S.
Government Printing Office, 2009).

163 *That answer would come at the end* Letter from Attorney General Eric
H. Holder Jr. to Morgan Frankel, Senate Legal Counsel, Re: *Witt v.
Department of Air Force*, April 24, 2009.

164 *The next day, June 30, 2010* C-SPAN 3 video of Elena Kagan confirmation
hearing before the Senate Judiciary Committee, June 30, 2010, http://
www.c-span.org/video/?294265-3/kagan-confirmation-hearing-day-3
-part-2.

166 *In his 2012 book* Jeffrey Toobin, *The Oath: The Obama White House and the
Supreme Court* (New York: Doubleday, 2012), 222–23.

17. OUTING GOLIATH

169 *Yet, because the highly decorated pilot and trainer* James Dao, "Officer Sues to
Block Discharge under Gay Ban," *New York Times*, August 11, 2010, http://
www.nytimes.com/2010/08/12/us/12ask.html?_r=1&scp=1&sq=Colonel
%20Fehrenbach&st=cse.

170–171 *In May 1992, Representative Schroeder* Nathaniel Frank, *Unfriendly Fire:
How the Gay Ban Undermines the Military and Weakens America* (New York:
Thomas Dunne, 2009), 62.

171 *Powell took umbrage that Schroeder* Ibid., 62–63.

172 *"Good morning, your honor," she greeted Judge Leighton* Major Margaret Witt
v. United States Department of the Air Force et al., Docket No. C06-5195
RBL, Tacoma, Washington, September 13, 2010, Transcript of Proceedings
before the Honorable Ronald B. Leighton, United States District Court
Judge, vol. 1.

18. TRUE STORIES

177 *In his opening statement on September 13* Major Margaret Witt v. United
States Department of the Air Force et al., Docket No. C06-5195 RBL, Tacoma, Washington, September 13, 2010, Transcript of Proceedings before
the Honorable Ronald B. Leighton, United States District Court Judge,
vol. 1.

178 *Within the first minute, Schaffer would disclose* Ibid., vol. 1.

181 *"It was kind of like extracting a parent* Ibid., vol. 3.

181 *Major Smidt said the news of Margie's* Ibid., vol. 3

181 *Major Krill said she was "horrified"* Ibid., vol. 3.

182 *"I'd hire her tomorrow," Mueller replied* Ibid., vol. 3.

183 *"I did not tell," she answered. "I tried very hard not to"* Ibid., vol. 1.

185 *He dreaded his roommate's reaction* Ibid., vol. 1.

191 *"General Rank asked me to specifically interview"* Ibid., vol. 4.

19. THE LAST DAYS OF SUMMER

193 *As the TV crews were packing up their cameras* Margarethe Cammermeyer with Chris Fisher, *Serving in Silence* (New York: Viking Adult, 1994), 6–7.

195 *"I figured they should hear it from me"* Major Margaret Witt v. United States Department of the Air Force et al., Docket No. C06-5195 RBL, Tacoma, Washington, September 13, 2010, Transcript of Proceedings before the Honorable Ronald B. Leighton, United States District Court Judge, vol. 5.

198 *Dunne: "Now, you've never met Major Witt before; is that correct?"* (and subsequent answers from General Stenner) Ibid., vol. 6.

204 *Stephens's column not only underscored General Laich's* Bret Stephens, "Why the GOP Should Repeal DADT," *Wall Street Journal*, September 21, 2010, http://www.wsj.com/articles/SB1000142405274870355660457550210 3316084526.

206 *"Mr. Lobsenz," Judge Leighton said, "I view"* Witt v. Department of the Air Force, trial transcript, September 21, 2010, vol. 6.

20. AN EXEMPLARY OFFICER

211 *In the week before the Witt trial got under way* Memorandum Opinion, Log Cabin Republicans v. United States of America et al., Case No. CV 04-08425-VAP (Ex), United States District Court, Central District of California, September 9, 2010.

211 *On September 23, the day before Judge Leighton* Rep. Jared Polis, Rep. Barney Frank, Rep. Tammy Baldwin, et al., to President Barack Obama, September 23, 2010. http://polis.house.gov/uploadedfiles/9-23_dadt_appeal _letter.pdf

214 *"The argument proves too much, however"* Witt v. Department of the Air Force, trial transcript, September 24, 2010, vol. 7.

21. HEARD

218 *"This is such an exciting day," Grethe Cammermeyer said* KOMO Staff and News Services, "Judge: Lesbian's Discharge from Air Force Unconstitutional," September 24, 2010, posted 2:07 p.m.

219 *"A bit of big breaking news late on a Friday"* The Rachel Maddow Show, "Another

Blow to DADT as Court Orders Reinstatement," September 24, 2010, http://www.nbcnews.com/video/rachel-maddow/39352146#39352146.

221–222　　*This was publicly confirmed in early February 2010*　*Hardball with Chris Matthews*, NBC News, "Vice President Biden on 'Andrea Mitchell Reports,' February 2nd, 2010," http://www.nbcnews.com/id/35203953/ns /msnbc-hardball_with_chris_matthews/t/vice-president-biden-andrea -mitchell-reports—february-nd/#.V4r5uo6vQ-8.

223　　*It was, he said, "a matter of urgency"*　Elisabeth Bumiller, "Pentagon Sees Little Risk in Allowing Gay Men and Women to Serve Openly," *New York Times*, November 30, 2010.

223　　*Although it passed 57–40, it was actually*　Liz Halloran, "Senate Defeat of 'Don't Ask, Don't Tell' Repeal Highlights Partisan Distrust," National Public Radio, December 9, 2010.

INDEX

177; unit culture of, 179–81; and Unit Training Assembly, 60. *See also Witt v. Air Force*

Friscia, Anna, 6–8

Gates, Robert, 156, 161–62, 165, 211, 221–24

gay marriage. *See* same-sex marriage

Gemberling, Jan: coaching Margie through rough spots, 114; and Laurie McChesney, 77–79, 83–86, 105; at Margie and Laurie's wedding, 238; on Margie as ideal plaintiff for DADT lawsuit, 95–97; and Margie's discharge hearing from Air Force, 138–40; and Margie's notice of discharge from Air Force, 93–100, 116; meets Margie and Tiffany Jensen, 63–64; and *Witt v. Air Force*, 156, 169, 213

geoducks, 19–20

Gibbons, Euell, 24

Gibson, Robert "Hoot," 50–51

Gomez, Karyn Ingebritsen. *See* Ingebritsen, Karyn (Gomez)

Gould, Ronald, 150–53, 210

Graber, Susan, 150

Green Ramp tragedy, 51–53

Gregoire, Chris, 235

Ham, Carter F., 222

Hampton, Julya, 141

Hansen, Thomas, 180, 182

Harvard Law School, 162–64

Holder, Eric, 163–66

Holmes, Andrew, 145

homosexuality: and AIDS, 56–57; the Bible on, 235; David's story, 26–27; decriminalization of, 96–97;

and home ownership, 64–65; as instrument of communism, 235; legal opinions of, 121; in the military, ix–xi, 39, 54, 103–4 (See also *specific legal cases*); physical characteristics of, x; as threat to morale and cohesion in military, 103–4, 124, 168, 171, 177. *See also* Don't Ask, Don't Tell

Hrivnak, Ed, 59–60, 68–71, 147–48, 190–92, 227

Hrivnak, Jennifer, 68, 71, 227

Human Rights Campaign, 155

Hussein, Saddam, 49, 69

Ingebritsen, Karyn (Gomez), 16–17, 25–27, 169, 193–94, 238

Inslee, Jay, 226

Jensen, Tiffany: Adam Toren's questions about, 90–92; background of, 4–5; end of relationship with Margie, 72–76, 78–79; in Hawaii with Margie, 63–64, 75–76; and home ownership with Margie, 64–65; meets and moves in with Margie, 63–64; outing Margie to Air Force, 90–91, 109; and parenthood, 5–6, 11–12, 65, 72–76, 78; pregnancy of, 79; and tension over Margie's reservist career, 65–66

Johnson, Claudia, 235

Johnson, Jeh, 162, 222

Johnson, Laurie. *See* McChesney, Laurie Johnson

Julian, Heather, 7, 180

Julian, Stacey, 6–8, 146–47, 180, 229–30, 238

Jumper, John, 90

she is gay, 108–9; in Oman with
446th AES, 6–15, 69–72; as operating room nurse at Tacoma General
Hospital, 34; ordered to leave 446th
AES and Air Force, 112–14; outed
to Air Force, immediate aftermath
of, 98–106; outed to Air Force, legal
options of, 93–97; outed to Air Force
by Pat McChesney and Tiffany
Jensen, 90–91; out to her parents,
116–18; out to Jim Schaffer, 11;
out to the world, 118–19; at Pacific
Lutheran University, 31–34; and
parenthood, 5–6, 11–12, 65, 72–76;
parents' expectations of, 23–25; pho-
tographed for Air Force recruiting
materials, 58–59; as physical therapist, 53, 61–62, 66, 76–77; on *The
Rachel Maddow Show*, 219–22, 227;
as rehabilitation coordinator at VA
hospital in Spokane, 234; as reservist in 446th AES (*See* 446th AES);
at same-sex marriage hearing in
Washington state, 235–36; at Scott
Air Force Base, 49–61; sense of
humor of, 21–22, 24, 32, 66, 77, 82,
99, 105, 194; sexual harassment by
men, 40–45; at Sheppard Air Force
Base, 35–36; shunned by Catholic
community, 85; as threat to morale
and cohesion in 446th AES, 103–4,
124, 168, 171, 177; and Tiffany
Jensen (*See* Jensen, Tiffany); at
trial of Matt Kane, 142–43; value to
446th AES, 3, 88–89; in Weisbaden,
Germany, 48–49; on Whidbey Island
with Grethe Cammermeyer, 127–29;
at White House DADT repeal

signing ceremony, 224–26; at White
House holiday reception, 232–33.
See also Don't Ask, Don't Tell; *Witt
v. Air Force*

Witt, Virginia, 19, 23–24, 107, 126, 238

Witt standard, xii, 152, 159–60, 170,
177, 211, 215, 219–20

Witt v. Air Force: ACLU national's concerns about, 140–42; and adultery,
91, 174, 177, 194, 196–97, 203, 206–
7; aftermath of, 217–28; beginning
of lawsuit, 116–19; en banc appeal
denial, 159; hearing appeal, 137,
140–42, 148–53, 156–58; hearing before Judge Ronald Leighton (2006),
120–26; hearing before Judge
Ronald Leighton (2006), ruling on,
133–37, 209; Supreme Court review
declined by Solicitor General Kagan, 159–67; at trial (2010), closing
arguments, 205–7; at trial (2010),
government's case, 197–207; at trial
(2010), Judge Leighton's closing remarks, 207–8; at trial (2010), Judge
Leighton's pretrial conference with
case lawyers, 176–77; at trial (2010),
Margie's testimony and cross-examination, 193–97; at trial (2010),
opening statements, 168–75; at trial
(2010), plaintiff's witnesses, 177–92;
trial verdict, 209–11, 212–17, 224,
226–27, 230, 232

World Trade Center, 1–3, 68

Yousef, Ramzi, 1

Zilly, Thomas, 132–33, 144–45, 171,
231